The Big Book of Scrappy Quilts

The
Big Book of
Scrappy Quilts

Crib-Size to King-Size

Martingale®
Create with Confidence

The Big Book of Scrappy Quilts: Crib-Size to King-Size
© 2015 by Martingale & Company®

Martingale®
19021 120th Ave. NE, Ste. 102
Bothell, WA 98011-9511 USA

ShopMartingale.com

Printed in China
20 19 18 17 16 15   8 7 6 5 4 3 2 1

Library of Congress Cataloging-in-Publication Data is available upon request.

ISBN: 978-1-60468-644-9

Mission Statement

Dedicated to providing quality products and service to inspire creativity.

Credits

PUBLISHER AND CHIEF VISIONARY OFFICER
Jennifer Erbe Keltner

EDITORIAL DIRECTOR
Karen Costello Soltys

ACQUISITIONS EDITOR
Karen M. Burns

TECHNICAL EDITOR
Mary V. Green

COPY EDITOR
Melissa Bryan

DESIGN DIRECTOR
Paula Schlosser

PRODUCTION MANAGER
Regina Girard

INTERIOR DESIGNER
Connor Chin

PHOTOGRAPHER
Brent Kane

ILLUSTRATORS
Lisa Lauch, Ann Marra, Brian Metz, Missy Shepler, Adrienne Smitke, Laurel Strand, Robin Strobel, and Rose Wright

TEXT LAYOUT
Dianna Logan / DBS

Contents

Introduction

Scrappy. What sort of images does that word evoke for you? Is it a happy assortment of fabric treasures combined into a single project? Is it odds and ends of fabrics you just couldn't bear to part with, all sewn together to make a cherished quilt? Or is it more controlled—bits and pieces of assorted creams and blues, or a variety of children's prints you've collected over the years? No matter what pictures your mind's eye conjures up when you hear the word scrappy, you're sure to find several quilts to suit your style in *The Big Book of Scrappy Quilts.*

We've compiled an array of scrappy quilts as diverse as the fabrics used in creating them! Love Log Cabin quilts? They're here. Crazy about Star blocks? You'll find several to choose from. Like to put your own spin on scrappy pinwheels? Your chance to do just that awaits inside. Delight in discovering ideas galore for making the most of all your fabric scraps.

The word scrappy is also defined as having a determined spirit. That fits well too when describing quilters. So relax, grab your favorite beverage, and get ready to enjoy page after page of spectacular scrappy quilts. And as a scrappy quilt lover, determine to select your next project (or two) from the patterns within this big book of ideas!

Open Season

Carrie's inspiration for this project was an antique two-color quilt in rusty orange and brownish gold. Obviously she didn't feel compelled to reproduce it exactly! Instead of using just two colors and straight, plain strips, Carrie made the quilt in her own great freewheeling style.

"Open Season," designed by Carrie Nelson, pieced by Judy Adams, quilted by Diane Tricka

Finished quilt: 68½" x 81½"   ◆   **Finished block:** 4" x 8"

▶ Materials

Yardage is based on 42"-wide fabric.

1⅞ yards of light print for blocks and sashing

58 assorted squares, 10" x 10", in a range of light, medium, and dark values for blocks, sashing, and border (Carrie used Layer Cakes.)

⅝ yard of fabric for binding

5¼ yards of fabric for backing

74" x 87" piece of batting

▶ Cutting

All measurements include ¼"-wide seam allowances.

From the light print, cut:
9 strips, 4⅞" x 42"; crosscut into 72 squares, 4⅞" x 4⅞"
6 strips, 2½" x 42"

From *each* of 18 assorted medium or dark squares, cut:
1 square, 9¼" x 9¼" (18 total)

From *each* of 32 assorted squares, cut:
1 strip, 5" x 10" (32 total), from the *lengthwise* grain
1 strip, 4" x 10" (32 total)

From *each* of the 8 remaining assorted squares, cut:
2 strips, 4" x 10" (16 total), from the *lengthwise* grain

From the binding fabric, cut:
2"-wide bias strips to make 310" of bias binding

Making the Blocks

Use a scant ¼"-wide seam allowance throughout. After sewing each seam, press the seam allowances in the direction indicated by the arrows, or press them open if you prefer.

1 Use Carrie's special technique for making four matching Flying Geese blocks at once. Choose four matching 4⅞" light squares and one 9¼" medium or dark square for each set. Draw a diagonal line on the wrong side of each light square. With right sides together, place two marked squares on opposite corners of the large square. The points of the small squares will overlap a bit and the drawn line will extend across the square from corner to corner.

2 Stitch a scant ¼" from each side of the drawn line. Cut the squares apart on the drawn line and press the seam allowances toward the small triangles.

3 With right sides together, place the remaining marked squares on the corners of both pieces. Stitch, cut, and press as shown. The blocks should measure 4½" x 8½". Make a total of 18 sets of four matching Flying Geese blocks (72 total).

Assembling the Quilt Top

1 Sort the blocks into four groups of 18 blocks each; there should be one Flying Geese block from each fabric in each group. Randomly sew the blocks in one group together as shown to make a strip measuring 8½" x 72½". Repeat to make a total of four Flying Geese strips. (The arrangement of the colors in each strip should be different, but all geese should point in one direction.)

Make 4.

2 Divide the 4" x 10" strips into six sets of eight strips each. Join the strips from one set end to end to make a continuous strip measuring approximately 76" long. Repeat to make a second 76"-long strip. Lay out the two strips side by side, offsetting the seamline positions in the two strips, and trim both strips to 72½" long. Repeat to make a total of three trimmed pairs of pieced strips.

3 Sew the 2½"-wide light strips together end to end. From the strip, cut three 72½"-long strips.

4 Sew a pair of pieced strips from step 2 to the long sides of a light strip from step 3 as shown. The strip should measure 9½" x 72½". Repeat to make a total of three sashing strips.

Make 3.

5 Lay out the Flying Geese strips and sashing strips, alternating them as shown in the quilt assembly diagram, at right. Sew the strips together, pressing the seam allowances toward the sashing strips. The quilt top should measure 59½" x 72½".

Adding the Border

1 Sort the 5" x 10" strips into four sets of eight strips each. Join the strips from one set end to end as shown to make a border strip. If you used a Layer Cake, keep the pinked edges on the outside. Press the seam allowances in one direction (or press them open). Repeat to make a total of four border strips, each approximately 76" long.

Make 4.

2 Trim two border strips to measure 72½" long and sew them to the sides of the quilt top. Press the seam allowances toward the border. Trim the remaining two border strips to measure 68½" long and sew them to the top and bottom of the quilt top. Press the seam allowances toward the border.

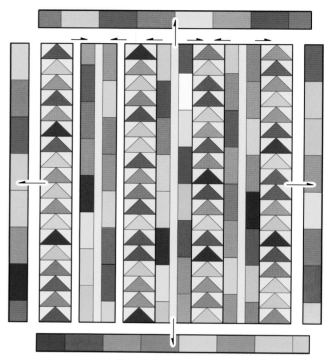

Quilt assembly

Finishing the Quilt

For help with any of the finishing steps, go to ShopMartingale.com/HowtoQuilt for free downloadable information.

1 Layer, baste, and quilt your quilt, or take it to your favorite long-arm machine quilter for finishing.

2 Using the 2"-wide bias strips, make and attach binding.

Double Windmill

When originally published in the **Spokane Daily Chronicle,** *Alice Brooks's Depression-era "Double Windmill" pattern was described as "simple." It is an easy quilt with only two pattern pieces, but it has the potential to be a showcase for a large collection of prints, feeding the eye of an appreciative viewer.*

"Double Windmill," pieced and quilted by Karen Earlywine

Finished quilt: 83" x 94"   ◆   Finished block: 11" x 11"

▶ Materials

Yardage is based on 42"-wide fabric except where noted.

6½ yards of unbleached muslin for blocks and borders

4 yards *total* of assorted 1930s reproduction prints for blocks and outer border

¾ yard of yellow print for binding

3 yards of 90"-wide unbleached muslin for backing*

89" x 100" piece of batting

Template plastic

*If using 42"-wide unbleached muslin, you'll need 8¼ yards (3 widths pieced horizontally).

▶ Cutting

All measurements include ¼"-wide seam allowances. Make a template for piece A using the pattern on page 13.

From the assorted 1930s reproduction prints, cut a *total* **of:**
146 squares, 3⅝" x 3⅝"; cut in half diagonally to yield 292 triangles
168 pieces with template A

From the unbleached muslin, cut on the *lengthwise* **grain:**
2 strips, 6" x 92"
2 strips, 6" x 70"

From the remaining unbleached muslin, cut:
21 strips, 3¼" x 42"; cut into 168 pieces with template A*
146 squares, 3⅝" x 3⅝"; cut in half diagonally to yield 292 triangles

From the yellow print, cut:
10 strips, 2¼" x 42"

*If you're using muslin or a solid fabric, you don't need to cut reverse pieces; however, if you substitute a fabric that has a right side and a wrong side, cut all 168 pieces with template A reversed.

Making the Blocks

1 Sew each muslin half-square triangle to a print A piece as shown. Press the seam allowances toward the A piece. Sew each print half-square triangle to a muslin A piece. Press the seam allowances toward the print triangle. Make 168 of each unit.

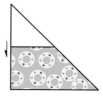 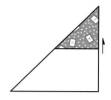

Make 168.   Make 168.

2 In a pleasing mix of colors, arrange eight units as shown. Pin and sew two units together along the long edges, matching the seams, to make a square unit. Be careful not to stretch the bias edges as you stitch. Press the seam allowances toward the print A piece. Make four square units for each block (168 total).

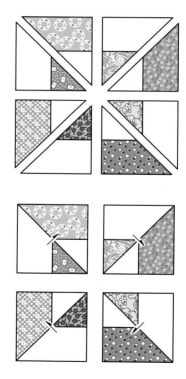

3 Using a ruler, trim each square unit to measure 6" x 6" by placing the 45° line on your ruler along the diagonal seam. Be sure to trim off the dog-ears.

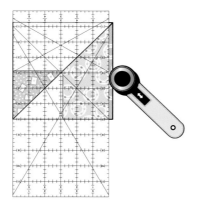

4 Sew the square units together in pairs to make a half block. Sew two half blocks together, matching the seams, to complete the block. Make a total of 42 blocks. Trim them to 11½" x 11½".

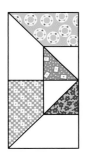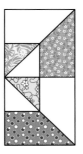

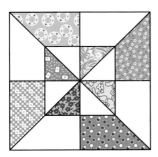

Make 42.

Assembling the Quilt Top

1 Arrange the blocks in seven rows of six blocks each as shown in the quilt assembly diagram. Rearrange the blocks until you are pleased with the color placement.

2 Sew the blocks into rows. Press the seam allowances in opposite directions from row to row. Stitch the rows together. Press the seam allowances in one direction.

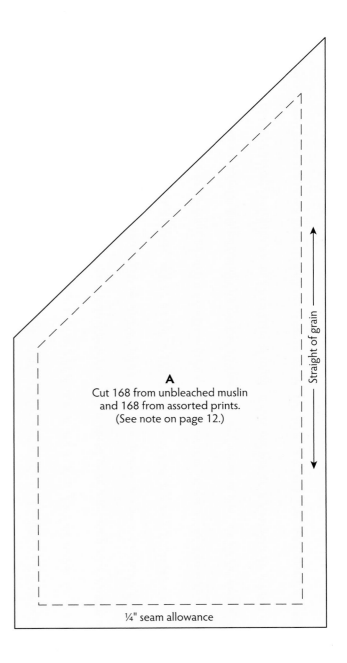

A
Cut 168 from unbleached muslin and 168 from assorted prints. (See note on page 12.)

Straight of grain

¼" seam allowance

Adding the Borders

1 Using the muslin 6"-wide strips, measure, cut, and sew the shorter strips to the top and bottom of the quilt top, and then repeat to add the longer strips to the sides of the quilt top. Press all seam allowances toward the border. The quilt top should measure 77½" x 88½" for the outer border to fit properly.

2 Sew the remaining print half-square triangles and muslin half-square triangles together along their long edges to make 124 half-square-triangle units. Press the seam allowances toward the print triangles.

3 Sew 30 half-square-triangle units together for the top border. Be sure all of the print triangles face in the direction shown in the quilt assembly diagram. Repeat to make a strip for the bottom border.

4 Sew 32 half-square-triangle units together in the same manner for a side border. Make two side-border strips.

5 Referring to the assembly diagram, pin and sew the strips from step 4 to the sides of the quilt top. Press the seam allowances toward the muslin border.

6 Sew the border strips from step 3 to the top and bottom of the quilt top. Press the seam allowances toward the muslin border.

Finishing the Quilt

For help with any of the finishing steps, go to ShopMartingale.com/HowtoQuilt for free downloadable information.

1 Layer, baste, and quilt your quilt, or take it to your favorite long-arm machine quilter for finishing.

2 Using the yellow 2¼"-wide strips, make and attach binding.

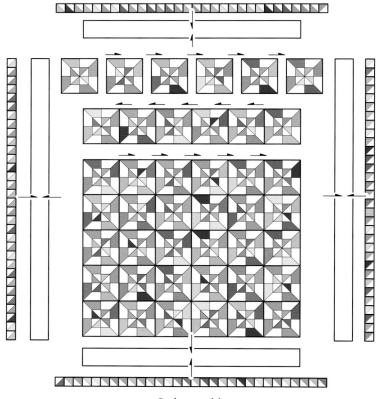

Quilt assembly

Sparkler

The pieced sashing strips make the half-square-triangle units in this quilt appear slightly asymmetrical, creating a bold, dynamic design. Use high-contrast fabrics for extra punch.

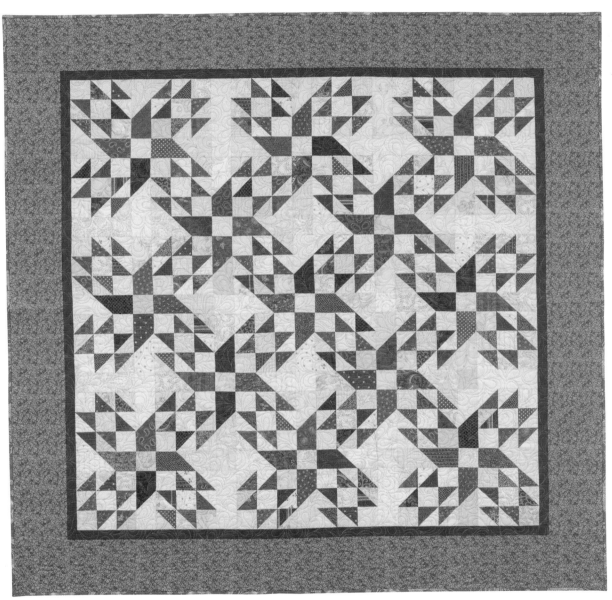

"Sparkler," designed and made by Kim Brackett

Finished quilt: 59½" x 59½"   ◆   **Finished block:** 6" x 6"

Materials

Yardage is based on 42"-wide fabric.

32 strips, 2½" x 42", of assorted cream prints for blocks and sashing

21 strips, 2½" x 42", of assorted red prints for blocks and sashing

1⅛ yards of medium-red print for outer border

⅓ yard of dark-red print for inner border

⅝ yard of red floral for binding

4¼ yards of fabric for backing

63½" x 63½" piece of batting

Cutting

All measurements include ¼"-wide seam allowances.

From *each* of 24 assorted cream strips, cut:
2 rectangles, 2½" x 4½" (48 total)
11 squares, 2½" x 2½" (264 total)

From *each* of the 8 remaining assorted light-cream strips, cut:
1 rectangle, 2½" x 6½" (8 total)
1 rectangle, 2½" x 4½" (8 total; 4 are extra)
11 squares, 2½" x 2½" (88 total; 3 are extra)

From *each* of 17 assorted red strips, cut:
3 rectangles, 2½" x 4½" (51 total)
10 squares, 2½" x 2½" (170 total)

From *each* of the 4 remaining assorted red strips, cut:
1 rectangle, 2½" x 4½" (4 total; 3 are extra)
13 squares, 2½" x 2½" (52 total; 6 are extra)

From the dark-red print, cut:
5 strips, 1½" x 42"

From the medium-red print, cut:
6 strips, 6" x 42"

From the red floral, cut:
7 strips, 2½" x 42"

Cutting from Scraps

If you prefer to use scraps, follow the instructions below. See "Cutting" at left for instructions on cutting the borders and binding.

From assorted red prints, cut:
216 squares, 2½" x 2½"
52 rectangles, 2½" x 4¼"

From assorted light prints, cut:
349 squares, 2½" x 2½"
8 rectangles, 2½" x 6½"
52 rectangles, 2½" x 4½"

Making the Blocks

1 Make a half-square-triangle unit using a red 2½" square and a cream 2½" square. Mark the diagonal on the wrong side of the cream square and sew ¼" to one side of the line. Trim, leaving a ¼" seam allowance. Press the seam allowances toward the red triangle. Make 216.

Make 216.

2 Sew two half-square-triangle units from step 1 to opposite sides of a cream 2½" square as shown. Press the seam allowances toward the cream square. Make 36.

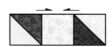

Make 36.

3 Sew together two half-square-triangle units from step 1 and a cream 2½" square. Press the seam allowances as shown. Make 72.

Make 72.

4 Sew together one unit from step 2 and two units from step 3 as shown. Press the seam allowances toward the units from step 2. Make 36 blocks.

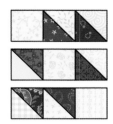 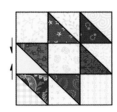

Make 36.

Making the Sashing Units

Using a red 2½" x 4½" rectangle and a cream 2½" x 4½" rectangle, make a split unit using the folded-corner method as shown. Place the two rectangles right sides together at right angles, matching the corners. Draw a diagonal line from corner to corner. Sew on the drawn line. Check to make sure you've sewn accurately, and then trim the excess corner fabric, leaving ¼" seam allowance. Press the seam allowances toward the red fabric. Make 52.

Make 52.

Assembling the Quilt Top

1 Arrange the blocks, pieced sashing units, cream 2½" x 6½" rectangles, and cream 2½" squares into horizontal rows as shown in the quilt assembly diagram below.

2 Sew the pieces together in rows, pressing the seam allowances as indicated. Sew the rows together. Press the seam allowances in one direction.

Adding the Borders

1 Sew the dark-red 1½"-wide strips to the quilt edges for the inner border.

2 Sew the medium-red 6"-wide strips to the quilt edges for the outer border.

Finishing the Quilt

For help with any of the finishing steps, go to ShopMartingale.com/HowtoQuilt for free downloadable information.

1 Layer, baste, and quilt your quilt, or take it to your favorite long-arm machine quilter for finishing.

2 Using the red-floral 2½"-wide strips, make and attach binding.

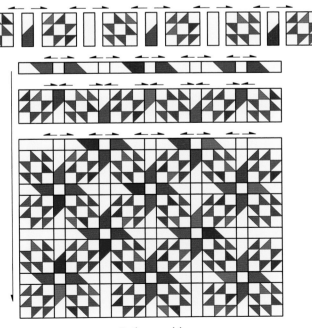

Quilt assembly

Autumn Splendor

You won't believe how easy this quilt is—it sure doesn't look it. Just sew the strips together, cut out the block from the strips, and the triangular shapes magically appear. You can use up lots of smaller scraps while getting ready for winter with this cozy quilt.

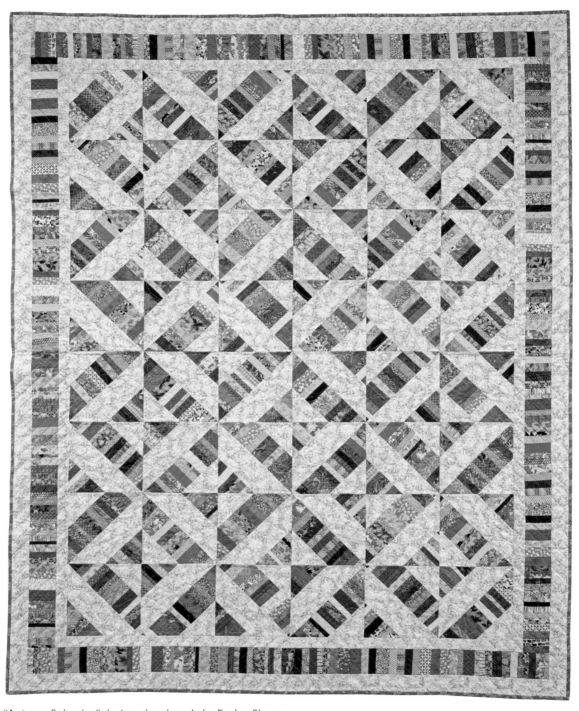

"Autumn Splendor," designed and made by Evelyn Sloppy

Finished quilt: 75" x 95" ◆ **Finished block: 10" x 10"**

▶ Materials

Yardage is based on 42"-wide fabric. Fat quarters are 18" x 21".

7¼ yards total of assorted autumn-colored scraps OR 29 fat quarters for blocks and middle border

4¼ yards of light-green print for blocks and inner and outer borders

¾ yard of fabric for binding

6¼ yards of fabric for backing

83" x 103" piece of batting

▶ Cutting

All measurements include ¼"-wide seam allowances.

From the assorted autumn-colored scraps or fat quarters, cut:

Approximately 1266 strips that vary in width from 1" to 2½" and are at least 5" long. You will need fewer strips if you use strips longer than 5". Strips that are at least 9" long will make 2 units, strips at least 13" long will make 3 units, and strips at least 17" long will make 4 units.

From the light-green print, cut:

24 strips, 4" x 42"
8 strips, 2" x 42"
9 strips, 3" x 42"

From the binding fabric, cut:

9 strips, 2½" x 42"

Making the Blocks

1 Sew the autumn-colored strips together along their long edges to make 24 string-pieced units that measure at least 5" wide and 40" long. Press the seam allowances in one direction. Trim each unit so that it measures exactly 4" wide.

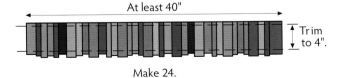

At least 40"

Trim to 4".

Make 24.

2 With right sides together, sew a 4"-wide light-green strip to each string-pieced unit from step 1

as shown. Press the seam allowances toward the green strip.

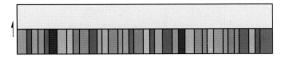

3 Place two units from step 2 right sides together, alternating the position of the green strips as shown. Stitch ¼" from both long edges. Repeat with the remaining units from step 2.

Place 2 units right sides together.

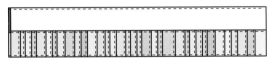

Stitch along both long edges.

4 Using a square ruler, line up the 10" mark on both sides of the ruler with the bottom seamline as shown; cut along both sides of the ruler. Rotate the ruler and continue cutting, rotating the ruler in the opposite direction with every cut. Each set of paired strips will yield 4 blocks. Cut 48 blocks.

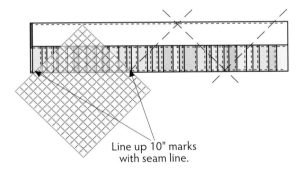

Line up 10" marks with seam line.

5 Remove any stitches at the point of each block. Open up each block and press the seam allowances toward the green strip. The blocks should measure 10" x 10".

Make 48.

Assembling the Quilt Top

1 Arrange the blocks in rows as shown, being sure to alternate the direction of each block.

2 Sew the blocks into rows. Press the seam allowances in opposite directions from row to row. Sew the rows together. Press the seam allowances in one direction.

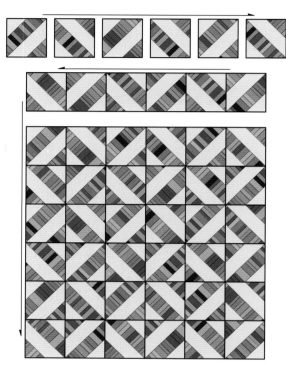

Quilt assembly

Adding the Borders

1 Sew the 2"-wide light-green strips to the quilt edges for the inner border.

2 Measure the length of the quilt top through the center and record the measurement. To make the pieced middle border, sew remaining autumn-colored strips together along the long edges, using as many as necessary to achieve a strip at least the length of the recorded measurement. Make two. Trim the strips to 4" wide and the correct length. Stitch the strips to the sides of the quilt. Press the seam allowances toward the inner border. In the same manner, measure the width of the quilt top through the center, including the borders you just added, and make two pieced strips for the top and bottom borders. Sew the strips to the top and bottom edges of the quilt. Press the seam allowances toward the inner border.

3 Sew the 3"-wide light-green strips to the quilt edges for the outer border.

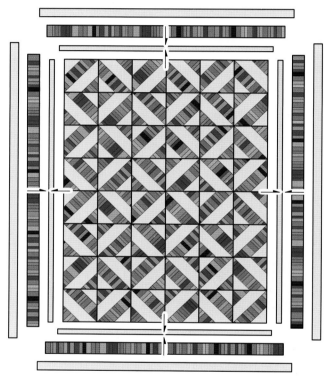

Adding the borders

Finishing the Quilt

For help with any of the finishing steps, go to ShopMartingale.com/HowtoQuilt for free downloadable information.

1 Layer, baste, and quilt your quilt, or take it to your favorite long-arm machine quilter for finishing.

2 Using the 2½"-wide strips, make and attach binding.

Plain Jane

Sparkling jewel-tone prints, a new twist on traditional blocks, and an abundance of quilting stitches come together to create this lap quilt that's anything but plain. Long on style and short on sewing time, this comfy quilt is one you'll want to keep within easy reach.

"Plain Jane," designed by Kim Diehl, pieced by Barbara Walsh and Kim Diehl, machine quilted by Deborah Poole

Finished quilt: 66½" x 72½" ◆ **Finished block:** 6" x 6"

▸ Materials

Yardage is based on 42"-wide fabric. Fat quarters are 18" x 21", fat eighths are 9" x 21", and chubby sixteenths are 9" x 11".

2 yards of blue print for border

30 chubby sixteenths of assorted medium and dark prints for Snowball Variation blocks

4 fat quarters of assorted light prints for Snowball Variation blocks

10 fat eighths of assorted light prints for Rail Fence Variation blocks

33 squares, 5" x 5", of assorted medium and dark prints for Rail Fence Variation blocks

3 squares, 2½" x 2½", of assorted medium and dark prints for Rail Fence Variation blocks

Enough 2½"-wide assorted medium- and dark-print strips in random lengths to equal 288" of binding when pieced together end to end

4¼ yards of fabric for backing

73" x 79" piece of batting

▸ Cutting

All measurements include ¼"-wide seam allowances. Cut all pieces across the width of the fabric except where noted.

From the *length* of each assorted-print chubby sixteenth, cut:
2 rectangles, 3½" x 11"; crosscut into 6 squares, 3½" x 3½" (combined total of 180)

From the *length* of each light-print fat quarter, cut:
6 strips, 2½" x 21"; crosscut into 45 squares, 2½" x 2½" (combined total of 180)

Cut the assorted-print 5" squares in half to yield:
2 rectangles, 2½" x 5" (combined total of 66)

From the *length* of each light-print fat eighth, cut:
3 strips, 2½" x 21"; crosscut into 9 rectangles, 2½" x 6½" (combined total of 90)

From the *lengthwise* grain of the blue print, cut:
2 strips, 6½" x 60½"
2 strips, 6½" x 66½"

Making the Snowball Variation Blocks

1 Use a pencil and an acrylic ruler to draw a diagonal line on the wrong side of each light 2½" square. Layer a prepared square over one corner of an medium- or dark-print 3½" square. Stitch the pair together on the drawn line. Press and trim the resulting corner triangle. Repeat to make a total of 180 pieced squares.

Make 180.

2 Lay out four pieced squares to make a Snowball Variation block. Join the squares in each row. Press the seam allowances in opposite directions. Join the rows. Press the seam allowances open. Repeat to make a total of 45 Snowball Variation blocks measuring 6½" square, including seam allowances.

Make 45.

Making the Rail Fence Variation Blocks

1 Select three assorted-print 2½" x 5" rectangles. Join the rectangles along the long edges to make a strip set. Press the seam allowances toward the middle rectangle. Crosscut the strip set at the center point to make two strip-set units measuring 2½" x 6½". Repeat to make a total of 44 strip-set units.

Cut each strip set in half.
Make 44 strip-set units.

2 Select one strip-set unit and two light 2½" x 6½" rectangles. Join a light rectangle to each long edge of the unit. Press the seam allowances toward the strip-set unit. Repeat to make a total of 44 Rail Fence Variation blocks measuring 6½" square, including seam allowances.

Make 44.

3 Sew together the three assorted-print 2½" squares to make a pieced rectangle. Press the seam allowances toward the center square. Use this pieced rectangle and the two remaining light rectangles to make one additional Rail Fence Variation block as instructed in step 2.

Assembling the Quilt Top

When laying out the Rail Fence Variation blocks to make the pieced rows, take care to rotate some or all of the blocks with a repeated pieced center rectangle so that the top and bottom positions are reversed. Doing this will give the illusion of using many more unique blocks and create added variety in the look of your patchwork.

1 Lay out five Snowball Variation blocks and four Rail Fence Variation blocks in alternating positions. Join the blocks to form row A. Press the seam allowances toward the Rail Fence blocks. Repeat to make a total of five A rows.

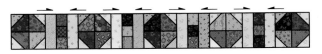

Row A.
Make 5.

2 Lay out five Rail Fence Variation blocks and four Snowball Variation blocks in alternating positions. Join the blocks to form row B. Press the seam allowances toward the Rail Fence blocks. Repeat to make a total of five B rows.

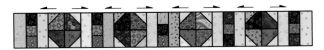

Row B.
Make 5.

3 Beginning with an A row, lay out the A and B rows in alternating positions. Join the rows. Press the seam allowances toward the B rows. The pieced quilt center should measure 54½" x 60½", including seam allowances.

Adding the Border

Join the blue 6½" x 60½" strips to the right and left sides of the quilt center. Press the seam allowances toward the blue print. Join the blue 6½" x 66½" strips to the top and bottom of the quilt center. Press the seam allowances toward the border. The pieced quilt top should now measure 66½" x 72½", including seam allowances.

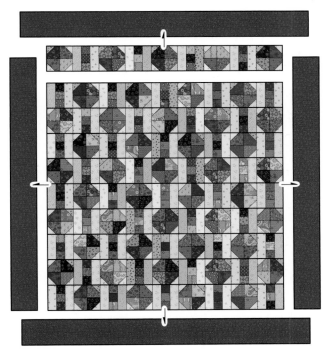

Quilt assembly

Finishing the Quilt

For help with any of the finishing steps, go to ShopMartingale.com/HowtoQuilt for free downloadable information.

1 Layer, baste, and quilt your quilt, or take it to your favorite long-arm machine quilter for finishing.

2 Join the 2½"-wide random lengths of assorted prints into one strip and use it to bind the quilt.

Churn Dash Weave

Many old-time quilt blocks were named for common household items, such as a butter churn. But what's a churn dash? Well, apparently **dash** signifies the sound of plunking or, in this case, the sound of the slurping that the plunger made when pounded into and pulled out of the butter churn. Here, the unifying light fabric weaves all the blocks together.

"Churn Dash Weave," designed and made by Mary Etherington and Connie Tesene

Finished quilt: 35½" x 45½"   ◆   **Finished block:** 5" x 5"

Materials

Yardage is based on 42"-wide fabric.

1¾ yards *total* of assorted dark-print scraps
   for blocks

1 yard *total* of assorted medium-print scraps
   for blocks

¾ yard *total* of assorted light-print scraps
   for blocks

⅓ yard of navy solid for binding*

1½ yards of fabric for backing

39" x 49" piece of batting

The quilt shown features a binding of blue velveteen.

Cutting

All measurements include ¼"-wide seam allowances.

Cutting for 1 Churn Dash Block

From *1* of the dark prints, cut:
2 squares, 2⅞" x 2⅞"; cut in half diagonally to yield
   4 triangles
4 squares, 1½" x 1½"

From *1* of the medium prints, cut:
2 squares, 2⅞" x 2⅞"; cut in half diagonally to yield
   4 triangles

From *1* of the light prints, cut:
5 squares, 1½" x 1½"

Cutting for Binding

From the navy solid, cut:
5 strips, 2¼" x 42"

Making the Blocks

Use one light, one medium, and one dark print for
each block.

1 Sew a medium 2⅞" triangle to a dark 2⅞" triangle.
Press the seam allowances toward the dark
triangle. Make four units.

Make 4.

2 Sew a light 1½" square to a dark 1½" square.
Press the seam allowances toward the dark
square. Make two units. Sew three light 1½" squares
and two dark 1½" squares into a row. Press the seam
allowances toward the dark squares.

Make 2.   Make 1.

3 Sew the units from steps 1 and 2 together. Press
the seam allowances as indicated. The block
should measure 5½" x 5½". Make 63 blocks.

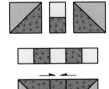

Make 63.

Assembling the Quilt Top

1 Arrange the blocks in nine rows of seven blocks each.

2 Sew the blocks together in rows, pressing the seam allowances in opposite directions from row to row. Join the rows. Press the seam allowances in one direction.

Finishing the Quilt

For help with any of the finishing steps, go to ShopMartingale.com/HowtoQuilt for free downloadable information.

1 Layer, baste, and quilt your quilt, or take it to your favorite long-arm machine quilter for finishing.

2 Using the navy 2¼"-wide strips, make and attach binding.

Quilt assembly

Neighbor's Fence

Made up of a variation on a classic Rail Fence *block, this quilt couldn't be any easier to piece! It's amazingly versatile: cozy in woodsy flannel prints and plaids, serene in Asian and textured tone-on-tone prints, or a real beach party in batiks. This quilt shines brightly in any fabric combination. Leftover blocks form a generous buffet runner or child's quilt.*

"Neighbor's Fence," designed by Anne Moscicki; pieced by Denise Bohbot, Laura Evans, Deb Hollister, Sybil Houghton, Karen Martinsson, Kyle McAvoy, Anne Moscicki, Kathy Roethle, Julia Teters, Mimi Teters, Cora Tunberg, and Linda Wyckoff; quilted by Celeste Marshall

Finished quilt: 62" x 74" ◆ **Finished block: 6" x 6"**

Materials

Yardage is based on 42"-wide fabric.

¼ yard *each* of 16 assorted prints for Duo blocks and Trio blocks

⅛ yard *each* of 8 assorted prints for Trio blocks

½ yard of gold fabric for stars and border corner squares

½ yard of fabric for inner border

1¼ yards of fabric for outer border

⅝ yard of fabric for binding

4 yards of fabric for backing

72" x 84" piece of batting

¾ yard of paper-backed fusible web

Cutting

All measurements include ¼"-wide seam allowances.

From *each* ¼-yard piece, cut:
1 strip, 2½" x 42" (16 total)
1 strip, 3½" x 42" (16 total)

From *each* ⅛-yard piece, cut:
1 strip, 2½" x 42" (8 total)

From the gold fabric, cut:
2 strips, 6" x 42"; crosscut into 12 squares, 6" x 6"
4 squares, 6½" x 6½"

From the inner-border fabric, cut:
9 strips, 1½" x 42"; crosscut 1 strip into 4 rectangles, 1½" x 6½"

From the outer-border fabric, cut:
6 strips, 6½" x 42"

From the binding fabric, cut:
7 strips, 2½" x 42"

Making the Duo Blocks

1. Arrange the 3½"-wide strips into eight pairs and sew the strips in each pair together. Press the seam allowances in either direction.

2. Crosscut each strip set into six 6½" squares until you have at least 40 Duo blocks.

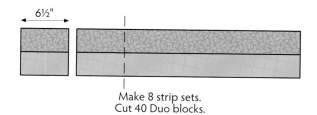

Make 8 strip sets.
Cut 40 Duo blocks.

Making the Trio Blocks

1. Arrange the 2½"-wide strips into eight sets of three strips each. Sew the strips in each set together. Press the seam allowances in either direction.

2. Crosscut each strip set into six 6½" squares until you have at least 40 Trio blocks.

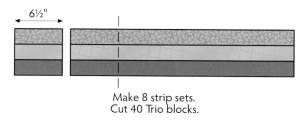

Make 8 strip sets.
Cut 40 Trio blocks.

Adding the Stars

1. Choose a dozen quilt blocks on which to fuse the stars. They may be either Duo blocks or Trio blocks.

2. To create your star template, begin by tracing or making a photocopy of the square pattern on page 30. Mark two dots anywhere on the bottom edge of the square, and mark one dot anywhere on each of the three remaining sides. Connect the dots as shown in the illustration following step 3. Cut out the star template on the lines.

3. Trace 12 star shapes onto the paper side of the fusible web. Cut out each shape slightly beyond the traced lines. Follow the fusible-web instructions to press each star, paper side up, onto the wrong side of a gold 6" square. Cut out the 12 stars on the lines.

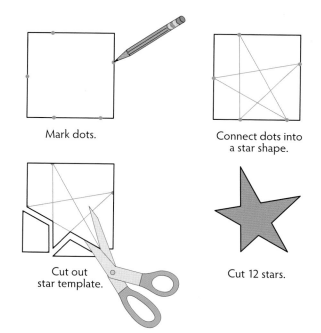

Mark dots.

Connect dots into a star shape.

Cut out star template.

Cut 12 stars.

4 Peel off the paper backing and arrange the stars at jaunty angles on your chosen blocks. Press. Secure the edges with a machine decorative stitch.

Assembling the Quilt Top

1 Lay out all the blocks on a bed or the floor, alternating the direction of the Duo blocks and the Trio blocks to form a checkerboard pattern. As you lay out the quilt, take time to distribute the stars in a pleasing way.

2 Sew the blocks into rows, pressing all seam allowances toward the Trio blocks to reduce bulk in the finished quilt top. Join the rows. Press the row seam allowances open.

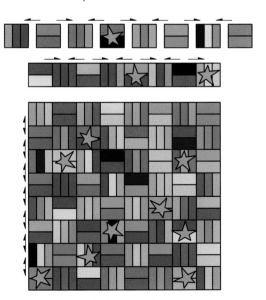

Quilt assembly

Adding the Borders

1 Sew the 6½"-wide outer-border strips together end to end. Measure the quilt top from side to side, and cut two strips to that measurement for the top and bottom of the quilt.

2 Sew a 1½" x 6½" rectangle of inner-border fabric to one side of each gold 6½" square to form a corner unit. Join a corner unit to each end of the top and bottom outer-border strips as shown in the diagram below.

3 Sew the 1½"-wide inner-border strips together end to end. Measure the quilt from top to bottom, and cut two strips each from the inner- and outer-border pieced strips to that measurement. Sew the side inner and outer borders to the quilt top.

4 Stitch the top and bottom inner borders to the quilt and trim the ends evenly. Add the top and bottom outer borders, pinning to match the vertical inner-border strips.

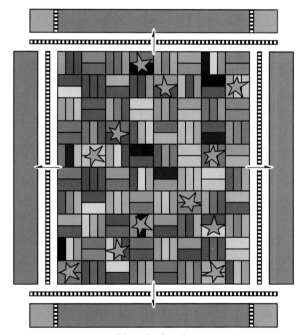

Adding the borders

Finishing the Quilt

For help with any of the finishing steps, go to ShopMartingale.com/HowtoQuilt for free downloadable information.

1 Layer, baste, and quilt your quilt, or take it to your favorite long-arm machine quilter for finishing.

2 Using the 2½"-wide strips, make and attach binding.

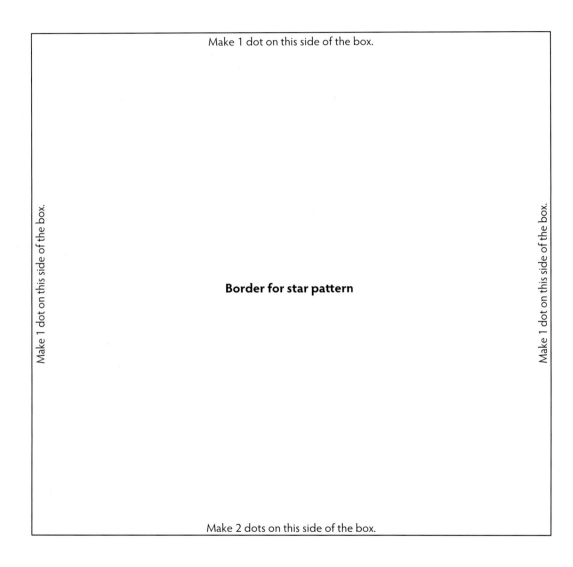

Make 1 dot on this side of the box.

Make 1 dot on this side of the box.

Border for star pattern

Make 1 dot on this side of the box.

Make 2 dots on this side of the box.

Oso

Carrie thought these looked like T blocks, but her mom thought they looked like Bear's Paw blocks. As Carrie says, "From June Cleaver to Mrs. Cunningham, moms are always right." So this quilt needed a Bear's Paw–appropriate name, and oso *is Spanish for "bear."*

"Oso," designed by Carrie Nelson, pieced by Judy Adams, machine quilted by Diane Tricka

Finished quilt: 76" x 91"   ◆   **Finished block:** 10½" x 10½"

Materials

Yardage is based on 42"-wide fabric.

1⅞ yards of cream print for block backgrounds

2¼ yards of tan print for block backgrounds and setting triangles

34 assorted squares, 10" x 10", for borders

32 assorted squares, 10" x 10", for blocks

¾ yard of fabric for binding

7½ yards of fabric for backing

84" x 99" piece of batting

Cutting

All measurements include ¼"-wide seam allowances.

From the cream print, cut:
5 strips, 10" x 42"; crosscut into 20 squares, 10" x 10"
3 strips, 4" x 42"; crosscut into 20 squares, 4" x 4"

From the tan print, cut:
3 strips, 10" x 42"; crosscut into 12 squares, 10" x 10"
2 strips, 16¾" x 42"; crosscut into:
    4 squares, 16¾" x 16¾"; cut into quarters diagonally to yield 16 side triangles (2 are extra)
    8 squares, 4" x 4"
1 strip, 8¾" x 42"; crosscut into:
    2 squares, 8¾" x 8¾"; cut in half diagonally to yield 4 corner triangles
    4 squares, 4" x 4"

From *each* of the 34 assorted squares for borders, cut:
1 strip, 4" x 10" (34 total; 4 are extra)
1 strip, 5" x 10" (34 total)

From the binding fabric, cut:
2"-wide bias strips to make 350" of bias binding

Making the Blocks

For each block, you'll need the following pieces:

    From cream or tan background: one 10" square and one 4" square

    From assorted squares: one 10" square

Use a scant ¼"-wide seam allowance throughout. After sewing each seam, press the seam allowances in the direction indicated by the arrows (or press them open if you prefer).

1 Use Carrie's special technique to make one large half-square-triangle unit and four small half-square-triangle units at the same time. Pair a 10" cream or tan background square with an assorted square. Draw a diagonal line from corner to corner on the wrong side of the lighter square. Draw a second diagonal line from one corner to the center of the square as shown.

2 Draw a horizontal line and a vertical line from the center of the square to the outer edge as shown. All of the drawn lines are cutting lines, not stitching lines.

3 Layer the marked square with the darker square, right sides together and raw edges aligned. Stitch a scant ¼" from each side of the diagonal lines as shown.

4 Cut the squares apart on the drawn lines. Trim the large half-square-triangle unit to measure 7½" square. Trim the small half-square-triangle units to measure 4" square. (Note: If you're making 12" blocks, trim the units to 8½" square and 4½" square.)

5 Lay out the units from step 4 and a 4" cream or tan background square as shown. Join the pieces into rows, and then sew the rows together to complete the block. The block should measure 11" x 11". Repeat to make a total of 20 cream blocks and 12 tan blocks.

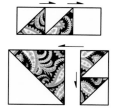 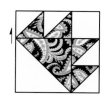

Make 20. Make 12.

Assembling the Quilt Top

1 Lay out the cream blocks, tan blocks, side triangles, and corner triangles in diagonal rows as shown. Sew the pieces together into rows. Press the seam allowances in opposite directions from row to row (or press them open).

2 Sew the rows together and press the seam allowances in one direction. And yes, the setting triangles have purposely been cut a bit oversized.

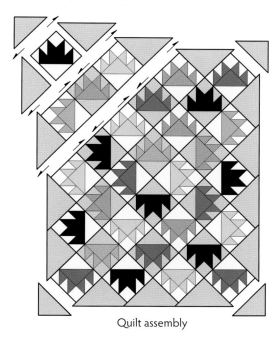

Quilt assembly

Adding the Borders

1 Before attaching the borders, trim and straighten the quilt top. Align the ¼" line on your long ruler with the outermost points of the blocks. Use a rotary cutter to trim any excess fabric, leaving a ¼" seam allowance and making sure the corners are square. (Carrie prefers to leave ⅜" to float the corners of the blocks just a bit.) The trimmed quilt should measure 60" x 75".

2 For the inner border, sort the 4" x 10" strips into the following groups:

Side borders: two groups of eight strips each

Top and bottom borders: two groups of seven strips each

Join each group of strips end to end to make four long strips. Press the seam allowances in one direction (or press them open). For the side borders, trim the longer strips to measure 4" x 75". For the top and bottom borders, trim the shorter strips to measure 4" x 67".

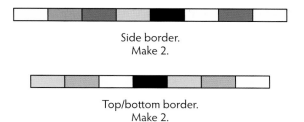

Side border.
Make 2.

Top/bottom border.
Make 2.

3 Sew the pieced inner-border strips to the sides, and then to the top and bottom edges of the quilt top. Press the seam allowances toward the inner border.

4 For the outer border, sort the 5" x 10" strips into the following groups:

Side borders: two groups of nine strips each

Top and bottom borders: two groups of eight strips each

Join each group of strips end to end to make four long strips. Press the seam allowances in one direction (or press them open). For the side borders, trim the longer strips to measure 5" x 82". For the top and bottom borders, trim the shorter strips to measure 5" x 76".

5 Sew the pieced outer-border strips to the sides, and then to the top and bottom edges of the quilt top. Press the seam allowances toward the outer border.

Finishing the Quilt

For help with any of the finishing steps, go to ShopMartingale.com/HowtoQuilt for free downloadable information.

1 Layer, baste, and quilt your quilt, or take it to your favorite long-arm machine quilter for finishing.

2 Using the 2"-wide bias strips, make and attach binding.

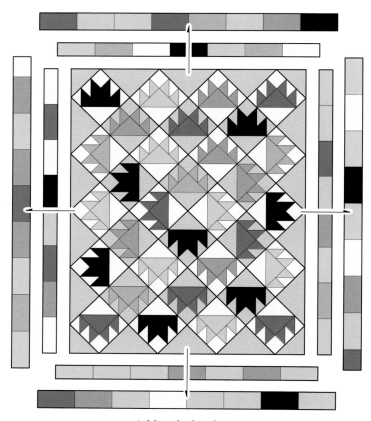

Adding the borders

Shoofly Pie

Whip together this quilt using two simple blocks—the Shoofly and the Half-Square Triangle. The blocks are created from either dark or light fabrics and arranged on the diagonal, resulting in a strong graphic design with a wonderful country appeal.

"Shoofly Pie," designed and pieced by Cheryl Wall, machine quilted by Linda Lang

Finished quilt: 70" x 70" ◆ **Finished block:** 6" x 6"

Materials

Yardage is based on 42"-wide fabric.

2⅞ yards *total* of assorted dark prints and plaids for blocks and setting triangles

2⅞ yards *total* of assorted light prints and plaids for blocks and setting triangles

1 yard of dark plaid for outer border

⅜ yard of light print for inner border

1 square, 10" x 10", of black print for border corner squares

⅝ yard of fabric for binding

4½ yards of fabric for backing

78" x 78" piece of batting

Cutting

All measurements include ¼"-wide seam allowances.

From the assorted dark prints and plaids, cut a *total* of:
24 sets of 5 matching squares, 2½" x 2½" (120 total)
24 sets of 8 matching squares, 2½" x 2½" (192 total)
7 squares, 5⅛" x 5⅛"; cut in half diagonally to yield 14 triangles
21 squares, 6⅞" x 6⅞"; cut 3 in half diagonally to yield 6 triangles

From the assorted light prints and plaids, cut a *total* of:
25 sets of 5 matching squares, 2½" x 2½" (125 total)
25 sets of 8 matching squares, 2½" x 2½" (200 total)
7 squares, 5⅛" x 5⅛"; cut in half diagonally to yield 14 triangles
21 squares, 6⅞" x 6⅞"; cut 3 in half diagonally to yield 6 triangles

From the light inner-border print, cut:
7 strips, 1½" x 42"

From the black print, cut:
4 squares, 4½" x 4½"

From the dark plaid for outer border, cut:
7 strips, 4½" x 42"

From the binding fabric, cut:
8 strips, 2¼" x 42"

Making the Shoofly Blocks

Directions are written for making one block at a time. After sewing each seam, press the seam allowances in the direction indicated by the arrows.

1 Choose five matching dark 2½" squares and eight matching 2½" squares from a contrasting dark fabric.

2 Pair four dark 2½" squares with four 2½" squares of a contrasting dark fabric, right sides together. Sew the pairs together to make four half-square-triangle units.

Make 4.

3 Arrange the half-square-triangle units and the remaining 2½" squares in rows as shown. Sew the squares in each row together, and then sew the rows together.

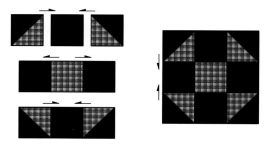

4 Repeat steps 1–3 to make 24 dark Shoofly blocks.

5 Repeat steps 1–3 using light fabrics to make 25 light Shoofly blocks.

Pleasing Pairings

When using two different dark or light fabrics in one block, you can create interest by pairing prints with stripes or plaids in different colors.

Making the Half-Square Triangle Blocks

1 With right sides together, pair one dark 6⅞" square with one 6⅞" square of a contrasting dark fabric. On the wrong side of one of the squares, draw a diagonal line with a fine pencil.

2 Sew ¼" from each side of the diagonal line. Cut apart along the line to make blocks. Press seam allowances toward the darker fabric.

 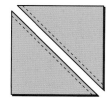

3 Repeat steps 1 and 2 to make 18 dark Half-Square Triangle blocks.

Make 18.

4 Repeat steps 1 and 2 using light fabrics to make 18 light Half-Square Triangle blocks.

Make 18.

Assembling the Quilt Top

1 Using triangles cut from 5⅛" squares, pair 12 dark and 12 light triangles as shown and sew them together, making six dark and six light pieced setting triangles.

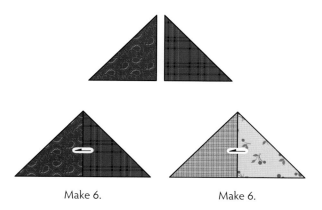

Make 6.   Make 6.

2 Arrange the blocks and setting triangles in diagonal rows as shown. The pieced setting triangles should be positioned along the top and bottom edges of the quilt.

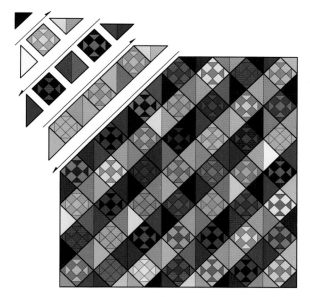

Quilt assembly

3 Sew the squares and setting triangles in each row together. When sewing the pieces in the upper rows together, sew from the bottom edge toward the top edge. When sewing the setting triangles to the blocks, begin sewing at the triangle's right-angle corner rather than from the triangle point.

4 Sew the rows together, matching the seam intersections.

5 Sew the remaining 5⅛" triangles to the corners. Handle the quilt top gently to avoid stretching the sides of the quilt. Square up the corners, if necessary.

Adding the Borders

1 Sew the light 1½"-wide inner-border strips together end to end. Measure the width of the quilt top through the center and cut two inner-border strips to that length. Sew the strips to the top and bottom edges of the quilt top.

2 Measure the length of the quilt top, including the borders just added, and cut two inner-border strips to that length. Sew the strips to the sides of the quilt top.

3 Sew the dark 4½"-wide outer-border strips together end to end. Measure the length and width of the quilt top through the center and cut four outer-border strips to those measurements. Sew the strips to the top and bottom edges of the quilt top.

4 Sew a black-print 4½" square to each end of the two remaining outer-border strips. Sew these strips to the sides of the quilt top, matching the seam intersections.

Finishing the Quilt

For help with any of the finishing steps, go to ShopMartingale.com/HowtoQuilt for free downloadable information.

1 Layer, baste, and quilt your quilt, or take it to your favorite long-arm machine quilter for finishing.

2 Using the 2¼"-wide strips, make and attach binding.

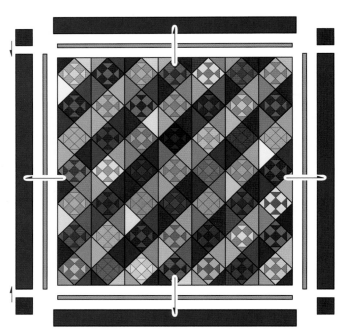

Adding the borders

Walled Garden

This quilt is essentially pink and brown with some green thrown in, a color scheme that seems to be a perennial favorite. Whatever colors you choose, try using a mixture of fat quarters, fat eighths, and leftovers from other projects to make good use of your stash and achieve a really scrappy look.

"Walled Garden," designed and made by Sheila Sinclair Snyder

Finished quilt: 80½" x 96½" ◆ **Finished block: 8" x 8"**

▶ Materials

Yardage is based on 42"-wide fabric.

½ yard *each* of 20 assorted pink prints for blocks and border

4½ yards *total* of assorted dark prints in green, brown, and burgundy for blocks and border

⅞ yard of fabric for binding

7½ yards of fabric for backing

86" x 102" piece of batting

Freezer paper or template plastic

▶ Cutting

All measurements include ¼"-wide seam allowances.

From *each* of the 20 assorted pink prints, cut:
8 squares, 4½" x 4½" (160 total)
2 strips, 2½" x 42"; crosscut into 20 squares, 2½" x 2½" (400 total)
2 squares, 4⅞" x 4⅞"; cut in half diagonally to yield 4 triangles (80 total)

From the assorted dark prints, cut a *total* of:
400 squares, 2½" x 2½" (80 sets of 4 matching squares for center blocks and 40 sets of 2 matching squares for border blocks)
48 strips, 1½" x 42"

From the binding fabric, cut:
9 strips, 2" x 42"

Making the Double Four-Patch Blocks

1 Sew two matching pink 2½" squares to two matching dark-print 2½" squares as shown to make a four-patch unit. Make two.

Make 2.

2 Arrange two matching pink 4½" squares with the units from step 1, noting the placement of the dark squares. Sew the squares and four-patch units together in rows. Press the seam allowances toward the pink squares. Sew the two rows together to form a Double Four-Patch block; press the seam allowances to one side.

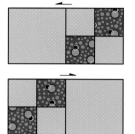 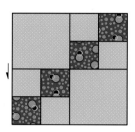

Make 80.

3 Repeat steps 1 and 2 to make a total of 80 Double Four-Patch blocks.

Making the Border Blocks

Each block used around the perimeter of the quilt is made from two pieced triangles. One triangle consists of a four-patch unit and two smaller triangles. The other, a Roman Stripe triangle, is made of strips. The border blocks are the same size as the Double Four-Patch blocks.

1 Arrange the dark-print 1½" x 42" strips into eight sets of six strips each, varying the color placement in each strip set. Sew the strip sets together and carefully press the seam allowances open. You might want to use spray starch or sizing at this step to help keep the strips straight and stabilized throughout the piecing process.

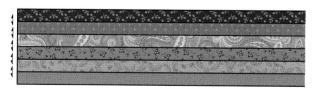

Make 8 strip sets.

Sheila loves the intricate look this border gives to the quilt. First, it finishes the visual effect of the diagonal patchwork chain by using a four-patch unit on one side of the blocks. Then the scrappy, strippy triangles on the other side of the blocks act as a darker zigzag frame around the whole quilt. Each border block is the same size as the blocks in the quilt center, so when you're done sewing the rows together, the border is already attached.

2 Make a guide for cutting the Roman Stripe triangle by drawing an 8⅞" square onto freezer paper or template plastic. Draw a line from corner to corner diagonally and cut out the resulting triangles. If you're using freezer paper, repeat to cut six or eight triangles; you can reuse each one several times.

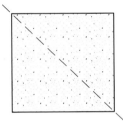

3 Press the freezer-paper triangles to the strip sets and cut the Roman Stripe triangles as shown using the freezer-paper triangles or a triangle ruler as a cutting guide. If you're using template plastic, draw around the triangle and cut on the drawn lines. You should be able to cut five triangles from each strip set. Cut 40 triangles.

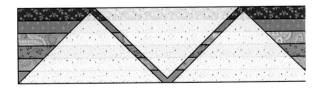

4 Sew two matching pink 2½" squares to two matching dark-print 2½" squares as shown to make a four-patch unit. Make 40.

Make 40.

5 Arrange and sew two matching pink 4⅞" triangles to each four-patch unit, noting the placement of the dark squares. Press the seam allowances toward the pink triangles. Make 40.

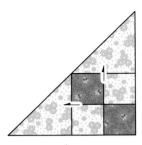

Make 40.

6 Sew a four-patch triangle to a Roman Stripe triangle to form a square block. Press the seam allowances toward the Roman Stripe. Handle the block carefully to avoid stretching the bias edges of the Roman Stripe triangle. Make 40 border blocks.

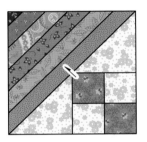

Make 40.

Check Your Ruler Stash

If you have a half-square-triangle ruler that goes up to the number 8 along the side, you can use that to cut triangles from the strip sets—no cutting guide or template needed! Simply place the long edge of the triangle ruler along the edge of the strip set and cut around the two short sides with your rotary cutter.

Assembling the Quilt Top

1 Arrange the Double Four-Patch blocks in 10 rows of eight blocks each, carefully positioning them so that the dark squares form a chain. Rearrange the blocks until you're satisfied with the placement.

2 Arrange the border blocks around the perimeter, referring to the quilt assembly diagram below. The Roman Stripe half of each block will create a stunning "border" around your quilt.

3 Sew the blocks together into rows. Press the seam allowances in opposite directions from row to row.

4 Sew the rows together. Press the seam allowances in one direction.

Finishing the Quilt

For help with any of the finishing steps, go to ShopMartingale.com/HowtoQuilt for free downloadable information.

1 Layer, baste, and quilt your quilt, or take it to your favorite long-arm machine quilter for finishing.

2 Using the 2"-wide strips, make and attach binding.

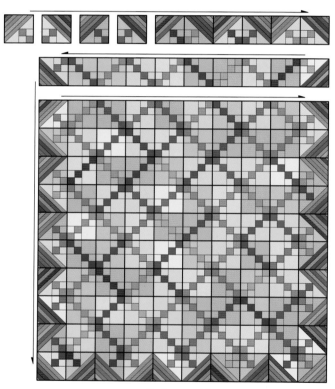

Quilt assembly

Scrappy Rectangles

Jo sometimes calls this quilt "2" x 3½" Scrappy Quilt" for the size of each piece used. She recommends making it from scraps. However, she's also made it with half-yard pieces of 18 different fabrics. Since there are 18 rectangles in each block, you can use a different fabric for each rectangle.

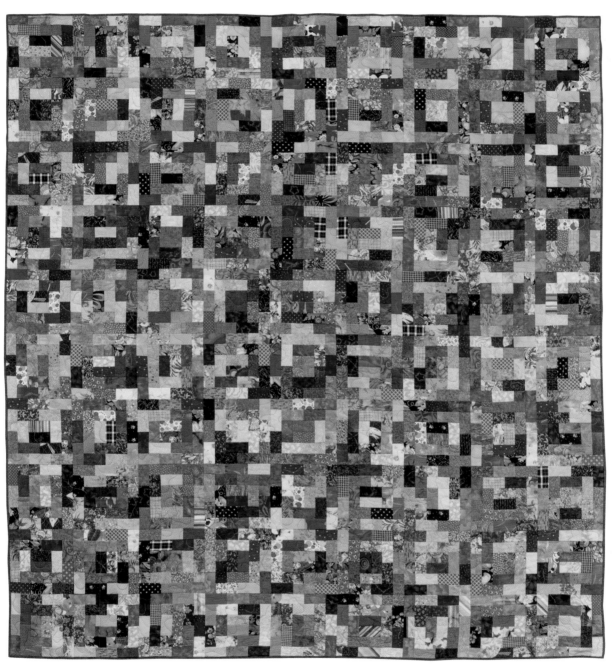

"Scrappy Rectangles," designed and made by Jo Parrott
Finished quilt: 81½" x 90½"   ◆   Finished block: 9" x 9"

▶ Materials

Yardage is based on 42"-wide fabric.

8⅝ yards *total* of assorted scraps for blocks

⅔ yard of fabric for binding

8 yards of fabric for backing*

87" x 96" piece of batting

If your backing fabric is 108" wide, you'll need only 2⅞ yards.

▶ Cutting

All measurements include ¼"-wide seam allowances.

From the assorted scraps, cut a *total* of:
1620 rectangles, 2" x 3½"

From the binding fabric, cut:
9 strips, 2¼" x 42"

Making the Blocks

Directions are for making one block. Repeat to make a total of 90 blocks. You may want to assembly-line sew the blocks in groups, making four or five blocks at a time. After sewing each seam, press the seam allowances as indicated by the arrows.

1 Sew two rectangles together along their long sides. Sew rectangles to the top and bottom.

 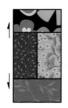

2 Sew two rectangles together end to end. Make two and sew them to the sides of the unit from step 1.

3 Sew two rectangles together end to end. Make two and sew them to the top and bottom of the unit from step 2.

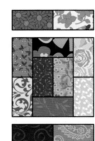 

4 Sew three rectangles together end to end. Make two and sew them to the sides of the unit from step 3. Make a total of 90 blocks.

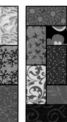  

Make 90.

Fabric Selection

You can tackle the fabric selection and cutting in a number of ways. When you cut out fabric for other quilt projects, immediately cut some 2" x 3½" rectangles from scraps as you go so that you'll have them for a quilt such as this one. If you don't have lots of scraps, fat quarters (which are 18" x 21") are a good option. You'll need 36 fat quarters to make all of the blocks. As you cut, just put all the rectangles in the same box and don't pay attention to which pieces you're sewing together.

You can easily make this quilt larger or smaller—just make more or fewer blocks. You'll need 30 blocks to make a 45" x 54" crib or lap quilt. For a king-size quilt, 108" x 108", make 144 blocks. To determine how many rectangles to cut, multiply the number of blocks by 18.

Assembling the Quilt Top

1 Arrange the blocks in 10 rows of nine blocks each, rotating every other block 90° as shown in the quilt assembly diagram.

2 Sew the blocks into rows. Press the seam allowances in opposite directions from row to row. Sew the rows together and press the seam allowances in one direction.

3 Baste around the quilt top ⅛" from the outer edge to stabilize the seams, being careful not to stretch the seams as you sew.

Finishing the Quilt

For help with any of the finishing steps, go to ShopMartingale.com/HowtoQuilt for free downloadable information.

1 Layer, baste, and quilt your quilt, or take it to your favorite long-arm machine quilter for finishing.

2 Using the 2¼"-wide strips, make and attach binding.

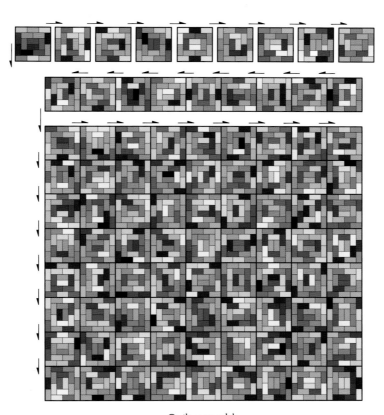

Quilt assembly

Generations

You can use the last tiny bits of some of your favorite fabrics in this quilt. Select high-contrast lights and darks to make sure the design doesn't become lost. Or use a single background fabric for even more definition.

"Generations," designed and pieced by Kim Brackett, quilted by Nancy Troyer

Finished quilt: 59½" x 75½" ◆ **Finished block:** 6" x 6"

▶ Materials

Yardage is based on 42"-wide fabric.

26 strips, 2½" x 42", of assorted dark prints in red, blue, brown, green, gold, and black for blocks and sashing

28 strips, 2½" x 42", of assorted light prints in tan, beige, and cream for blocks and sashing

1⅓ yards of blue print for outer border

1 yard of brown print for inner border and binding

4¼ yards of fabric for backing

64" x 80" piece of batting

▶ Cutting

All measurements include ¼"-wide seam allowances.

From *each of 18* assorted dark-print strips, cut:
4 rectangles, 2½" x 4½" (72 total)
8 squares, 2½" x 2½" (144 total)

From *each of 8* assorted dark-print strips, cut:
3 rectangles, 2½" x 4½" (24 total)
10 squares, 2½" x 2½" (80 total; 5 are extra)

From *each of 21* assorted light-print strips, cut:
3 rectangles, 2½" x 6½" (63 total)
2 rectangles, 2½" x 4½" (42 total)
4 squares, 2½" x 2½" (84 total)

From *each of 7* assorted light-print strips, cut:
3 rectangles, 2½" x 6½" (21 total; 2 are extra)
1 rectangle, 2½" x 4½" (7 total; 1 is extra)
5 squares, 2½" x 2½" (35 total; 5 are extra)

From the brown print, cut:
6 strips, 1½" x 42"
8 strips, 2½" x 42"

From the blue print, cut:
7 strips, 6" x 42"

Making the Blocks

1 Sew a dark 2½" x 4½" rectangle to a light 2½" square. Press the seam allowances toward the dark rectangle. Make two.

Make 2.

2 Sew a light 2½" x 4½" rectangle to a dark 2½" square. Press the seam allowances toward the light rectangle.

Make 1.

3 Sew the units from steps 1 and 2 together as shown to make the block. Press the seam allowances toward the unit from step 2. Make a total of 48 blocks.

Make 48.

Making the Sashing Units

1 Make a folded-corner unit as shown by sewing a dark 2½" square to a light 2½" x 6½" rectangle along the diagonal of the square. Trim the excess fabric from the corner, leaving a ¼" seam allowance, and press the unit open. Make 10.

Make 10.

Cutting from Scraps

If you prefer to use scraps, follow the instructions below. See "Cutting" above left for instructions on cutting the borders and binding.

From assorted dark prints, cut:
96 rectangles, 2½" x 4½"
219 squares, 2½" x 2½"

From assorted light prints, cut:
82 rectangles, 2½" x 6½"
48 rectangles, 2½" x 4½"
114 squares, 2½" x 2½"

2 Make a folded-corner unit as shown using a light 2½" x 6½" rectangle and two dark 2½" squares. Press. Make 72.

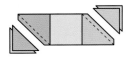

Make 72.

Assembling the Quilt Top

1 Arrange the blocks, pieced sashing units, and remaining light and dark 2½" squares in rows as shown.

2 Sew the units together in horizontal rows, pressing the seam allowances as shown. Join the rows. Press the seam allowances toward the sashing rows.

Adding the Borders

1 Join the brown 1½"-wide strips end to end. Measure the quilt top and cut two inner side borders to this length. Sew them to the quilt top. Measure the width of the quilt top, cut two border strips to this length, and add them to the top and bottom of the quilt top. Press all seam allowances toward the borders.

2 Repeat to add the blue 6"-wide outer border to the quilt top.

Finishing the Quilt

For help with any of the finishing steps, go to ShopMartingale.com/HowtoQuilt for free downloadable information.

1 Layer, baste, and quilt your quilt, or take it to your favorite long-arm machine quilter for finishing.

2 Using the brown 2½"-wide strips, make and attach binding.

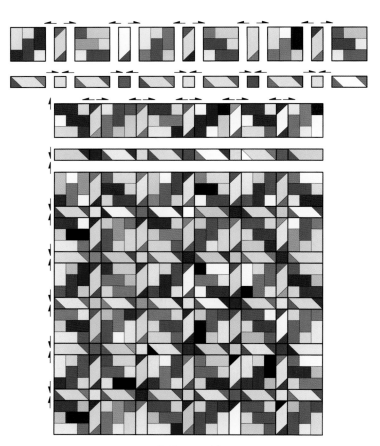

Quilt assembly

Faded Homesteads on the Prairie

This quilt was inspired by faded, well-worn blocks from a tattered quilt that had been cut up into individual blocks for sale at a quilt show. When Joanna and her friend both pulled out blocks from the same quilt from the sale bin, they know the blocks would provide wonderful inspiration for future projects.

"Faded Homesteads on the Prairie," designed by Joanna Figueroa, appliquéd by Denise Sheehan, quilted by Lynne Todoroff

Finished quilt: 86" x 86" ◆ Finished block: 16" x 16"

Materials

Yardage is based on 42"-wide fabric.

⅓ yard *each* of 13 assorted fabrics for roofs

½ yard *each* of 8 assorted light-colored fabrics for house backgrounds

⅝ yard *each* of 6 assorted light-colored fabrics for alternate block backgrounds

¼ yard *each* of 13 assorted fabrics for house fronts, sides, and chimneys

1 yard of fabric for border

⅛ yard *each* of 6 to 8 assorted wools for leaf and stem appliqués

⅔ yard of fabric for binding

8½ yards of fabric for backing

94" x 94" piece of batting

Template plastic

Roxanne's Glue-Baste-It water-soluble glue

Cutting

All measurements include ¼"-wide seam allowances. Make templates for pieces M, N, O, and the leaf from the patterns on pages 54 and 55.

From *each* of the 13 assorted front, side, and chimney fabrics, cut:

1 strip, 2½" x 42"; crosscut into:
 1 piece (13 total), 2½" x 9½" (A)
 2 pieces (26 total), 2½" x 6½" (B)
 3 pieces (39 total), 2½" x 4½" (C)
 2 pieces (26 total), 2" x 2½" (D)
2 pieces (26 total), 2" x 4½" (E)
1 piece (13 total), 1½" x 9½" (F)

From *each* of the 8 light-colored fabrics for house backgrounds, cut*:

2 strips, 2½" x 42"; crosscut into:
 6 pieces (48 total), 2½" x 4½" (G)
 4 pieces (32 total), 2½" x 3½" (H)
 2 pieces (16 total), 2½" x 7½" (I)
2 strips, 1½" x 42"; crosscut into:
 2 pieces (16 total), 1½" x 9½" (J)
 2 pieces (16 total), 1½" x 8½" (K)
 2 pieces (16 total), 1½" x 10" (L)
2 template M pieces (16 total)
2 template M reversed pieces (16 total)

From *each* of the 13 assorted fabrics for roofs, cut:

1 template N piece (13 total)
1 template O piece (13 total)

From the 6 light-colored fabrics for alternate block backgrounds, cut a *total* of:

12 squares, 16½" x 16½"

From the assorted wools, cut a *total* of:

12 pairs of matching stems, ½" x 13½"
12 sets of 16 matching leaves

From the border fabric, cut:

9 strips, 3½" x 42"

From the binding fabric, cut:

9 strips, 2¼" x 42"

*The amounts given are enough for 16 blocks. The excess will allow you more fabric combinations as you assemble the houses. Discard the extra pieces or set them aside for a future project.

Don't Forget: Offset

When joining two pieces with diagonal edges, always offset the pieces by ¼" so that the edges of the finished piece will align.

Making the House Blocks

1 Arrange the A–O pieces for one block into three sections as shown, using the same fabric for the front, side, and chimney pieces; the same fabric for the background pieces; and the same fabric for the roof pieces.

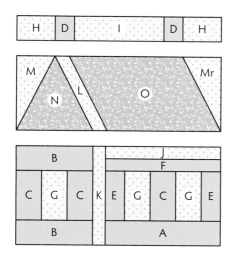

2 For the chimney section, sew the D, H, and I pieces together as shown. Press the seam allowances toward the D pieces.

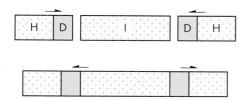

3 To make the roof section, center and sew the L piece to the right edge of the N piece (L is longer than necessary). Press the seam allowances toward the L piece. Trim the ends of the L piece even with the point and the lower edge of the N piece as shown.

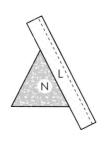 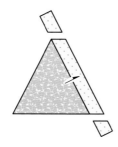

4 Add the O piece to the right edge of the L piece. Position the O piece so that it extends ¼" above the L piece at the upper edge. Press the seam allowances toward the O piece. Trim the wings.

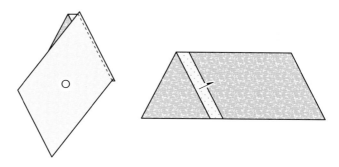

5 Add an M piece to the left edge of the step 4 piece and an M reversed piece to the right edge, offsetting the pieces (see "Don't Forget: Offset"). Press the seam allowances toward the M pieces. Trim the wings.

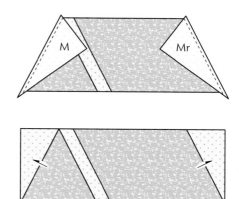

6 To make the side unit, sew the C, E, and G pieces together as shown. Press the seam allowances toward the G pieces.

 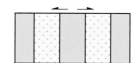

7 Add the F piece to the top of the unit from step 6 and the A piece to the bottom. Press the seam allowances toward the F and A pieces. Sew the J piece to the top of the unit. Press the seam allowances toward the F piece.

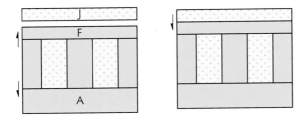

8 To make the front unit, sew the C pieces to the sides of the G piece as shown. Press the seam allowances toward the G piece. Add the B pieces to the top and bottom of this unit. Press the seam allowances toward the B pieces. Sew the K piece to the right edge of the unit. Press the seam allowances away from the K piece.

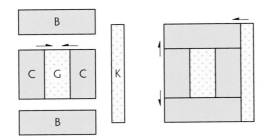

9 Sew the front unit to the left edge of the side unit to complete the bottom section. Press the seam allowances toward the front unit.

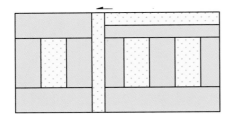

10 Sew the chimney, roof, and bottom sections together as shown, matching seam allowances where indicated, to complete the block. Press the seam allowances away from the roof section.

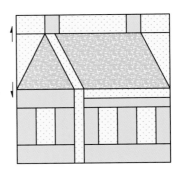

11 Repeat steps 1–10 to make a total of 13 blocks.

Making the Appliquéd Blocks

1 Select one pair of matching stems. Cut one of the stems into two pieces, ½" x 6½". Repeat with one stem of each of the remaining pairs.

2 Press the light-colored 16½" squares in half diagonally in each direction, right sides together.

3 Center the matching stem pieces on the diagonal lines of each background square as shown. Glue-baste and then appliqué the pieces in place.

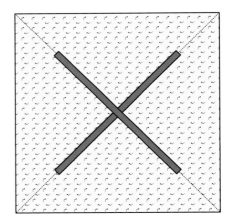

4. Arrange one set of leaves on each block as shown. Glue-baste and then appliqué the pieces in place to complete the blocks. Make 12.

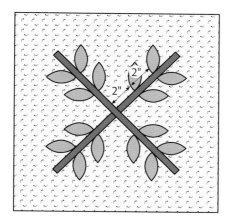

Assembling the Quilt Top

1. Arrange the blocks into five rows of five blocks each as shown in the quilt assembly diagram, alternating the House blocks and appliquéd blocks in each row and from row to row.

2. Sew the blocks in each row together. Press the seam allowances toward the appliquéd blocks. Sew the rows together. Press the seam allowances in one direction.

3. Add the 3½"-wide border strips to the quilt top, piecing the strips as necessary. Press the seam allowances toward the border.

Finishing the Quilt

For help with any of the finishing steps, go to ShopMartingale.com/HowtoQuilt for free downloadable information.

1. Layer, baste, and quilt your quilt, or take it to your favorite long-arm machine quilter for finishing.

2. Using the 2¼"-wide strips, make and attach binding.

Quilt assembly

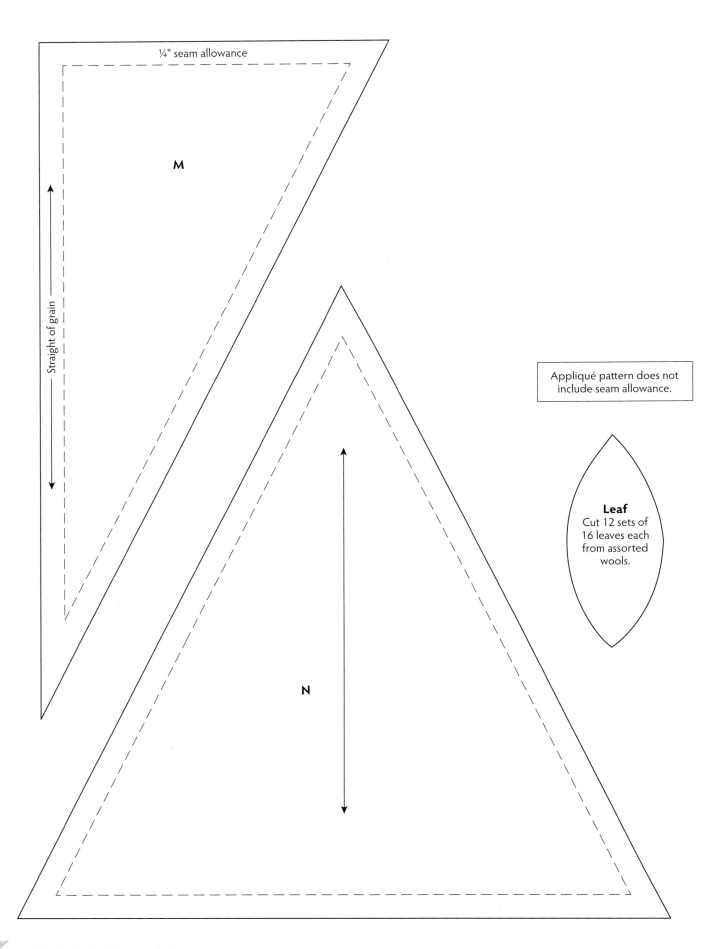

¼" seam allowance

M

Straight of grain

N

Appliqué pattern does not include seam allowance.

Leaf
Cut 12 sets of 16 leaves each from assorted wools.

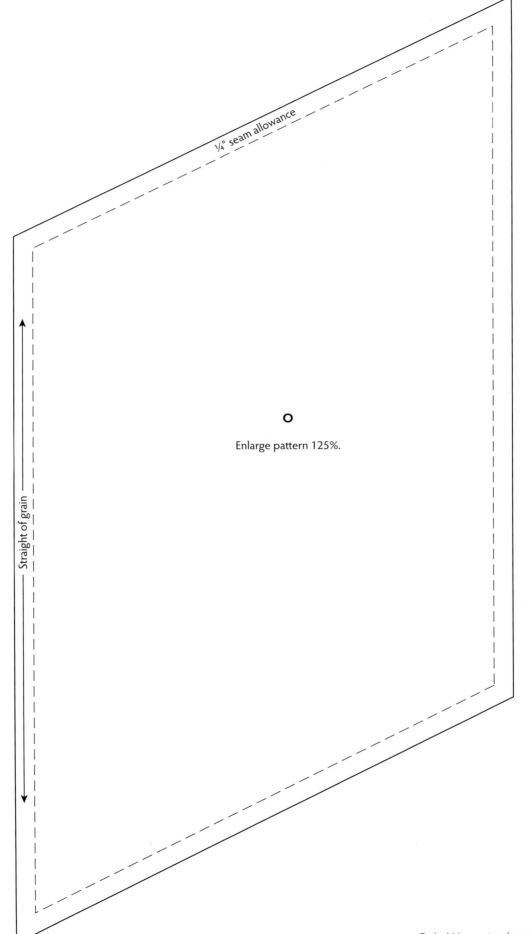

¼" seam allowance

Straight of grain

Enlarge pattern 125%.

Michael's Victory

Carol made this quilt to celebrate all the times
that her youngest son, Michael, has given his best and
achieved his goals both on and off the sports field.

"Michael's Victory," designed and made by Carol Hopkins

Finished quilt: 28" x 36½"   ◆   **Finished block:** 3" x 3"

Materials

Yardage is based on 42"-wide fabric.

48 scraps, at least 8" x 8", of assorted medium or dark prints for blocks and pieced border

1⅜ yards of light print for blocks, setting squares, setting triangles, and pieced border

⅓ yard of brown print for binding

1⅓ yards of fabric for backing

33" x 42" piece of batting

Cutting

All measurements include ¼"-wide seam allowances.

From the light print, cut:
48 squares, 4" x 4"
35 squares, 3½" x 3½"
6 squares, 5½" x 5½"; cut into quarters diagonally to yield 24 side triangles
2 squares, 3" x 3"; cut in half diagonally to yield 4 corner triangles

From *each* of the assorted medium- or dark-print scraps, cut:
1 square, 4" x 4" (48 total)
1 square, 2½" x 2½" (48 total)

From the brown print, cut:
4 strips, 2" x 42"

Making the Blocks

Instructions are for making one block. The light print is paired with a different medium or dark print in each block.

1 Pair a 4" medium or dark square with a 4" light square, right sides together. Without moving the fabrics, cut the layered squares in half vertically, horizontally, and diagonally from corner to corner as shown.

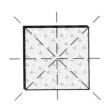

2 Sew each pair of triangles together to make eight half-square-triangle units. Press the seam allowances toward the darker fabric. Trim each unit to measure 1½" square.

Make 8.

3 Set aside three half-square-triangle units to use for the pieced border. Lay out five half-square-triangle units and a matching 2½" medium or dark square as shown.

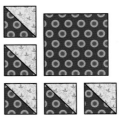

4 Sew two half-square-triangle units together, and then sew them to the larger square. Press the seam allowances open.

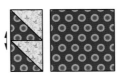 

5 Sew three half-square-triangle units together and sew them to the bottom of the unit from step 4. Press the seam allowances open.

6 Repeat steps 1–5 to make a total of 48 blocks, each measuring 3½" square.

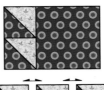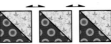 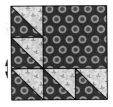

Make 48.

Assembling the Quilt Top

1 Lay out the blocks, 3½" light squares, light side triangles, and light corner triangles in diagonal rows. Notice that the blocks change direction in alternating vertical columns, so make sure you arrange the blocks as shown in the diagram following step 3.

2 Sew the blocks, setting squares, and side triangles together in diagonal rows, pressing the seam allowances open.

3 Sew the rows together, pressing the seam allowances open after adding each row. Add the corner triangles and press the seam allowances toward the triangles.

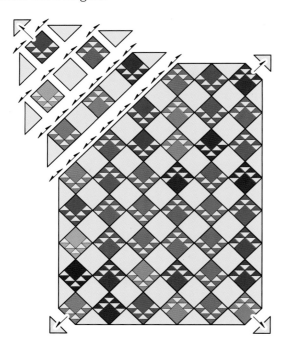

Adding the Border

1 Trim and square up the quilt top as needed, making sure to leave ¼" beyond the points of all the blocks for seam allowance.

2 Using the half-square-triangle units set aside for the pieced border, randomly sew together 34 units as shown to make a side border strip. Press the seam allowances open. Make two side borders.

Make 2.

3 Randomly sew together 27 half-square-triangle units as shown to make a top border strip. Note that one unit is rotated. Press the seam allowances open. Repeat to make a bottom border strip.

Make 2.

4 Sew the pieced strips from step 2 to the left and right sides of the quilt as shown, paying careful attention to the direction the triangles are facing. Press the seam allowances open.

5 Sew the pieced strips from step 3 to the top and bottom of the quilt, again being careful to orient the triangles as shown, and easing the borders to fit as needed. Press the seam allowances open.

Quilt assembly

Finishing the Quilt

For help with any of the finishing steps, go to ShopMartingale.com/HowtoQuilt for free downloadable information.

1 Layer, baste, and quilt your quilt, or take it to your favorite long-arm machine quilter for finishing.

2 Using the 2"-wide brown strips, make and attach binding.

Mending Basket

Gather a plethora of prints and dive into some fun as
you piece this scrappy back-to-basics patchwork project. Full
of old-fashioned appeal, this quilt will beckon you to curl up
and dream sweet dreams for many nights to come.

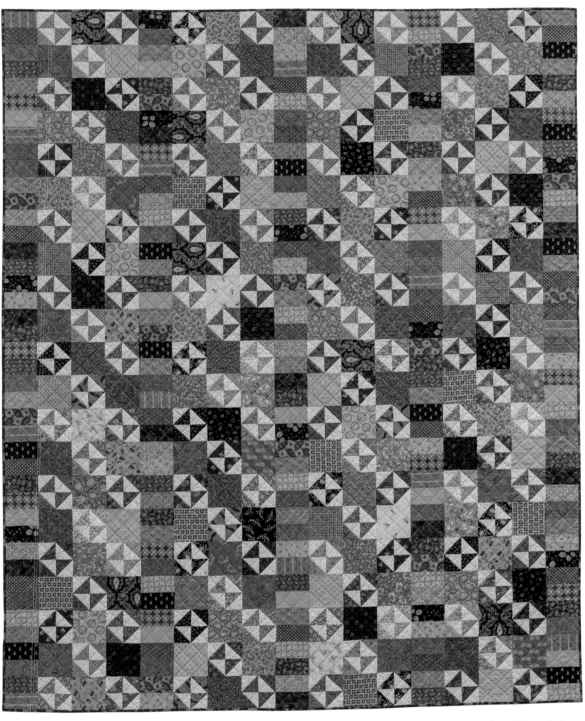

"Mending Basket," designed by Kim Diehl, pieced by Pat Peyton, machine quilted by Deborah Poole

Finished quilt: 68½" x 84½" ◆ **Finished block:** 12" x 12"

▶ Materials

Yardage is based on 42"-wide fabric. Fat quarters are 18" x 21" and fat eighths are 9" x 21".

11 fat quarters of assorted prints for block setting squares

19 fat eighths of assorted prints for X units

18 fat eighths of assorted prints for pieced sashing strips

1⅞ yards of tan print for X units

⅔ yard of complementary print for binding

5 yards of fabric for backing

74" x 90" piece of batting

▶ Cutting

All measurements include ¼"-wide seam allowances. Cut all strips across the width of the fabric in the order given unless otherwise indicated.

From the tan print, cut:
21 strips, 2⅞" x 42"; crosscut into 266 squares, 2⅞" x 2⅞". Cut in half diagonally to yield 532 triangles.

From *each* of the 19 fat eighths of assorted prints designated for X units, cut:
14 squares, 2⅞" x 2⅞"; cut in half diagonally to yield 28 triangles (combined total of 532). Keep the triangles organized by print.

From *each* of the 18 fat eighths of assorted prints designated for pieced sashing strips, cut:
12 rectangles, 2½" x 4½" (combined total of 216)

From *each* of the 11 fat quarters of assorted prints, cut:
12 squares, 4½" x 4½" (combined total of 132)

From the binding print, cut:
8 strips, 2½" x 42"

Making the Blocks

1 Select an assorted-print triangle and a tan triangle. Stitch the pair together along the long diagonal edges. Press the seam allowances toward the assorted-print triangle. Trim away the dog-ear points. Repeat for a total of 532 pieced half-square-triangle units measuring 2½" square, including seam allowances. Keep the units organized by print for greater ease in assembling the blocks.

Make 133 sets of 4.

2 Select four pieced half-square-triangle units sewn from a matching print. Lay out the units in two horizontal rows of two units each as shown. Join the units in each row. Press the seam allowances open. Join the rows. Press the seam allowances open. Repeat for a total of seven pieced X units from *each* of the 19 assorted prints (combined total of 133). The units should measure 4½" square, including seam allowances.

Make 133.

Perfect Triangles

Here's a great tip for piecing the half-square-triangle units for this quilt. After cutting your fabrics, choose one perfectly cut triangle and tape it to a square of paper to keep by your sewing machine. As you layer triangles together for stitching, use this triangle template to check the size of any layered pairs that don't match up perfectly. This enables you to see possible discrepancies and makes it easy to adjust your piecing accordingly to compensate.

3 Lay out five pieced X units and four assorted-print 4½" setting squares in three horizontal rows as shown. Join the pieces in each row. Press the seam allowances toward the setting squares. Join the rows. Press the seam allowances toward the middle row. Repeat for a total of 16 pieced A blocks measuring 12½" square, including seam allowances.

4 Lay out four pieced X units and five assorted-print 4½" setting squares in three horizontal rows as shown. Join the pieces in each row. Press the seam allowances toward the setting squares. Join the rows. Press the seam allowances away from the middle row. Repeat for a total of 12 pieced B blocks measuring 12½" square, including seam allowances. You'll have five unused X units and eight unused setting squares; these have been included for added versatility as you piece the blocks.

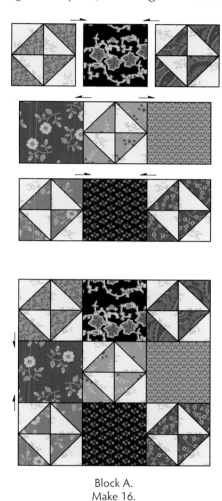

Block A.
Make 16.

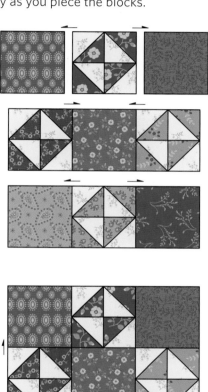

Block B.
Make 12.

Making the Sashing Strips

1 Select two assorted-print 2½" x 4½" rectangles. Join the pair along the long edges. Press the seam allowances to one side. Repeat for a total of 108 pieced sashing units measuring 4½" square, including seam allowances.

Make 108.

2 Join three pieced sashing units as shown. Press the seam allowances away from the middle unit. Repeat for a total of 35 pieced sashing strips measuring 4½" x 12½", including seam allowances. You'll have three unused units; these have been included for added versatility as you piece the strips.

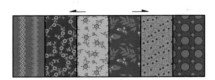

Make 35.

Easily Transporting Patchwork Units

Many of us use flannel-backed tablecloth fabric that's been cut into squares to help keep our in-progress patchwork and appliqué blocks organized as we work with them. Here's another clever use for tablecloth fabric: after arranging patchwork row units on a design wall, use a 12" width-of-fabric strip cut from a tablecloth remnant (with the flannel side up) to transport the pieces to your sewing machine.

Assembling the Quilt Top

1 Lay out five pieced sashing strips and four A blocks in alternating positions as shown. Join the pieces. Press the seam allowances toward the sashing strips. Repeat for a total of four pieced A rows measuring 12½" x 68½", including seam allowances.

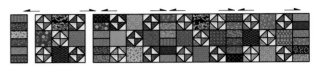

Row A.
Make 4.

2 Lay out five pieced sashing strips and four pieced B blocks in alternating positions as shown. Join the pieces. Press the seam allowances toward the sashing strips. Repeat for a total of three pieced B rows measuring 12½" x 68½", including seam allowances.

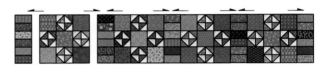

Row B.
Make 3.

3 Referring to the quilt photo on page 59, lay out the pieced A and B rows in alternating positions. Join the rows. Press the seam allowances toward the B rows. The pieced quilt top should now measure 68½" x 84½", including seam allowances.

Finishing the Quilt

For help with any of the finishing steps, go to ShopMartingale.com/HowtoQuilt for free downloadable information.

1 Layer, baste, and quilt your quilt, or take it to your favorite long-arm machine quilter for finishing.

2 Using the 2½"-wide strips, make and attach binding.

Precious Stones

Patchwork squares create the look of an interlocking maze across this quilt, inviting you to really have fun with your fabric selections. You can use lots of variety, both in the scale of your prints and with colors. The quilt shown features a neutral background fabric, but you could easily substitute a subtle print that contrasts well with the other fabrics.

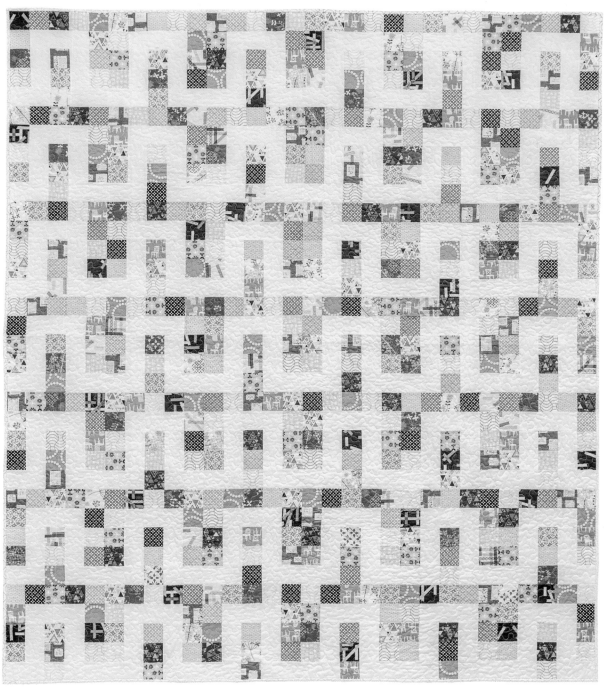

"Precious Stones," designed and made by Elizabeth Dackson

Finished quilt: 60" x 70" ◆ **Finished block: 10" x 10"**

Materials

Yardage is based on 42"-wide fabric. Fat quarters are 18" x 21".

14 fat quarters of assorted prints for blocks

2¼ yards of white fabric for background

⅝ yard of medium-scale print for binding

3⅞ yards of fabric for backing

68" x 78" piece of batting

Cutting

All measurements include ¼"-wide seam allowances.

From *each* of the 14 fat quarters, cut:
42 squares, 2½" x 2½" (588 total)

From the white fabric, cut:
29 strips, 2½" x 42"; crosscut into:
   126 squares, 2½" x 2½"
   84 rectangles, 2½" x 8½"

From the binding fabric, cut:
7 strips, 2½" x 42"

If Bigger Is Better

If you prefer a queen-size version of this quilt, you'll need to make 90 blocks, set 9 x 10, for a 90" x 102½" finished size.

Materials
30 fat quarters of assorted prints for blocks
5 yards of white fabric for background
⅞ yard of fabric for binding
8½ yards of fabric for backing
98" x 111" piece of batting

Making the Blocks

Use a scant ¼" seam allowance and press seam allowances open after sewing each seam.

1 Sew three 2½" squares of assorted prints together into a column. Make 126 of these three-square units, chain piecing them for efficiency.

Make 126.

2 Sew a white 2½" square to each of the three-square units from step 1.

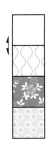

Make 126.

3 Sew three units from step 2 and two white 2½" x 8½" rectangles together, orienting the units from step 2 as shown. Make 42.

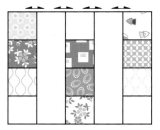

Make 42.

4 Sew five 2½" squares of assorted prints together to create a horizontal patchwork strip. Sew the strip to the top of a unit from step 3. Repeat to make a total of 42 blocks.

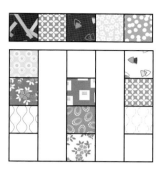

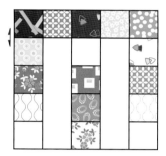

Make 42.

Assembling the Quilt Top

1 Arrange your blocks into seven rows of six blocks each in an order that is pleasing to your eye.

2 Sew the blocks in each row together, pressing seam allowances open as you go. Sew the rows together to complete the quilt top. You may find it helpful to sew the rows together in pairs first and then sew the pairs together. Press.

Finishing the Quilt

For help with any of the finishing steps, go to ShopMartingale.com/HowtoQuilt for free downloadable information.

1 Layer, baste, and quilt your quilt, or take it to your favorite long-arm machine quilter for finishing.

2 Using the 2½"-wide strips, make and attach binding.

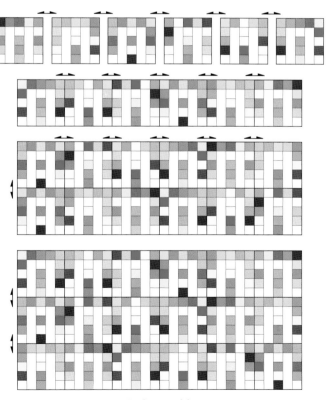

Quilt assembly

Spring Fling

Kaleidoscope is a traditional block, and this is a classic quilt in timeless colors. The illusion of overlapping dark and light circles continually draws your eyes across the surface. There are actually two variations of the block in this quilt, with the lights and darks placed in opposite positions. The center units are identical, but one block has light corners, and the other has dark corners.

"Spring Fling," designed and pieced by Robin Strobel, quilted by Pam Clarke

Finished quilt: 57½" x 72" ◆ **Finished block:** 7¼" x 7¼"

Materials

Yardage is based on 42"-wide fabric.

1⅜ yards of large-scale floral for outer border

⅜ yard of dark-blue fabric for inner border

¼ yard *each* of 16 different light fabrics for blocks (Fat quarters, which are 18" x 21", work well.)

¼ yard *each* of 16 different dark fabrics for blocks (Fat quarters work well.)

½ yard of fabric for binding

3½ yards of fabric for backing

62" x 76" piece of batting

Template plastic or a "kaleidoscope" ruler (available in most quilt shops)

Cutting

All measurements include ¼"-wide seam allowances. Strips are cut across the width of the fabric unless otherwise indicated.

From *each* of the 16 light and 16 dark fabrics, cut:
1 strip, 4½" x 42" (If using fat quarters, cut 2 strips, 4½" x 21", from each.)

From the dark-blue fabric, cut:
6 strips, 1¾" x 42"

From the large-scale floral, cut:
6 strips, 6" x 42" (If your outer-border fabric is not a full 42" wide, cut 7 strips.)

From the binding fabric, cut:
7 strips, 2¼" x 42"

Successful Fabric Selection

The relative value of the fabrics is the element that creates the design in this quilt. The greater the difference in value between the lights and darks, the more striking the pattern. To keep the secondary pattern from being too strong, the "dark" fabrics are prints that are more medium than dark in value. What is important is that the "dark" fabrics look darker in value than the "light" fabrics. You can use fewer fabrics—in fact this quilt is very striking made with only one light and one dark fabric.

Making the Blocks

Each block is made using the following units:

4 light and 4 dark center triangles

4 light or dark corner triangles

1 From each strip (or strips) of light and dark fabric, cut 12 large triangles using either a template made from the pattern provided on page 69, or a "kaleidoscope" ruler. Layer several strips and cut about six triangles at a time. You will have a total of 192 dark triangles and 192 light triangles.

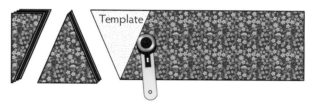

Cut 192 dark triangles and 192 light triangles.

2 From the remainder of each light and dark strip, cut three 3½" squares. You will have a total of 48 light squares and 48 dark squares. Cut each square in half on the diagonal. Set aside.

Cut 96.

Cut 96.

3 Randomly select a large light and a large dark triangle cut in step 1 and place right sides together. Stitch along one long bias edge. Repeat to sew each large light triangle to a large dark triangle. It doesn't matter if you sew with the light or the dark fabric on the top, but you need to be consistent. Keep the same value of fabric on the top! Press toward the dark fabric, being careful not to stretch the bias edges. Trim the dog-ears.

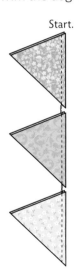

Start.

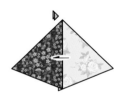

Press toward dark.
Trim dog-ears.

4 Randomly pair two of the units made in step 3. The light and dark triangles should alternate, and the pressed seam allowances should nestle together, making it easier to match the seams at the points. Stitch along one long edge. Press toward the dark fabric. Repeat with the remaining units made in step 3. Make 96 units.

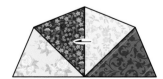

Make 96.

5 Sew together two of the units made in step 4. This is the trickiest step in constructing the blocks, because you have to match the points of eight different triangles. Press the seam allowances open to reduce bulk. You will get a "pie-plate" shape of eight triangles that will become the center of a block. Repeat with the remaining large triangle units to make 48 center units.

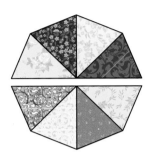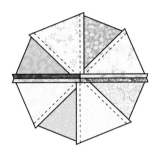

Make 48.

6 Roughly center a small dark triangle cut in step 2 against a large light triangle of a center unit and sew as shown. The corners of the small triangle will extend past the sides of the center unit. (It is difficult to perfectly center the corner triangles, so they are cut oversized and the corners will be trimmed.) Stitch ¼" from the edge. Repeat, sewing a small dark triangle to each of the remaining three large light triangles in the center unit. Press toward the small triangles. Trim the corners even with the center unit, being careful to leave a ¼" seam allowance where the seams cross. Your block should measure approximately 7¼". (Do not panic if your measurements are a little off. Fabric stretches!) Repeat this step on half of the center units to make 24 blocks with dark corners.

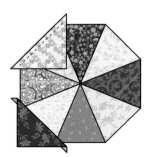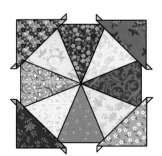

7 Repeat step 6, this time sewing four small light corner triangles to the large dark triangles. Press and trim. Make 24 blocks with light corners.

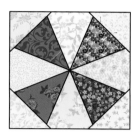

Make 24.

Assembling the Quilt Top

1 Arrange the blocks into eight rows of six blocks each, alternating light-cornered and dark-cornered blocks.

2 Sew the blocks into rows, matching points where triangles join. Press seam allowances in alternate directions from row to row. Sew the rows together, again matching triangle points. Press.

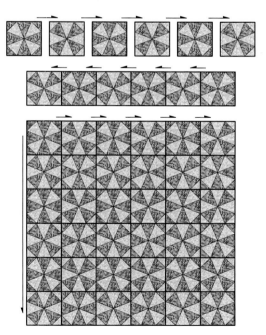

Quilt assembly

Adding the Borders

1 Sew the 1¾"-wide dark-blue inner-border strips end to end to make one long strip. Press. Measure the length of the quilt top through the center and cut two border strips to this size. Sew the strips to the sides of the quilt top, matching centers and easing as needed. The points in the quilt top will be easier to match if you sew with the quilt on top and the border strips underneath. Press toward the border. Measure the width of the quilt top through the center and cut two border strips to this size. Sew the strips to the top and bottom of the quilt, matching centers and easing as needed. Press toward the border.

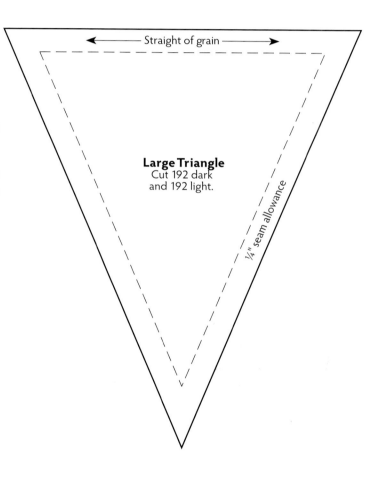

←———— Straight of grain ————→

Large Triangle
Cut 192 dark
and 192 light.

¼" seam allowance

2 Sew the 6"-wide floral outer-border strips end to end to make one long strip. Press. Measure the length of the quilt top through the center and cut two border strips to this size. Sew the strips to the sides of the quilt top. Press toward the outer border. Measure the width of the quilt top through the center and cut two border strips to this size. Sew the strips to the top and bottom of the quilt. Press toward the outer border.

Finishing the Quilt

For help with any of the finishing steps, go to ShopMartingale.com/HowtoQuilt for free downloadable information.

1 Layer, baste, and quilt your quilt, or take it to your favorite long-arm quilter for finishing.

2 Using the 2¼"-wide strips, make and attach binding.

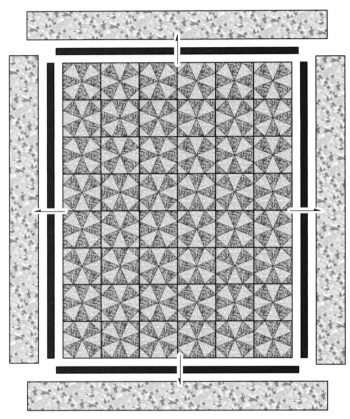

Adding the borders

Snowy Peaks

Crisp and clear as a snow-capped mountain on a winter day, these diamonds are a girl's best friend. A simple strip-piecing technique makes quick work of the pieced diamonds—this technique is sure to become a quilter's best friend as well.

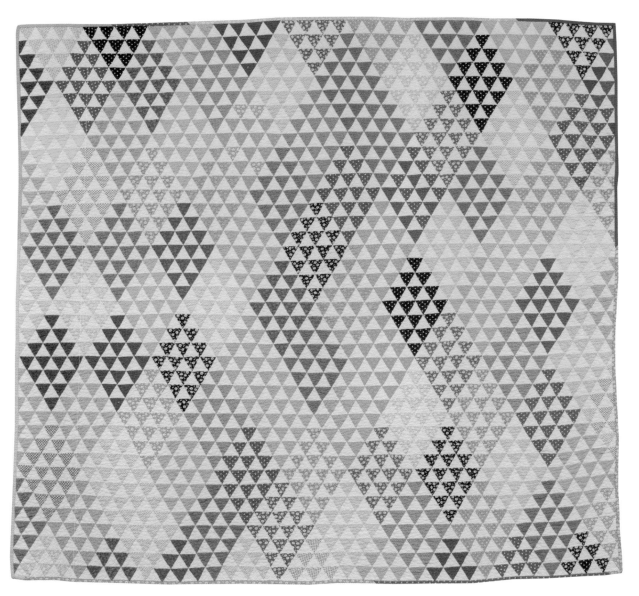

"Snowy Peaks," designed and made by Sandy Klop

Finished quilt: 74¾" x 73" ◆ Finished block: 8" x 14½" diamond

Materials

Yardage is based on 42"-wide fabric.

3¾ yards of unbleached muslin for blocks

1¾ yards *total* of blue prints for blocks

1½ yards *total* of pink and red prints for blocks

1½ yards *total* of green prints for blocks

1¼ yards *total* of yellow and gold prints for blocks

¾ yard *total* of orange and peach prints for blocks

½ yard *total* of black prints for blocks

⅝ yard of fabric for binding*

4½ yards of fabric for backing

77" x 79" piece of batting

Equilateral-triangle ruler**

You can also cut strips from leftover fabrics and make a scrappy pieced binding as Sandy did in the quilt shown.

**If you don't have one of these, they're available at www.AmericanJane.com.*

Cutting

All measurements include ¼"-wide seam allowances.

From the unbleached muslin, cut:
59 strips, 2½" x 42"

From the assorted prints, cut a *total* of:
59 strips, 2½" x 42"

From the binding fabric, cut:
8 strips, 2¼" x 42"

Making the Diamonds

1 Layer each muslin strip with a print strip, right sides together. Sew both long sides using a ¼" seam allowance until you have 57 pairs sewn. Leave the remaining two pairs unsewn.

2 Align the 2½" line on an equilateral-triangle ruler with the bottom raw edge of the sewn strips. Cut on both sides.

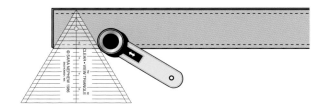

3 Move the ruler over to the right, keeping the 2½" line on the bottom raw edge and the lower-left side at the point of your previous cut. Repeat to the end of the strip and for all remaining pairs of strips, including the unsewn strips. Set aside the cut triangles from the unsewn strips until later.

4 Use a seam ripper to open the tips of the sewn triangles to create a diamond. Press the seam allowances toward the print triangles.

Making the Large Diamond Blocks

To make one Large Diamond block, sew 16 small diamonds of the same color into pairs, keeping the light triangles toward the top. Sew the pairs into four diagonal rows. Sew the rows together in pairs. Match the dog-ear seam points to help align the diamonds. Press toward the prints. Sew the rows together to complete the block. Construct a total of 76 Large Diamond blocks.

Make 76.

Making Half Blocks for the Sides

You will need five half blocks for the left side and five half blocks for the right side of the quilt.

1 For each half block, sew a row of four diamonds, a row of three diamonds, and a row of two diamonds as shown, matching the colors.

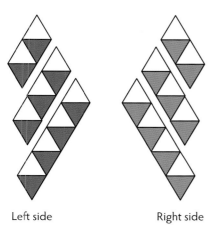

Left side   Right side

2 Sew the rows together and add a single diamond to the top corner of the 10 half blocks as shown. You will trim off the long edge of the half Diamond blocks after final assembly.

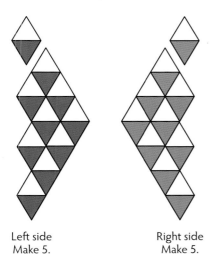

Left side   Right side
Make 5.   Make 5.

Making Half Blocks for the Top and Bottom

You'll need nine half blocks for the top and nine half blocks for the bottom of the quilt.

1 For each of the top half blocks, sew together a row of three diamonds and a row of two diamonds, starting from the right and matching the colors. Add a single diamond, and then add a single print triangle (set aside earlier) to the top of each row and one additional triangle to the upper-left corner. Sew the rows together to complete a top half block. Repeat to make nine.

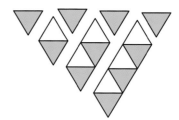 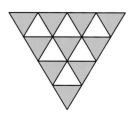

Top half Diamond block.
Make 9.

2 For each of the bottom half blocks, sew together a row of three diamonds and a row of two diamonds, starting from the left and matching the colors. Add a single diamond, and then add a single muslin triangle to the bottom of each row and one additional muslin triangle to the lower-right corner. Sew the rows together to complete a bottom half block. Repeat to make nine.

 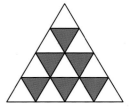

Bottom half Diamond block.
Make 9.

Assembling the Quilt Top

1 Arrange the blocks on a design wall or a large piece of flannel. Sew the blocks into diagonal rows, and then sew the rows together.

2 Trim the half blocks on the left and right sides of the quilt top to make straight edges.

Finishing the Quilt

For help with any of the finishing steps, go to ShopMartingale.com/HowtoQuilt for free downloadable information.

1 Layer, baste, and quilt your quilt, or take it to your favorite long-arm machine quilter for finishing.

2 Using the 2¼"-wide strips, make and attach binding.

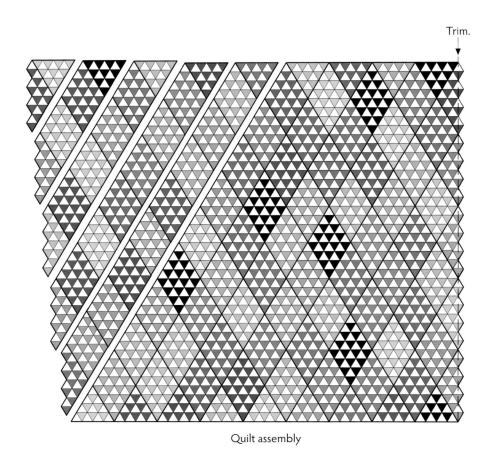

Trim.

Quilt assembly

Gelato

Scoop up an assortment of precut 5" squares in a rainbow of colors and you're on your way to whetting your appetite for a fun and refreshing treat.

"Gelato," designed and pieced by Gerri Robinson, machine quilted by Rebecca Segura.

Finished quilt: 52" x 62½"   ◆   Finished block: 8" x 8"

Materials

Yardage is based on 42"-wide fabric. Fat eighths are 9" x 21".

40 squares, 5" x 5", of assorted bright prints for blocks

2 yards of white solid for block backgrounds, pieced sashing, and inner border

1⅝ yards of floral for outer border

⅞ yard of green solid for blocks

1 fat eighth *each* of blue, pink, red, and yellow solids for pieced sashing

½ yard of cream-and-green diagonal stripe for binding

3¾ yards of fabric for backing

62" x 72" piece of batting

Cutting

All measurements include ¼"-wide seam allowances.

From the assorted bright squares, cut a *total* of:
80 rectangles, 2½" x 4½"

From the white solid, cut:
31 rectangles, 2½" x 8½"
40 squares, 2⅞" x 2⅞"
160 squares, 2½" x 2½"
4 strips, 1½" x 42"

From the green solid, cut:
40 squares, 2⅞" x 2⅞"
80 squares, 2½" x 2½"

From *each* of the blue, pink, red, and yellow fat eighths, cut:
3 squares, 2½" x 2½" (12 total)
24 squares, 1½" x 1½" (96 total)

From the floral, cut on the *lengthwise* grain:
2 strips, 6½" x 54"
2 strips, 6½" x 56"

From the cream-and-green diagonal stripe, cut:
7 strips, 2½" x 42"

Making the Blocks

1 Draw a diagonal line on the wrong side of a white 2⅞" square. Place the square right sides together with a green 2⅞" square. Sew ¼" from each side of the drawn line. Cut on the drawn line, open the unit, and press toward the green fabric. The half-square-triangle units should measure 2½" square. Make a total of 80 units.

Make 80.

2 Make flying-geese units using the folded-corner method. Draw a diagonal line on the wrong side of a green 2½" square and a white 2½" square. Layer one square right sides together on a bright-print 2½" x 4½" rectangle, matching corners. Sew on the drawn line. Trim the excess fabric, leaving ¼" seam allowance. Open the unit and press the triangle toward the corner. Repeat with the second square on the opposite corner. The unit should measure 2½" x 4½". Make a total of 80 units.

Make 80.

3 Sew a white 2½" square to a half-square-triangle unit as shown. Press the seam allowances toward the green triangle. Sew the pieced unit to the top of a flying-geese unit to make a quadrant. Press the seam allowances in the directions indicated. Make 80 quadrants.

Make 80.

4 Sew four quadrants together to make a block. Press the seam allowances in the directions indicated. The block should measure 8½" square. Make a total of 20 blocks.

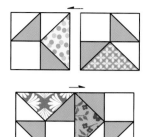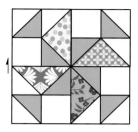

Make 20.

Making the Sashing Units

1 Draw a diagonal line on the wrong side of a blue 1½" square. Place the square right side down on one corner of a white 2½" x 8½" rectangle. Sew on the diagonal line, trim the excess fabric, and press the blue triangle toward the corner. Repeat on the opposite corner to make a single pieced-sashing unit. Make a total of five blue, four pink, three red, and two yellow units.

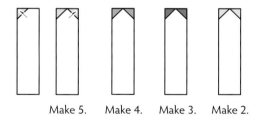

Make 5.   Make 4.   Make 3.   Make 2.

2 In the same manner, sew two blue 1½" squares and two pink 1½" squares to the ends of a white 2½" x 8½" rectangle as shown to make a double pieced-sashing unit. Make two blue/pink units. Repeat to make three blue/red units, two blue/yellow units, two pink/red units, four pink/yellow units, and four yellow/red units.

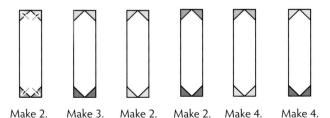

Make 2.   Make 3.   Make 2.   Make 2.   Make 4.   Make 4.

Assembling the Quilt Top

1 Lay out the blocks, the pieced sashing units, and the blue, pink, red, and yellow 2½" squares as shown in the quilt assembly diagram below, making sure to orient the sashing units as shown. The triangle corners should make small stars when the strips are positioned correctly. Once you're satisfied with the arrangement, sew the pieces together into rows. Press the seam allowances toward the sashing units.

2 Join the rows and press the seam allowances toward the sashing rows. The quilt top should measure 38½" x 48½".

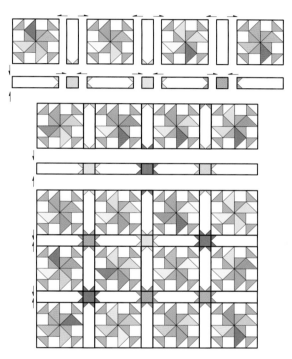

Quilt assembly

Adding the Borders

1 Join the 1½"-wide white strips end to end to make a long strip. Measure the quilt, cut strips to the required measurements, and sew them to the quilt top for the inner border. Press the seam allowances toward the border.

2 Repeat to add the floral outer-border strips to the quilt top. Press the seam allowances toward the outer border.

Finishing the Quilt

For help with any of the finishing steps, go to ShopMartingale.com/HowtoQuilt for free downloadable information.

1 Layer, baste, and quilt your quilt, or take it to your favorite long-arm machine quilter for finishing.

2 Using the cream-and-green 2½"-wide strips, make and attach binding.

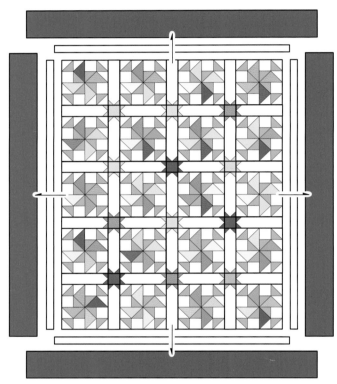

Adding the borders

Sherbet Punch

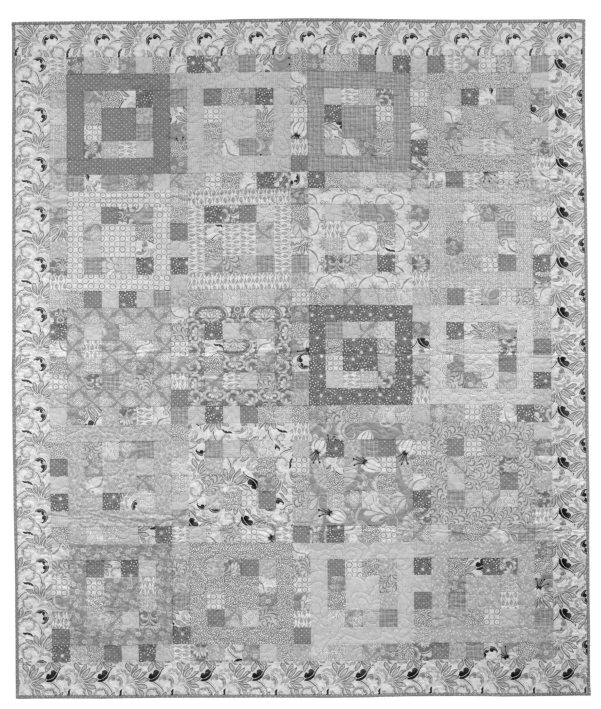

Collecting the fat quarters for this quilt is half the fun, especially if you do it a little at a time. Just pick a color scheme and look for those colors at each quilt shop you visit. When you look at the finished quilt, you'll remember where you got each fabric!

"Sherbet Punch," designed and pieced by Tracy Overturf, machine quilted by Lynn Reppas

Finished quilt: 66½" x 80½" ◆ **Finished block:** 12" x 12"

Materials

Yardage is based on 42"-wide fabric. Fat quarters are 18" x 21".

20 assorted fat quarters for blocks and sashing*

1⅛ yards of fabric for border

⅔ yard of fabric for binding

5 yards of fabric for backing

73" x 87" piece of batting

Don't prewash the fabrics in this case; you'll need the full size of the unwashed fat quarters to cut the pieces needed.

Cutting

All measurements include ¼"-wide seam allowances.

From *each* assorted fat quarter, cut:

1 strip, 5" x 21"; from each strip, cut 1 square, 4½" x 4½" (20 total). Cut the remainder of the strip *lengthwise* into 2 strips, 2½" wide.
   From *each* strip, cut:
   1 rectangle, 2½" x 12½" (40 total), and 1 square, 2½" x 2½" (40 total).
   1 strip, 2½" x 21"; crosscut into 2 rectangles, 2½" x 8½" (40 total), and 1 square, 2½" x 2½" (20 total)
4 strips, 2½" x 21" (80 total; 4 are extra)

From the border fabric, cut:

8 strips, 4½" x 42"

From the binding fabric, cut:

8 strips, 2½" x 42"

Making the Blocks

1 Sew two 2½" x 21" assorted strips together to make a strip set; repeat to make a total of 10 strip sets. Press the seam allowances toward the darker fabric in each set. Cut each strip set into eight units, 2½" x 4½", for a total of 80 units.

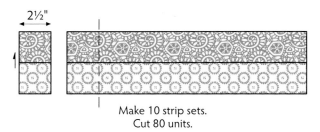

Make 10 strip sets.
Cut 80 units.

2 Sew units from step 1 to opposite sides of a 4½" square, making sure to use different-colored units. Press the seam allowances toward the center square. Make 20.

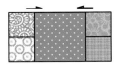

Make 20.

3 From the remaining 2½" x 21" strips, create five groups of four strips each, making sure to use four different fabrics in each set. Sew the strips in each set together and press the outer seam allowances outward and the inner seam allowances in either direction. Cut each strip set into eight units, 2½" x 8½", for a total of 40 units.

Make 5 strip sets.
Cut 40 units.

4 Sew units from step 3 to the remaining sides of each unit from step 2, making sure to vary the fabrics. Press the seam allowances toward the top and bottom units.

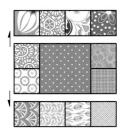

Organizing Strip Sets

To make block assembly easier, group your strip sets into sets of two strips, four strips, and six strips, and make a separate group of 2½" squares.

5 Sew 2½" x 8½" rectangles that match the center square to opposite sides of each block. Press the seam allowances toward the rectangles. Sew matching 2½" x 12½" rectangles to the top and bottom of each block. Press the seam allowances toward the rectangles. The blocks should measure 12½" x 12½".

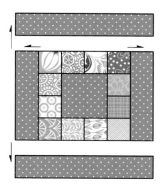

Make 20.

Making the Sashing Units

Make six strip sets of six assorted 2½" x 21" strips each. Cut each strip set into eight units, 2½" x 12½", for a total of 48 sashing units. Press the seam allowances on each end inward and press the remaining seam allowances in either direction.

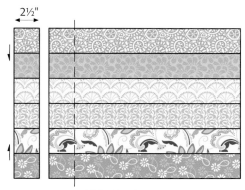

Make 6 strip sets.
Cut 48 units.

Not Enough Variety in Your Sashing?

You can take units apart and recombine the pieces to make new units, or make new sets by using pairs or singles. You'll have enough extra segments to allow you to keep squares of the same fabric from being too close together.

Assembling the Quilt Top

1 Arrange the blocks and sashing units into a horizontal row as shown. Sew one sashing unit to the left side of each block and to the left and right sides of the last block in the row. Press the seam allowances toward the blocks. Sew the blocks and sashing units together. Press the seam allowances toward the blocks. Make five rows.

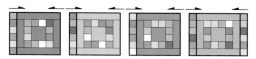

Make 5.

2 Randomly sew leftover strip sets of six and two squares, along with single squares, into six sashing strips of 29 pieces each.

Make 6.

3 Sew the sashing strips to the top of each row and to the top and bottom of the last row. Join the rows. Press the seam allowances toward the block rows.

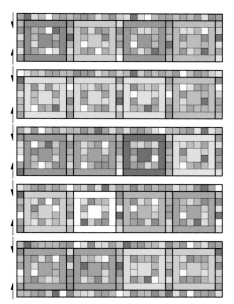

Quilt assembly

Adding the Border

1 Sew two 4½" x 42" strips together; repeat to make four long strips. From those strips, cut two 72½"-long strips and sew them to the sides of the quilt top. Press the seam allowances toward the border.

2 Cut two 66½"-long strips and sew them to the top and bottom of the quilt top. Press the seam allowances toward the border.

Finishing the Quilt

For help with any of the finishing steps, go to ShopMartingale.com/HowtoQuilt for free downloadable information.

1 Layer, baste, and quilt your quilt, or take it to your favorite long-arm machine quilter for finishing.

2 Using the 2½"-wide strips, make and attach binding.

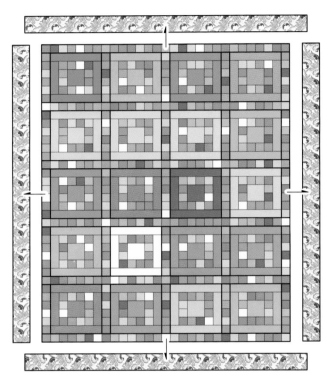

Adding the border

Fireworks

This quilt, made up in bright prints, is reminiscent of a profusion of fireworks exploding in the sky.

"Fireworks," designed and made by Kate Henderson

Finished quilt: 51" x 68" ◆ **Finished block:** 17" x 17"

Materials

Yardage is based on 42"-wide fabric.

36 strips, 2½" x 42", of assorted bright prints for blocks

1⅞ yards of white solid for blocks

⅝ yard of blue print for binding

3¼ yards of fabric for backing

57" x 74" piece of batting

Cutting

All measurements include ¼"-wide seam allowances.

From *each* of the 36 print strips, cut:
1 strip, 2½" x 27" (36 total)

From the leftovers of 12 print strips, cut a *total* of:
12 squares, 2½" x 2½"

From the white solid, cut:
6 strips, 2½" x 42"; crosscut into:
    24 rectangles, 2½" x 6½"
    24 squares, 2½" x 2½"
3 strips, 9¾" x 42"; crosscut into 12 squares,
    9¾" x 9¾". Cut into quarters diagonally to yield
    48 triangles.
3 strips, 5⅛" x 42"; crosscut into 24 squares,
    5⅛" x 5⅛". Cut in half diagonally to yield
    48 triangles.

From the blue print, cut:
7 strips, 2½" x 42"

Making the Blocks

1 Sew white 2½" squares to opposite sides of a print 2½" square. Press the seam allowances open.

2 Sew white 2½" x 6½" rectangles to the top and bottom of the unit from step 1. Press the seam allowances open. Make 12 units.

3 Organize the print 2½" x 27" strips into 12 piles of three strips each. Sew each group of strips together along their long edges. Press the seam allowances open. Cut each strip set into four squares, 6½" x 6½" (48 total).

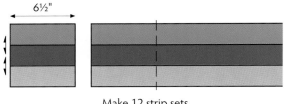

Make 12 strip sets.
Cut 4 squares from each.

4 Arrange a unit from step 2, four matching units from step 3, four half-square triangles (corners), and four quarter-square triangles (top, bottom, and sides) as shown to make a block. Sew into diagonal rows and press the seam allowances open. Sew the rows together and press the seam allowances open. Make 12 blocks.

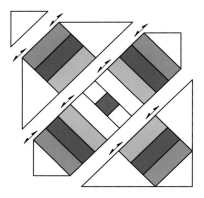

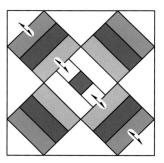

Make 12.

Assembling the Quilt Top

1 Arrange the blocks in four rows of three blocks each. Sew the blocks together in rows and press the seam allowances open.

2 Sew the rows together. Press the seam allowances open.

Finishing the Quilt

For help with any of the finishing steps, go to ShopMartingale.com/HowtoQuilt for free downloadable information.

1 Layer, baste, and quilt your quilt, or take it to your favorite long-arm machine quilter for finishing.

2 Using the blue 2½"-wide strips, make and attach binding.

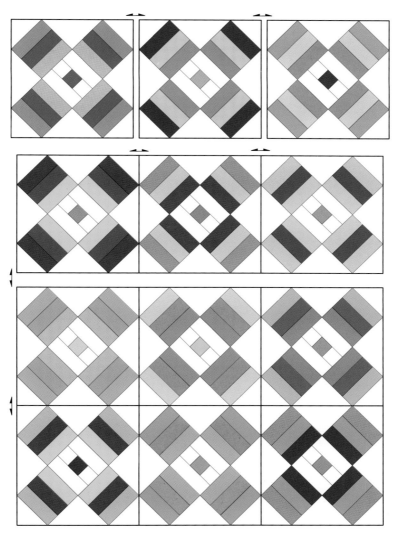

Quilt assembly

Scrappy Nines

The blending of a black-and-tan color palette with a scrappy fabric selection makes this quilt fun to create, and packs it with a big WOW factor. You'll hear oohs and aahs when you show this quilt to your friends!

"Scrappy Nines," designed by Pat Wys, pieced by Teresa Wade, quilted by Leisa Wiggley

Finished quilt: 66½" x 78½"   ◆   **Finished block:** 12" x 12"

Materials

Yardage is based on 42"-wide fabric.

1⅜ yards *each* of 4 assorted light-value neutral fabrics for blocks and pieced border

⅝ yard *each* of 5 assorted dark-value neutral fabrics for blocks and pieced border

¾ yard of fabric for binding

5 yards of fabric for backing

74" x 86" piece of batting

Cutting

All measurements include ¼"-wide seam allowances.

From *each* of the light-value fabrics, cut:
3 strips, 6½" x 42" (12 total; 1 is extra); crosscut into:
    82 rectangles, 3½" x 6½"
    15 squares, 6½" x 6½"
3 strips, 4" x 42" (12 total; 3 are extra); crosscut into:
    60 rectangles, 2" x 4"
    60 squares, 4" x 4"; cut in half diagonally to yield
    120 triangles
7 strips, 1½" x 42"; cut in half to yield 14 strips,
    1½" x 21" (56 total; 4 are extra)

From *each* of the dark-value fabrics, cut:
7 strips, 1½" x 42"; cut in half to yield 14 strips,
    1½" x 21" (70 total; 5 are extra)
12 squares, 4" x 4" (60 total)
3 squares, 2" x 2" (15 total)

From the binding fabric, cut:
2½"-wide bias strips to make 300" of bias binding

No Limits Here!

The yardage listed is sufficient to make this quilt using four different lights and five different darks. However, if you want an even scrappier quilt, use as many light- and dark-value fabrics as you can get your hands on. The sky is the limit. Get scrappy, you'll be happy!

Making the Nine-Patch Units

Both of the blocks, as well as the pieced border, incorporate nine-patch units that measure 3½" square.

1. Randomly join two dark 1½"-wide strips and one light 1½"-wide strip along their long edges to make strip set A as shown. Press the seam allowances open to reduce bulk. Repeat to make a total of 26 strip sets. From the strip sets, cut 336 segments, 1½" wide.

Strip set A.
Make 26. Cut 336 segments.

2. In the same manner, make strip set B using two light strips and one dark strip. Press the seam allowances open. Make a total of 13 strip sets. From these strip sets, cut 168 segments, 1½" wide.

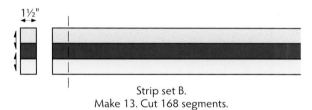

Strip set B.
Make 13. Cut 168 segments.

3. Sew a B segment between two A segments to make a nine-patch unit. Press the seam allowances open. Make a total of 168 units.

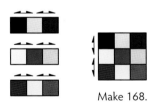

Make 168.

Pressing for Perfection

When making the nine-patch units, you may find it helpful to press the seam allowances open. The seams within the units will match up more easily, and joining the completed blocks will be easier too.

Making the Nines in the Corners Blocks

1 For each block, lay out four nine-patch units, four light 3½" x 6½" rectangles, and one light 6½" square.

2 When you're pleased with the value placements, sew the pieces together into rows. Press the seam allowances away from the rectangles. Sew the rows together and press the seam allowances away from the center. Make 15 blocks.

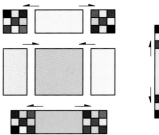 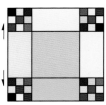

Make 15.

Making the Scrappy Nines Blocks

1 Lay out four dark 4" squares, four light 2" x 4" rectangles, and one dark 2" square as shown. Sew the pieces together into rows, and then sew the rows together. Press all the seam allowances open. Make 15 center units.

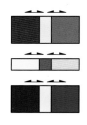

Make 15.

2 To make the pieced triangle units, sew 4" light triangles to adjacent sides of a nine-patch unit as shown. Press the seam allowances toward the triangles. The triangles are slightly oversized and will be trimmed in the next step. Make 60 of these units.

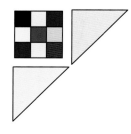 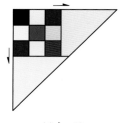

Make 60.

3 Trim the triangle units, leaving a ¼" seam allowance beyond the intersection of the nine-patch unit and triangles.

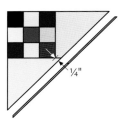

¼"

4 Sew triangle units to opposite sides of a center unit, aligning the point of the nine-patch unit with the center of the narrow rectangle. Press the seam allowances toward the center unit. Trim the tips of the triangles.

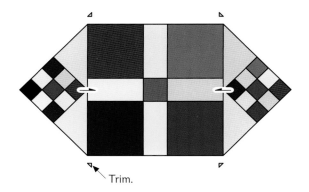

Trim.

5 Sew triangle units to the top and bottom of the unit from step 4 to complete the Scrappy Nines block. Press the seam allowances toward the center. Make 15. The blocks should measure 12½" square.

Make 15.

Assembling the Quilt Top

1 Lay out the Nines in the Corners blocks and the Scrappy Nines blocks in six rows of five blocks each, alternating the blocks as shown in the quilt assembly diagram. Rows 1, 3, and 5 begin and end with Nines in the Corners blocks. Rows 2, 4, and 6 begin and end with Scrappy Nines blocks.

2 When you're satisfied with the arrangement, sew the blocks together into rows. Press the seam allowances toward the Nines in the Corners blocks. Sew the rows together and press the seam allowances in one direction.

Quilt assembly

Adding the Border

At first glance, it appears that this quilt doesn't have a border. But by sewing small Nine Patches and plain rectangles around the perimeter, you're adding an extra element that makes the design look finished. The border will use the 48 remaining nine-patch units.

1 Set four nine-patch units aside. Sew the remaining nine-patch units together in pairs. Make 22 pairs.

2 Lay out six light 3½" x 6½" rectangles, five nine-patch pairs, and two nine-patch units as shown to make a side border. Press the seam allowances toward the rectangles. Make two side borders. Sew

these border strips to the left and right sides of the quilt top.

Make 2.

3 Join six nine-patch pairs and five light 3½" x 6½" rectangles, alternating them as shown to make the top border. Repeat to make the bottom border. Press the seam allowances toward the rectangles.

Make 2.

4 Sew the border strips to the top and bottom edges of the quilt top. Press the seam allowances toward the borders.

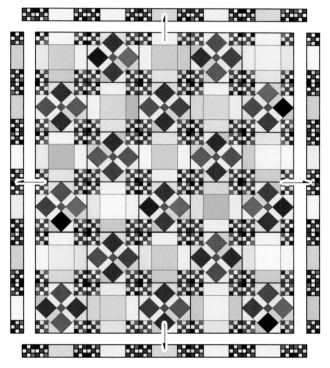

Adding the border

Finishing the Quilt

For help with any of the finishing steps, go to ShopMartingale.com/HowtoQuilt for free downloadable information.

1 Layer, baste, and quilt your quilt, or take it to your favorite long-arm machine quilter for finishing.

2 Using the 2½"-wide bias strips, make and attach binding.

Rose Window

This quilt brings to mind the hot-pink roses of early summer and the fresh greens of the leaves. The glowing center of the quilt is like the sun streaming through the trees. The design features striking complementary tones of red-purple and yellow-green.

"Rose Window," designed by Sharon Peterson and Ionne McCauley, pieced by Sharon Peterson

Finished quilt: 41½" x 41½" ◆ **Finished block:** 6" x 6"

▶ Materials

Yardage is based on 42"-wide fabric.

1 yard *total* of assorted medium yellow-green prints
for blocks

⅞ yard *total* of assorted red-purple prints
for blocks

⅝ yard of red-purple print for inner border and
binding

½ yard of muddy yellow-green print for
outer border

¼ yard *total* of assorted light yellow-green prints
for blocks

⅛ yard of black print for blocks

2¾ yards of fabric for backing

46" x 46" piece of batting

▶ Cutting

All measurements include ¼"-wide seam allowances.

From the assorted medium yellow-green prints, cut:
128 squares, 2½" x 2½"
36 squares, 3" x 3"

From the assorted light yellow-green prints, cut:
12 squares, 2½" x 2½"
4 squares, 3" x 3"

From the assorted red-purple prints, cut:
96 squares, 2½" x 2½"
32 squares, 3" x 3"

From the black print, cut:
16 squares, 2½" x 2½"

From the red-purple print for border and binding, cut:
2 strips, 1" x 36½"
2 strips, 1" x 37½"
5 strips, 2½" x 42"

From the muddy yellow-green print, cut:
2 strips, 2¾" x 37½"
3 strips, 2¾" x 40"

Making the Blocks

1 Mark a diagonal line on the wrong side of a 3" light
yellow-green square. Place the square right sides
together with a 3" medium yellow-green square. Sew
¼" from each side of the drawn line. Cut on the line,

press the seam allowances toward the darker fabric,
and trim the units to 2½" x 2½". Make 8 half-square-
triangle units with light yellow-green and medium
yellow-green fabrics, and 64 units with red-purple
and medium yellow-green fabrics.

Make 8.   Make 64.

2 Using the 2½" squares and the half-square-
triangle units from step 1, make 36 divided Nine
Patch blocks as shown.

Make 12.   Make 4.   Make 20.

Assembling the Quilt Top

1 Arrange the blocks on a design wall, referring
to the quilt assembly diagram. Sew the blocks
together in rows. Press the seam allowances in
alternate directions from row to row.

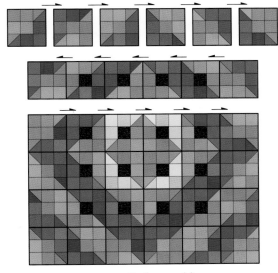

Quilt assembly

2 Sew the rows together and press the seam
allowances open or in one direction as desired.

Adding the Borders

1 Sew the 1" x 36½" red-purple pieces to the sides of the quilt. Press seam allowances toward the border.

2 Sew the 1" x 37½" red-purple pieces to the top and bottom of the quilt. Press seam allowances toward the border.

3 Sew the 2¾" x 37½" muddy yellow-green pieces to the sides of the quilt. Press seam allowances toward the inner border.

4 Sew the three remaining 2¾" x 40" muddy yellow-green pieces together end to end. From this pieced strip, cut two strips, 2¾" x 42", and sew them to the top and bottom of the quilt. Press seam allowances toward the inner border.

Finishing the Quilt

For help with any of the finishing steps, go to ShopMartingale.com/HowtoQuilt for free downloadable information.

1 Layer, baste, and quilt your quilt, or take it to your favorite long-arm machine quilter for finishing.

2 Using the 2½"-wide red-purple strips, make and attach binding.

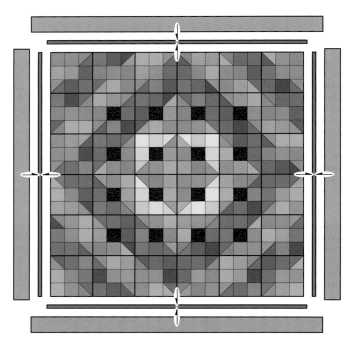

Adding the borders

BFF

BFF—Best Friends Forever! Quilting sisters Barbara and Mary love Pinwheel and Four Patch blocks, and the combination turned out fabulous in this whimsical quilt. Using black was a first for them, but this border fabric had so many appealing colors in it, they couldn't resist. Make this fun quilt with your BFF!

"BFF," designed and made by Barbara Groves and Mary Jacobson
Finished quilt: 64" x 80" ◆ **Finished block:** 8" x 8"

Materials

Yardage is based on 42"-wide fabric.

96 coordinating squares, 5" x 5", for blocks

2⅜ yards of black print for Pinwheel blocks and outer border

1 yard of white with red dot for Pinwheel blocks

1 yard of black with white dot for inner border and binding

5¼ yards of fabric for backing

72" x 88" piece of batting

Cutting

All measurements include ¼"-wide seam allowances.

From the white with red dot, cut:
6 strips, 4⅞" x 40"; crosscut into 48 squares, 4⅞" x 4⅞"

From the black print, cut:
6 strips, 4⅞" x 40"; crosscut into 48 squares, 4⅞" x 4⅞"
7 strips, 6¾" x 40"

From the black with white dot, cut:
6 strips, 2" x 40"
8 strips, 2¼" x 40"

Making the Pinwheel Blocks

1 Draw a diagonal line on the wrong side of each white-with-red-dot 4⅞" square.

2 Layer one marked square and one black-print 4⅞" square right sides together, with the marked square on top. Stitch ¼" from each side of the drawn line, cut apart on the drawn line, and press the seam allowances toward the black print triangles. The half-square-triangle units should measure 4½" x 4½". Make 96.

Make 96.

3 Arrange and sew four half-square-triangle units into a Pinwheel block as shown. The block should measure 8½" x 8½". Make 24 Pinwheel blocks.

Make 24.

Making the Four Patch Blocks

1 Divide the 96 coordinating 5" squares into 48 pairs, combining two contrasting colors or contrasting values (light and dark).

2 Layer each pair of squares right sides together. Stitch along two opposite sides of the squares as shown.

3 Cut down the center of the squares as shown and press the seam allowances open. Make a total of 96 two-patch units.

Cut.

2½" 2½"

Make 96.

4 Divide the units from step 3 into 48 new combinations of contrasting pairs.

5 With right sides together, layer the two-patch units, aligning the seams. Stitch along two opposite sides, making sure to stitch across the previous seamlines as shown.

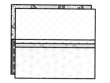

6 Cut down the center of the sewn units as shown and press the seam allowances open. Make a total of 96 Four Patch blocks.

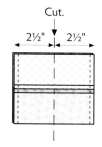

Make 96.

7 Arrange and sew four of the Four Patch blocks together into a Sixteen Patch block as shown. The block should measure 8½" x 8½". Make 24 Sixteen Patch blocks.

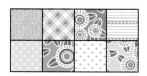 

Make 24.

Assembling the Quilt Top

1 Referring to the quilt assembly diagram, arrange the blocks in eight rows of six blocks each, alternating them as shown. Sew the blocks into rows, pressing the seam allowances toward the pinwheel blocks.

Quilt assembly

2 Sew the rows together and press in one direction. The quilt should now measure 48½" x 64½".

Adding the Borders

1 Piece the black-with-white-dot 2" x 40" strips together end to end.

2 Measure the quilt from top to bottom through the middle to determine the length of the side inner borders. From the pieced strip, cut two border strips to the needed length and attach them to the sides of the quilt.

3 Measure the quilt from side to side through the middle, including the side borders, to determine the length of the top and bottom borders. From the

pieced strip, cut two border strips to the needed length and attach them to the top and bottom of the quilt. The quilt should now measure 51½" x 67½".

4 Piece the seven black-print 6¾" x 40" strips together end to end.

5 Repeat the measuring and cutting process to add the black-print outer border. The quilt should now measure 64" x 80".

Finishing the Quilt

For help with any of the finishing steps, go to ShopMartingale.com/HowtoQuilt for free downloadable information.

1 Layer, baste, and quilt your quilt, or take it to your favorite long-arm machine quilter for finishing.

2 Using the black-with-white-dot 2¼"-wide strips, make and attach binding.

Quilt layout

Broken Dishes

Quilt blocks made by our ancestors were often named after common household items and everyday things. This quilt was inspired by the Civil War period in US history, when much more than dishes were broken as sons, brothers, fathers, and uncles marched off to battle.

"Broken Dishes," designed and made by Mary Etherington and Connie Tesene

Finished quilt: 36½" x 36½" ◆ **Finished block:** 6" x 6"

Materials

Yardage is based on 42"-wide fabric.

1½ yards *total* of assorted light prints for blocks and sashing

1½ yards *total* of assorted medium and dark prints for blocks

⅓ yard of red print for binding

1¼ yards of fabric for backing

40" x 40" piece of batting

Cutting

All measurements include ¼"-wide seam allowances.

Cutting for 1 Broken Dishes Block

From *1* of the assorted light prints, cut:
1 square, 3¼" x 3¼"; cut into quarters diagonally to yield 4 triangles
6 squares, 1⅞" x 1⅞"; cut in half diagonally to yield 12 triangles
4 rectangles, 1½" x 2½"

From *1* of the assorted medium or dark prints, cut:
2 squares, 2⅞" x 2⅞"; cut in half diagonally to yield 4 triangles
1 square, 2½" x 2½"
6 squares, 1⅞" x 1⅞"; cut in half diagonally to yield 12 triangles

Cutting for Sashing and Stars

From the assorted light prints, cut:
40 rectangles, 2" x 6½"

From the assorted medium and dark prints, cut:
16 squares, 2" x 2"
8 matching connector squares, 1¼" x 1¼", to match each 2" square (128 total)

Cutting for Binding

From the red print, cut:
4 strips, 2¼" x 42"

Making the Blocks

Use one light and one dark (or medium) print for each block.

1 Sew four light 3¼" triangles to the sides of a dark 2½" square. Press the seam allowances toward the dark square.

2 Sew four dark 2⅞" triangles to the sides of the unit from step 1. Press the seam allowances toward the dark triangles.

3 Sew a light 1⅞" triangle to a dark 1⅞" triangle to make a half-square-triangle unit. Make 12 units.

Make 12.

4 Join four light 1½" x 2½" rectangles, the unit from step 2, and the 12 units from step 3. Press the seam allowances as indicated. The block should measure 6½" x 6½". Make 25 blocks.

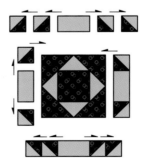 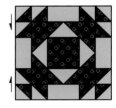

Make 25.

Assembling the Quilt Top

1 Draw a diagonal line on the wrong side of each dark 1¼" connector square.

2 Arrange five Broken Dishes blocks and four light 2" x 6½" sashing rectangles in a row. Make five. Arrange five light 2" x 6½" sashing rectangles and four dark 2" squares in alternating rows. When you have a pleasing arrangement, pin a marked connector square to each corner of the 24 sashing rectangles in the quilt center, right sides together, making sure the connector squares match the adjacent 2" dark squares. Pin two connector squares to each of the 16 sashing rectangles around the perimeter of the quilt. Again, the pieces in each star should be the same fabric.

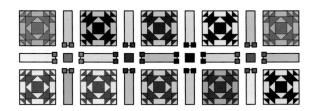

3 Sew on the drawn line of one of the connector squares. Trim the outside corner *of the connector square only*, ¼" from the stitching line. Press the seam allowances toward the corner. Repeat with remaining squares pinned on all rectangles.

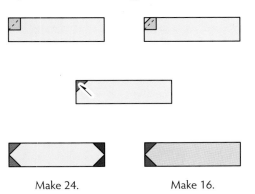

Make 24.   Make 16.

4 Sew the blocks and sashing units together in rows. Press the seam allowances toward the sashing units. Sew the sashing units and 2" dark squares together in rows. Press the seam allowances toward the sashing units. Join the rows. Press the seam allowances toward the sashing rows.

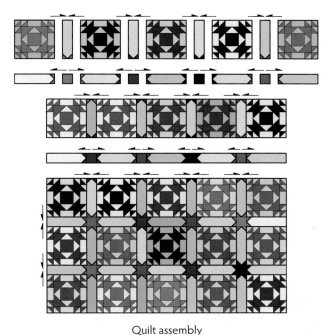

Quilt assembly

Finishing the Quilt

For help with any of the finishing steps, go to ShopMartingale.com/HowtoQuilt for free downloadable information.

1 Layer, baste, and quilt your quilt, or take it to your favorite long-arm machine quilter for finishing.

2 Using the red 2¼"-wide strips, make and attach binding.

Twist and Turn

Combine two simple blocks and your favorite fabrics to create this fun, scrappy quilt! It lends itself easily to any color scheme or fabric style.

"Twist and Turn," designed and pieced by Cheryl Wall, machine quilted by Mary Flynn

Finished quilt: 68½" x 72½" ◆ **Finished block:** 8" x 12"

Materials

Yardage is based on 42"-wide fabric.

3 yards *total* of assorted medium prints and plaids for blocks and border corner squares

1 yard of tan stripe for outer border

⅔ yard *total* of assorted black prints for blocks and border corner squares

⅔ yard *total* of assorted light prints and plaids for blocks

½ yard of black print for inner border

⅝ yard of fabric for binding

4½ yards of fabric for backing

76" x 80" piece of batting

Cutting

All measurements include ¼"-wide seam allowances.

From the assorted black prints, cut a *total* of:
36 pairs of matching squares, 2½" x 2½" (72 total)
36 squares, 2½" x 2½"
4 matching squares, 4½" x 4½"

From the assorted light prints and plaids, cut a *total* of:
36 pairs of matching squares, 2½" x 2½" (72 total)
36 squares, 2½" x 2½"

From the assorted medium prints and plaids, cut a *total* of:
17 squares, 4½" x 4½"
104 rectangles, 2½" x 8½"
70 rectangles, 2½" x 4½"
4 matching squares, 2½" x 2½"

From the black print for inner border, cut:
6 strips, 2½" x 42"

From the tan stripe, cut:
7 strips, 4½" x 42"

From the binding fabric, cut:
8 strips, 2¼" x 42"

Pick and Choose

This is a great project for using precut 2½"-wide strips, available at your local quilt shop. Supplement them with scraps from your stash to make the quilt uniquely yours!

Making the Four Patch Blocks

After sewing each seam, press the seam allowances in the direction indicated by the arrows.

1 Select two matching black 2½" squares and two matching light 2½" squares. Sew the black and light squares together in pairs. Sew the pairs together to form a four-patch unit. Make 36.

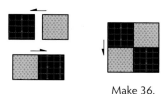

Make 36.

2 Sew two four-patch units together as shown.

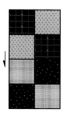

3 Select two different black 2½" squares, two different light 2½" squares, and two different medium 2½" x 4½" rectangles. Sew a light square and a black square to each end of the two rectangles.

4 Select two different medium 2½" x 8½" rectangles and sew them to the sides of the four-patch unit from step 2. Sew the units from step 3 to the top and bottom, keeping the black and light squares in a consistent pattern.

 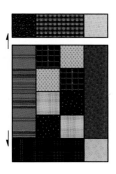

5 Repeat steps 2–4 to make 18 blocks.

Making the Courthouse Steps Blocks

1 Select one medium 4½" square, two different medium 2½" x 4½" rectangles, and two different medium 2½" x 8½" rectangles. Sew the 2½" x 4½" rectangles to the top and bottom of the square, and then sew the longer rectangles to the sides of the unit.

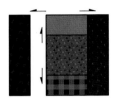

2 Select two different medium 2½" x 8½" rectangles and sew them to the top and bottom of the step 1 unit.

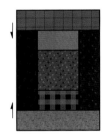

3 Repeat steps 1 and 2 to make 17 Courthouse Steps blocks.

Assembling the Quilt Top

1 Arrange the blocks in five rows of seven blocks each, alternating them as shown.

2 Sew the blocks in each row together, and then sew the rows together.

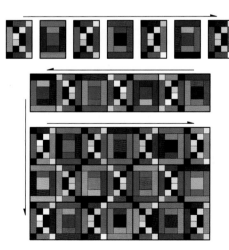

Quilt assembly

Adding the Borders

1 Sew the black 2½"-wide inner-border strips together end to end. Cut two strips, 56½" long, and two strips, 60½" long. Sew the 56½"-long strips to the top and bottom edges of the quilt top.

2 Sew a medium 2½" square to each end of the 60½"-long strips. Sew these strips to the sides of the quilt top.

3 Sew the tan 4½"-wide outer-border strips together end to end. Cut two strips, 60½" long, and two strips, 64½" long. Sew the 60½"-long strips to the top and bottom of the quilt.

4 Sew a black 4½" square to each end of the 64½"-long strips. Sew these strips to the sides of the quilt.

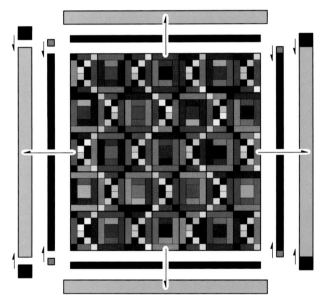

Adding the borders

Finishing the Quilt

For help with any of the finishing steps, go to ShopMartingale.com/HowtoQuilt for free downloadable information.

1 Layer, baste, and quilt your quilt, or take it to your favorite long-arm machine quilter for finishing.

2 Using the 2¼"-wide strips, make and attach binding.

Maize and Blue

A wide range of blues, soft buttery yellows, golds, and tans give this quilt a universal appeal. The zigzag setting strips and flying-geese border add extra pizzazz. The block, called Our Editor, was found in Once More around the Block *by Judy Hopkins (Martingale & Company, 2003).*

"Maize and Blue," designed and made by Laurie Simpson
Finished quilt: 99" x 99" ◆ **Finished block:** 12" x 12"

Materials

Yardage is based on 42"-wide fabric.

5 yards *total* of assorted medium- and dark-blue prints for blocks and borders

4¾ yards *total* of assorted light-yellow and gold prints for blocks and borders

2 yards *each* of 2 dark fabrics for zigzag setting strips

⅝ yard of medium-blue print for pieced outer border

⅞ yard of fabric for binding

9⅝ yards of fabric for backing

105" x 105" piece of batting

Cutting

All measurements include ¼"-wide seam allowances. Since the blocks are scrappy, cutting instructions are given for one block. Repeat the cutting for 25 blocks— 23 full blocks and 4 half blocks. For ease of construction, the cutting for the 4 half blocks will produce two pairs of identical half blocks. This is slightly different from the quilt shown in the photograph, in which the 4 half blocks are all different.

Cutting for 1 Block

From 1 light print, cut:
1 square, 7¼" x 7¼"; cut into quarters diagonally to yield 4 triangles
4 squares, 3⅞" x 3⅞"; cut in half diagonally to yield 8 triangles

From 1 dark print, cut:
1 square, 7¼" x 7¼"; cut into quarters diagonally to yield 4 triangles
4 squares, 3⅞" x 3⅞"; cut in half diagonally to yield 8 triangles

Cutting for Setting Strips, Borders, and Binding

From 1 dark print for zigzag setting strips, cut:
6 squares, 18¼" x 18¼"; cut into quarters diagonally to yield 24 triangles (2 are extra)
3 squares, 9⅜" x 9⅜"; cut in half diagonally to yield 6 triangles

From the other dark print for zigzag setting strips, cut:
6 squares, 18¼" x 18¼"; cut into quarters diagonally to yield 24 triangles (2 are extra)
3 squares, 9⅜" x 9⅜"; cut in half diagonally to yield 6 triangles

From the light prints, cut:
180 squares, 2⅞" x 2⅞"; cut in half diagonally to yield 360 triangles
Cut the rest of the light prints into 1"-wide strips of random lengths to equal at least 800" when pieced together end to end.

From the medium- and dark-blue prints, cut:
45 squares, 5¼" x 5¼"; cut into quarters diagonally to yield 180 triangles
32 squares, 4¼" x 4¼"; cut into quarters diagonally to yield 128 triangles
Cut the rest of the dark prints into 1"-wide strips of random lengths to equal at least 400" when pieced together end to end.

From the medium-blue print for outer border, cut:
33 squares, 4¼" x 4¼"; cut into quarters diagonally to yield 132 triangles

From the binding fabric, cut:
11 strips, 2¼" x 42"

A Note about the Borders

To simplify the fitting of the pieced outer border, the directions include an additional ½" dark border before the final border of blue quarter-square triangles. This differs slightly from the quilt shown in the photograph.

Making the Blocks

After sewing each seam, press the seam allowances in the direction indicated by the arrows.

1 Sew two pairs of light and dark quarter-square triangles together as shown. Sew the pairs together to make the center of the block.

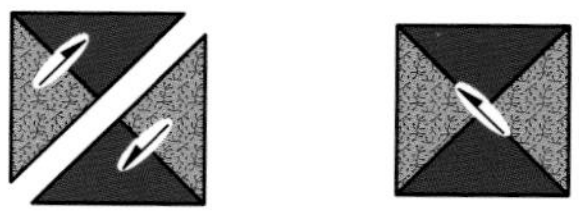

2 Sew two light half-square triangles to a dark quarter-square triangle as shown. Make two. Repeat to make two units with light quarter-square triangles and dark half-square triangles.

Make 2 of each.

3 Sew a light half-square triangle to a dark half-square triangle. Make four.

Make 4.

4 Sew the units from steps 1–3 together in rows as shown. Repeat for a total of 23 blocks.

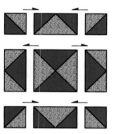 

Make 23.

5 Make four half blocks as shown using the remaining half-square and quarter-square triangles.

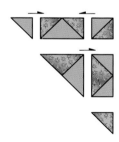 

Make 4.

Assembling the Quilt Top

1 Arrange the blocks and setting triangles into five vertical rows as shown in the quilt assembly diagram.

2 Sew the blocks and triangles into rows. Press seam allowances toward the triangles. Sew the rows together. Press the seam allowances to one side.

Quilt Assembly

Adding the Border

1 Sew the 1" light strips together so that you have eight strips of the following lengths: two 85½" strips, two 86½" strips, two 94½" strips, and two 95½" strips. Press the seam allowances to one side.

2 Sew the 85½" strips to the top and bottom of your quilt. Press the seam allowances toward the strips. Sew the two 86½" strips to the sides. Press toward the strips.

3 Sew a light 2⅞" half-square triangle to each side of a dark 5¼" quarter-square triangle. Press the seam allowances to one side. Repeat to make 180 flying-geese units for the borders.

Make 180.

4 Sew 43 of the flying-geese units into a strip. Press the seam allowances to one side. Make two. Sew these strips to the sides of your quilt. The triangles should point toward the top on the left and toward the bottom on the right.

▷▷▷▷▷▷▷▷▷▷▷▷▷▷▷▷▷▷▷▷▷▷

Side.
Make 2.

5 Sew 47 of the flying-geese units into a strip. Note how the geese are arranged in the corners. Press the seam allowances to one side. Make two.

Top

Bottom

6 Sew the strips from step 5 to the top and bottom of your quilt, making sure the triangles are oriented correctly. Press the seam allowances toward the narrow light border.

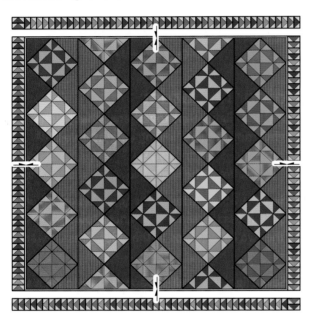

Adding the border

7 Sew the 1" x 94½" light strips to the top and bottom of your quilt. Press the seam allowances toward the strips.

8 Sew the 1" x 95½" strips to the sides of your quilt. Press toward the strips.

9 Sew the random-length 1" dark strips together to make two strips 95½" long and two strips 96½" long. Press the seam allowances in one direction.

10 Sew the 95½" dark strips to the top and bottom of your quilt. Press the seam allowances toward the strips. Sew the 96½" dark strips to the sides of the quilt. Press.

11 Sew 32 assorted medium- to dark-print and 33 medium-blue print 4¼" quarter-square triangles into a strip, alternating the fabrics as shown. Repeat to make four strips. Press the seam allowances to one side.

Make 4.

12 Sew a strip from step 11 to each side of the quilt. Press the seam allowances toward the strips. Miter the diagonal seams at each corner; to do this, fold the quilt on the diagonal to align the raw edges. Begin sewing at the inside corner and stitch to the outer corner.

Quilt layout

Finishing the Quilt

For help with any of the finishing steps, go to ShopMartingale.com/HowtoQuilt for free downloadable information.

1 Layer, baste, and quilt your quilt, or take it to your favorite long-arm machine quilter for finishing.

2 Using the 2¼"-wide strips, make and attach binding.

Around the Town

This quilt features a coordinated collection of polka dots and paisley prints. The dark and light units alternate to make a simple 12" block. When set together, some of the blocks are rotated, forming a barn raising–type arrangement. This quilt is proof that simple blocks can create a stunning design.

"Around the Town," designed and pieced by Nancy J. Martin, quilted by Frankie Schmitt.

Finished quilt: 60" x 60" ◆ **Finished block:** 12" x 12"

Materials

Yardage is based on 42"-wide fabric.

36 strips, 2½" x 22", of light prints for blocks

36 strips, 2½" x 22", of dark prints in teal, brown, and rose for blocks

1⅞ yards of floral for border and binding

3⅞ yards of fabric for backing

68" x 68" piece of batting

Cutting

All measurements include ¼"-wide seam allowances.

From 18 of the light strips, cut a *total* of:
72 rectangles, 2½" x 4½"

From 18 of the dark strips, cut a *total* of:
72 rectangles, 2½" x 4½"

From the floral, cut on the *lengthwise* grain:
2 strips, 6¼" x 48½"
2 strips, 6¼" x 60"

From the binding fabric, cut:
2¼"-wide bias strips to make 250" of bias binding

Making the Blocks

1 Stitch a light 2½"-wide strip to a dark 2½"-wide strip along the long edges to make a strip set. Press the seam allowances toward the dark strip. Make a total of 18 strip sets and cut into 144 segments, 2½" wide.

Make 18 strip sets.
Cut 144 segments.

2 Stitch a light and dark strip-set segment to each 2½" x 4½" light rectangle and dark rectangle as shown.

Make 72 of each.

3 Arrange five dark and four light units as shown and sew together to make a block. Make eight blocks. These will be referred to as dark blocks.

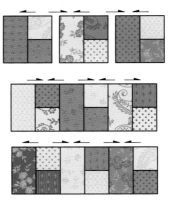

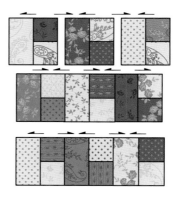

Make 8.

4 Arrange four dark and five light units as shown and sew together to make a block. Make eight blocks. These will be referred to as light blocks.

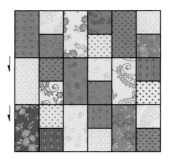

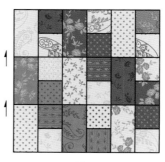

Make 8.

Assembling the Quilt Top

1 To create a barn raising–type design, arrange the light and dark blocks as shown in the layout diagram. There should be four dark blocks at the center of the quilt and one at each corner.

2 Sew the blocks into rows, pressing the seam allowances in opposite directions from row to row. Sew the rows together and press.

3 Using the 6¼"-wide border strips, add the borders to the sides and then to the top and bottom of the quilt top. Press the seam allowances toward the border.

Finishing the Quilt

For help with any of the finishing steps, go to ShopMartingale.com/HowtoQuilt for free downloadable information.

1 Layer, baste, and quilt your quilt, or take it to your favorite long-arm machine quilter for finishing.

2 Using the 2¼"-wide bias strips, make and attach binding.

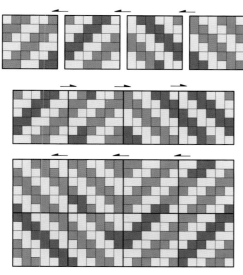

Quilt assembly

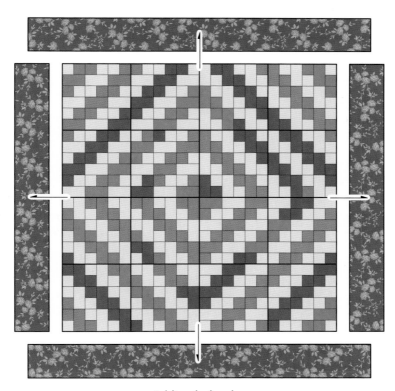

Adding the border

Ohio Star and Courthouse Steps

Raid your stash to gather all the fabrics needed for this delightful combination of Ohio Star and Courthouse Steps blocks. You can easily make circles appear in the design by using darker-value light fabrics for the background of some of the Ohio Star blocks, placing them in the spaces where the dark sides of the Courthouse Steps blocks meet.

"Ohio Star and Courthouse Steps," designed and pieced by Sally Schneider, quilted by Marilyn Gore

Finished quilt: 91½" x 91½" ◆ **Finished block:** 9" x 9"

▶ Materials

Yardage is based on 42"-wide fabric.

4⅓ yards *total* of assorted light fabrics for blocks

3⅛ yards *total* of assorted dark fabrics for blocks

2 yards *total* of assorted medium fabrics for blocks

½ yard of fabric for inner border

1⅓ yards of fabric for outer border

¾ yard of fabric for binding

8½ yards of fabric for backing

96" x 96" piece of batting

Magic Triangle Ruler (optional)

▶ Cutting

All measurements include ¼"-wide seam allowances. The yardages given for assorted darks and mediums are estimates only, based on using darks for the Ohio Star block center and star points and mediums within the star. As with any scrap quilt, varying the value placement makes the quilt more interesting, so feel free to play with that aspect of the quilt design. As long as there is contrast with the background, the values will work in any position.

From the assorted light fabrics, cut:
61 rectangles, 4" x 5"
41 sets of 4 matching squares, 3½" x 3½" (164 total)
80 rectangles, 1½" x 3½"
80 rectangles, 1½" x 5½"
80 rectangles, 1½" x 7½"

Cutting for the Ohio Star Blocks

From the assorted dark fabrics, cut:
41 sets of 2 matching rectangles, 4" x 5" (82 total), and 1 square, 3½" x 3½" (41 total)

From the assorted medium fabrics, cut:
41 rectangles, 4" x 5"

Cutting for the Courthouse Steps Blocks

From the assorted dark and medium fabrics, cut:
20 rectangles, 4" x 5"
80 rectangles, 1½" x 5½"
80 rectangles, 1½" x 7½"
80 rectangles, 1½" x 9½"

Cutting for Borders and Binding

From the inner-border fabric, cut:
9 strips, 1½" x 42"

From the outer-border fabric, cut:
9 strips, 4½" x 42"

From the binding fabric, cut:
10 strips, 2¼" x 42"

Making the Ohio Star Blocks

Directions are for making one block. For each Ohio Star block, choose two matching dark 4" x 5" rectangles, one matching dark 3½" square, one light 4" x 5" rectangle, four matching light 3½" squares, and one medium-value 4" x 5" rectangle.

1 Use Sally's special technique for making quarter-square-triangle units. Mark the wrong side of the light- and medium-value 4" x 5" rectangles using a square ruler with a 45° line through the center. Align the diagonal line of the ruler with the short side of the rectangle. Draw a diagonal line from the corner of the rectangle to the long side. Rotate the rectangle and

repeat from the opposite corner. You will have two parallel lines ½" apart. Place each marked rectangle right sides together with a dark 4" x 5" rectangle. Sew on the drawn lines, and then cut between them. Press the seam allowances toward the dark fabric.

2 Place a dark/medium half-square-triangle unit right sides together with a dark/light half-square-triangle unit, arranging the pieces so that the dark triangles are opposite light- or medium-value triangles. Draw a line diagonally across the half-square-triangle unit, crossing the seam. Sew ¼" from each side of the line, and then cut on the line.

Make 4.

3 Square up the quarter-square-triangle units to 3½" x 3½". Press the seam allowances toward the dark/medium side. Trim the dog-ears. Make four matching quarter-square-triangle units for each block.

4 Arrange the four quarter-square-triangle units with a dark 3½" square and four matching light 3½" squares as shown. Sew the pieces together in rows. Join the rows, matching the intersecting seams. Press the seam allowances in the directions indicated. Make 41 blocks.

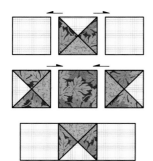 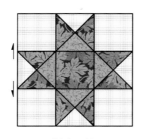

Make 41.

Making the Courthouse Steps Blocks

Directions are for making one block. The Courthouse Steps blocks are completely scrappy. The dark and light triangles in the center quarter-square-triangle units do not match in most of the blocks.

1 Follow the directions in step 1 of "Making the Ohio Star Blocks" to mark parallel lines on the wrong side of two light 4" x 5" rectangles. Place each marked rectangle right sides together with a dark 4" x 5" rectangle. Sew on the drawn lines, and then cut between them. Press the seam allowances toward the dark fabric.

2 Place the resulting half-square-triangle units right sides together, arranging the pieces so that the dark triangles are opposite light triangles. Draw a line diagonally across the half-square-triangle unit, crossing the seam. Sew ¼" from each side of the line, and then cut on the line.

3 Square up the quarter-square-triangle units to 3½" x 3½". Press the seam allowances to one side. Trim the dog-ears.

4 Sew light 1½" x 3½" rectangles to the two opposite light sides of a quarter-square-triangle unit. Press the seam allowances toward the rectangles.

5 Sew dark- or medium-value 1½" x 5½" rectangles to the two opposite dark sides of the unit. Press the seam allowances toward the rectangles that were just added.

6 Repeat steps 4 and 5 using light 1½" x 5½" rectangles and dark- or medium-value 1½" x 7½" rectangles.

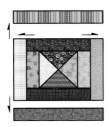

7 For the last round, repeat steps 4 and 5 using light 1½" x 7½" rectangles and dark- or medium-value 1½" x 9½" rectangles. Press seam allowances toward the rectangles just added. Make 40 blocks.

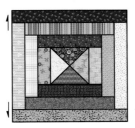

Make 40.

Assembling the Quilt Top

1 Arrange the Ohio Star and Courthouse Steps blocks in rows, alternating the blocks and placing an Ohio Star block in each corner. Refer to the quilt layout diagram on page 114 and make sure the Courthouse Steps blocks are turned in the right direction.

2 Sew the blocks together in rows, pressing the seam allowances in opposite directions from row to row.

3 Join the rows, pressing the seam allowances in one direction.

Adding the Borders

1 Sew the inner-border strips together end to end to make one long strip. Measure the quilt through the center from top to bottom and cut two strips that length.

2 Sew the trimmed border strips to the sides of the quilt top. Press the seam allowances toward the border strips.

3 Measure the quilt through the center from side to side, including the borders just added. Cut two strips that length.

4 Sew the trimmed border strips to the top and bottom of the quilt top. Press the seam allowances toward the border strips.

5 Repeat steps 1–4 to add the outer-border strips.

Finishing the Quilt

For help with any of the finishing steps, go to ShopMartingale.com/HowtoQuilt for free downloadable information.

1 Layer, baste, and quilt your quilt, or take it to your favorite long-arm machine quilter for finishing.

2 Using the 2¼"-wide strips, make and attach binding.

Quilt layout

Labyrinth

This quilt has a great flea market-type appeal. To achieve this look, don't try to match fabrics; just stitch them together randomly. This quilt is quick and fun.

"Labyrinth," designed by Julie Popa, pieced by Tina Fonnesbeck and Julie Popa, quilted by Paula Murray

Finished quilt: 64½" x 86"

Materials

Yardage is based on 42"-wide fabric.

2⅝ yards *total* of assorted prints for pieced panels

1⅓ yards of red print for sashing, inner border, and binding

1⅝ yards of brown solid for sashing

1⅓ yards of brown floral for outer border

5⅝ yards of fabric for backing

72" x 93" piece of batting

Cutting

All measurements include ¼"-wide seam allowances. Cut strips across the width of the fabric unless otherwise indicated.

From the assorted prints, cut a *total* of:
2 to 3 strips, 6½" wide, in random lengths to equal at least 60" when pieced together
2 to 3 strips, 5½" wide, in random lengths to equal at least 60" when pieced together
2 to 3 strips, 4½" wide, in random lengths to equal at least 60" when pieced together
3½"-wide strips in random lengths to equal at least 300" when pieced together
2½"-wide strips in random lengths to equal at least 360" when pieced together

From the brown solid, cut on the *lengthwise* grain:
6 strips, 4½" x 50½"
5 rectangles, 4½" x 10"

From the red print, cut:
10 strips, 2" x 42"
8 strips, 2½" x 42"
5 rectangles, 4½" x 10"

From the brown floral, cut:
7 strips, 6" x 42"

Making the Pieced Panels

1 Sew several assorted-print 2½"-wide strips of varied lengths together end to end to make a pieced strip 60" long, trimming the strip as needed to achieve the required length. Repeat with the remaining 2½"-wide strips to make a total of six pieced strips.

Make 6.

2 Repeat step 1 to make five 60"-long pieced strips from the 3½"-wide strips, and one 60"-long pieced strip *each* from the 4½"-, 5½"-, and 6½"-wide strips.

3 Sew the pieced strips together along the long edges in the order shown to make two strip sets, each measuring 21½" x 60". From the strip sets, cut a *total* of 10 segments, 10" wide.

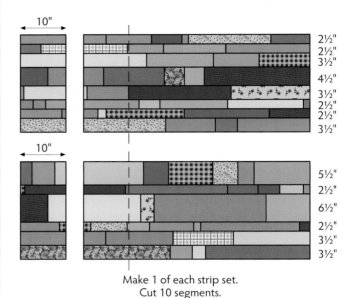

Make 1 of each strip set.
Cut 10 segments.

4 Arrange the segments into five rows of two segments each. Mix up the segments as much as possible by turning some of them upside down and/or moving them to opposite sides so that you spread out the colors across the quilt. When you are pleased with the arrangement, sew the segments in each row together.

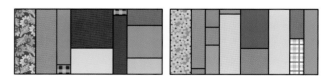

Assembling the Quilt Top

1 Refer to the quilt assembly diagram below to sew the red and brown 4½" x 10" sashing rectangles to the ends of the rows as shown. Press the seam allowances toward the rectangles. Sew the rows together, inserting a brown 4½" x 50½" sashing strip between each one. Press the seam allowances toward the sashing.

2 Sew the red 2" x 42" inner-border strips together and press the seam allowances to one side. Measure the quilt top lengthwise through the center, cut two strips to the correct length, and sew them to the sides of the quilt top. In the same manner, measure the width of the quilt top, cut two strips to that length, and sew them to the top and bottom of the quilt top.

3 Repeat step 2 with the brown-floral 6" x 42" strips to add the outer border and press.

Finishing the Quilt

For help with any of the finishing steps, go to ShopMartingale.com/HowtoQuilt for free downloadable information.

1 Layer, baste, and quilt your quilt, or take it to your favorite long-arm machine quilter for finishing.

2 Using the red 2½"-wide strips, make and attach binding.

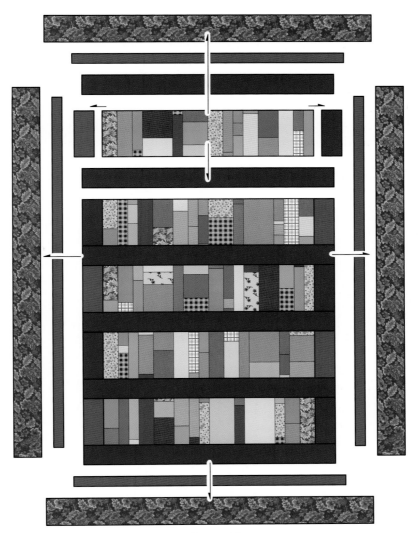

Quilt assembly

Pineapple Nine Patch

The blocks in this quilt masquerade as the classic Pineapple block but are pieced together in nine-patch fashion. Whether you use scraps or a planned assortment of fabrics, you'll be delighted at how quickly your quilt comes together.

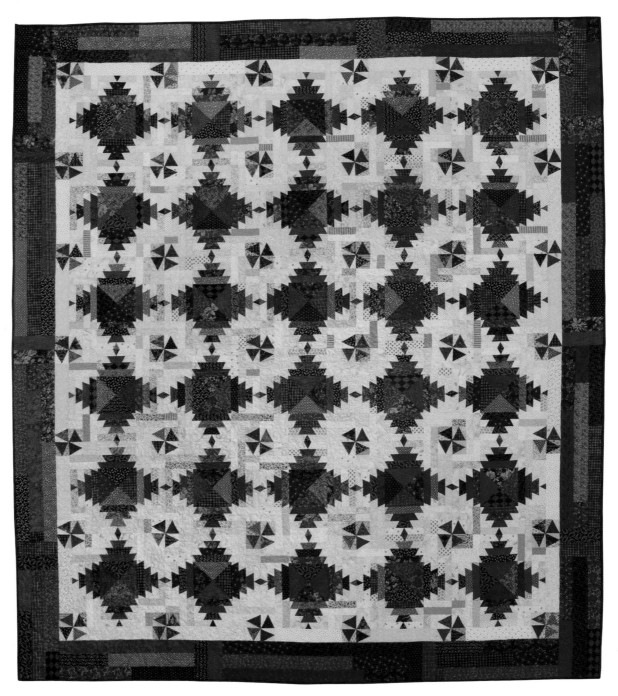

"Pineapple Nine Patch," designed and pieced by Cathy Wierzbicki, machine quilted by Bonnie Gibbs

Finished quilt: 84" x 97½"   ◆   **Finished block: 13½" x 13½"**

Materials

Yardage is based on 42"-wide fabric.

6 yards *total* of assorted dark fabrics (Cathy recommends ½ yard *each* of 12 fabrics) for blocks and borders

5½ yards *total* of assorted light fabrics (Cathy recommends ½ yard *each* of 11 fabrics) for blocks and borders

¾ yard of fabric for binding

8 yards of fabric for backing

92" x 106" piece of batting

See-through template plastic or Tri-Recs Tools (available at quilt and fabric shops)

Cutting

All measurements include ¼"-wide seam allowances. Before you begin cutting, if you are not using the Tri-Recs Tools, make templates for pieces A–D using template plastic and the patterns on page 122. Be sure to include all of the markings. You will be using both sides of these templates to cut your block pieces, so flip each template over and mark the reverse side with an R. To make the best use of your strips when cutting the pieces, invert the template every other cut. If you are using the Tri-Recs Tools, match the patterns on page 122 with the tool to find the corresponding letter for each piece.

From the assorted dark fabrics, cut a *total* of:
12 strips, 6" x 42"; from the strips, cut 120 pieces using template A
6 strips, 6¾" x 42"; crosscut into 30 squares, 6¾" x 6¾". Cut into quarters diagonally to yield 120 triangles (E).
32 strips, 2½" x 42"; from 7 of the strips, cut 168 pieces using template C. Set aside the remaining 25 strips.

From the assorted light fabrics, cut a *total* of:
12 strips, 6" x 42"; from the strips, cut*:
   120 pieces using template B
   120 pieces using template B reversed
15 strips, 2½" x 42"; from the strips, cut*:
   168 pieces using template D
   168 pieces using template D reversed
22 rectangles, 2½" x 10"
44 strips, 1½" x 42"

From the fabric for binding, cut:
10 strips, 2¼" x 42"

*If you cut from folded strips, each cut will yield 1 regular piece and 1 reversed piece.

Making the Blocks

After sewing each seam, press the seam allowances in the direction indicated by the arrows.

1 Sew one B piece and one B reversed piece to each A piece. The units should measure 6" square.

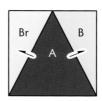

Make 120.

2 Cut each unit horizontally into four 1½"-wide slices. Invert each slice, and then separate the slices from all of the units into stacks of like pieces.

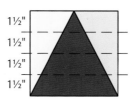 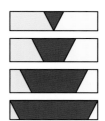

3 Sew the slices back together in their inverted positions to make unit 1, selecting one piece from each stack. Choose four different fabrics for each unit.

Unit 1.
Make 120.

4 To make unit 2, sew one D piece and one D reversed piece to each of the C pieces. The units should measure 2½" square.

Make 168.

5 Sew two assorted light 1½" x 42" strips together along the long edges to make a strip set. Repeat to make a total of 22 strip sets. Crosscut the strip sets into 120 segments, 2½" wide, and 120 segments, 4½" wide.

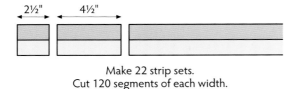

Make 22 strip sets.
Cut 120 segments of each width.

6 Sew a 2½"-wide segment to the triangle-point side of a unit from step 4. Add a 4½"-wide segment to the upper long edge of the unit. Make a total of 120 units, being careful to always orient the dark triangle in the same direction. These units should measure 4½" square. Set aside the remaining units from step 4 for the border.

Unit 2.
Make 120.

7 To make unit 3, select four assorted E triangles. Sew the triangles into pairs, and then sew the pairs together. Repeat to make a total of 30 units.

Unit 3.
Make 30.

8 Select and arrange four *each* of units 1 and 2 and one unit 3 into three horizontal rows. Sew the units in each row together, and then sew the rows together. Repeat to make a total of 30 blocks. The blocks should measure 14" square.

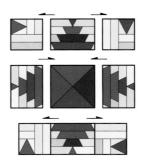
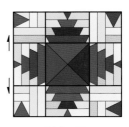

Make 30.

Assembling the Quilt Top

1 Refer to the quilt assembly diagram on page 121 to lay out the blocks in six rows of five blocks each.

2 Sew the blocks in each row together, and then sew the rows together.

Adding the Borders

1 Sew C/D units to the ends of a light 2½" x 10" rectangle, orienting the triangles as shown. Repeat to make a total of 22 units.

Make 22.

2 Sew together five units from step 1 to make the top inner-border section. Repeat to make the bottom inner-border section. Refer to the assembly diagram to sew these border strips to the top and bottom of the quilt top, making sure the triangles are oriented correctly. Sew together six units from step 1. Add one of the remaining C/D units to each end of the strip. Repeat to make a total of two side inner borders. Add the borders to the sides of the quilt top.

Top/bottom border.
Make 2.

Side border.
Make 2.

3 To make the pieced outer border, sew two different dark 2½" x 42" strips together along the long edges to make a strip set. Repeat to make a total of two strip sets. Crosscut the strip sets into 10 segments, 6½" wide.

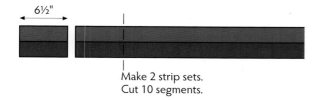

Make 2 strip sets.
Cut 10 segments.

4 Cut the remaining dark 2½" x 42" strips into random lengths from 5" to 22". For each strip set, you will need three pieces that are at least 22" long. Sew pieces together end to end with a straight seam to achieve the needed length. Make a total of 42 strips, 22" long. Sew three strips together along the long edges to make a strip set. Repeat to make a total of 14 strip sets. Trim eight strip sets to 21¾", leaving the remaining six strip sets at 22".

Make 8.   Make 6.

5 Alternately sew together two 6½" segments from step 3 and three 22" segments from step 4. Repeat to make a total of two borders. Trim the borders to fit the width of your quilt, which should be 72". Sew these borders to the top and bottom edges of the quilt top.

6 Sew together three 6½" segments and four 21¾" segments. Repeat to make a total of two borders. Sew these borders to the sides of the quilt top.

Finishing the Quilt

For help with any of the finishing steps, go to ShopMartingale.com/HowtoQuilt for free downloadable information.

1 Layer, baste, and quilt your quilt, or take it to your favorite long-arm machine quilter for finishing.

2 Using the 2¼"-wide strips, make and attach binding.

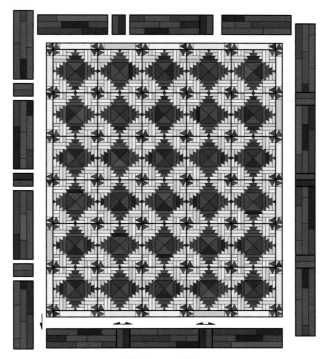

Quilt assembly

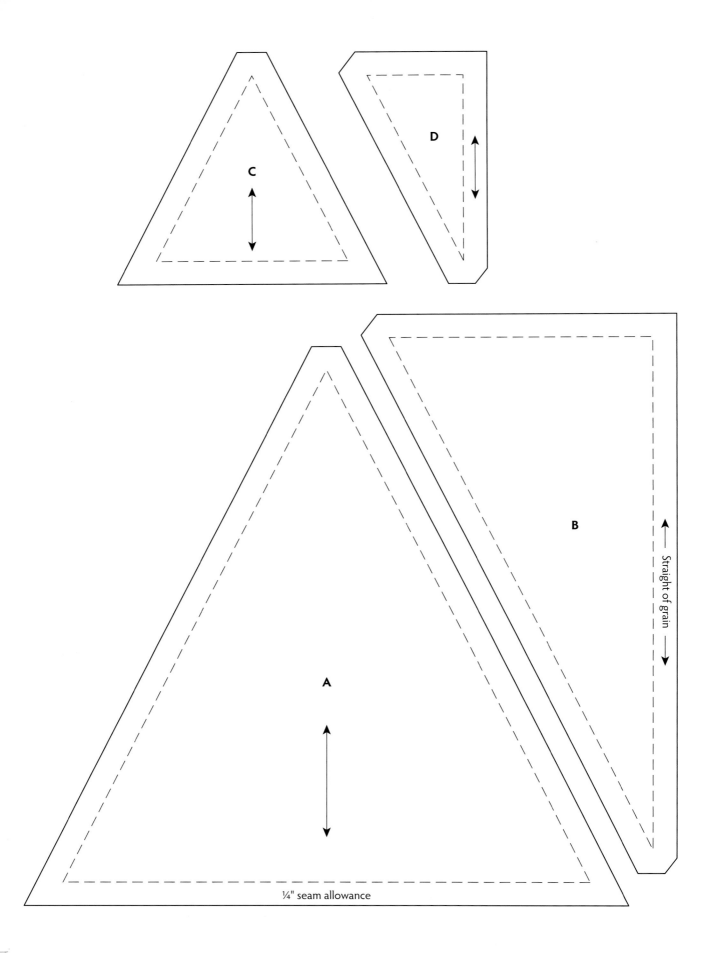

C

D

B

Straight of grain

A

¼" seam allowance

Road Trip

What could be better than a road trip? A road trip with terrific quilting friends! You can hear the chatter now: "Which way are we going?" "Let's have some chocolate!" "Where is the GPS?" "RECALCULATING!" "How much money did you spend?" Let this quilt remind you of some of the great trips you've taken with friends.

"Road Trip," designed by Pat Wys, pieced by Marty Miller, quilted by Leisa Wiggley

Finished quilt: 65½" x 81½"   ◆   **Finished block:** 10" x 10"

Materials

Yardage is based on 42"-wide fabric.

2¾ yards *total* of assorted dark neutral prints for blocks and setting triangles

1¾ yards *total* of assorted medium neutral prints for blocks and setting triangles

1⅔ yards of white print for sashing

1½ yards *total* of assorted light neutral prints for blocks and setting triangles

1¼ yards *total* of assorted black tone on tones for blocks, sashing cornerstones, and setting triangles

⅞ yard of fabric for binding*

5 yards of fabric for backing

73" x 89" piece of batting

Optional; the quilt shown uses black scraps for the binding.

Cutting

All measurements include ¼"-wide seam allowances.

From the assorted light prints, cut a *total* of:
284 squares, 2½" x 2½"

From the assorted dark prints, cut a *total* of:
142 squares, 4½" x 4½"

From the assorted medium prints, cut a *total* of:
320 squares, 2½" x 2½"

From the assorted black tone on tones, cut a *total* of:
32 squares, 2½" x 2½"
9 squares, 7" x 7"; cut into quarters diagonally to yield 36 triangles
4 squares, 4⅛" x 4⅛"; cut into quarters diagonally to yield 16 triangles (2 are extra)
2 squares, 2⅜" x 2⅜"; cut in half diagonally to yield 4 triangles
49 squares, 2" x 2"

From the white print, cut:
21 strips, 2" x 42"; crosscut into 80 rectangles, 2" x 10½"

From the binding fabric, cut:
2½"-wide bias strips to make 306" of bias binding

Making the Blocks and Setting Triangles

1 Draw a diagonal line from corner to corner on the wrong side of the light 2½" squares.

2 Place two marked light 2½" squares on opposite corners of a dark 4½" square. Stitch on the drawn lines. Press the triangle corners toward the outside edges of the large square. Check to make sure your triangle corners line up precisely with the edges of the larger square, and then trim away the bottom two layers of the triangle corners, leaving a ¼" seam allowance. Make 142.

Make 142.

3 Sew two medium 2½" squares together to make a pair. Make 160 pairs.

Make 160.

4 Arrange four units from step 2 and four pairs from step 3 together in three rows with a black tone-on-tone 2½" square as shown. Sew the units into rows. Press the seam allowances as indicated by the arrows. Sew the rows together. Make 32 blocks.

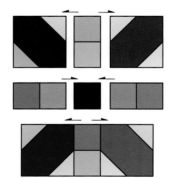

Make 32.

5 Arrange two pairs from step 3 together with one unit from step 2, two black tone-on-tone 7" triangles, and one black tone-on-tone 4⅛" triangle as shown. Sew the units together in rows, pressing the seam allowances as indicated. Sew the rows together. Make 14 pieced side setting triangles.

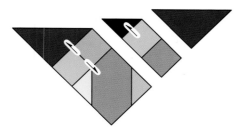

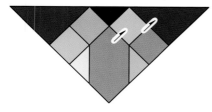

Make 14.

6 Arrange a pair from step 3 together with two black tone-on-tone 7" triangles and one black tone-on-tone 2⅜" triangle as shown. Sew the larger black triangles to the left and right sides of the squares. Press the seam allowances toward the triangles. Then add the smaller black triangle and press. Make four corner setting triangles.

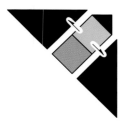 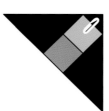

Make 4.

Make Use of the Waste

If you like to make small quilts, you can make bonus half-square-triangle units when sewing the small squares to the corners of the larger squares. Simply sew another line of stitching ½" from the first stitched line. Cut between the two stitched lines and press the seam allowances toward the darker fabric.

Assembling the Quilt Top

1 Referring to the quilt assembly diagram below, arrange the blocks, sashing strips, and sashing squares in diagonal rows.

2 Sew the block and sashing rows, including the side setting triangles, as shown. Join the rows. Press the seam allowances toward the sashing.

3 Add the corner triangles to the quilt. Press the seam allowances toward the sashing.

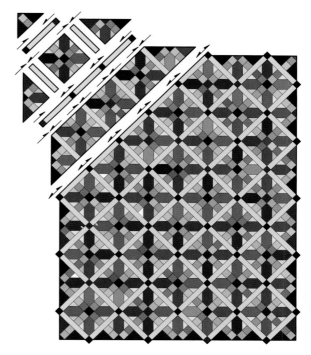

Quilt assembly

4 Trim the sashing squares along the edges of the quilt and square up the corners.

Finishing the Quilt

For help with any of the finishing steps, go to ShopMartingale.com/HowtoQuilt for free downloadable information.

1 Layer, baste, and quilt your quilt, or take it to your favorite long-arm machine quilter for finishing.

2 Using the 2½"-wide bias strips, make and attach binding.

Diamond Crosses

An amazing variety of quilt blocks and shapes can be made from 10" precut squares. This block incorporates two favorite shapes—diamonds and crosses. Choosing three high-contrast fabrics for each block will make the design pop.

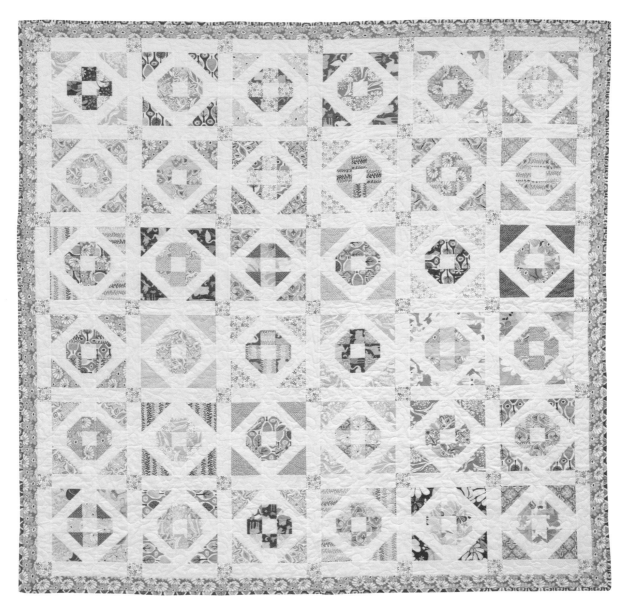

"Diamond Crosses," designed and made by Kate Henderson

Finished quilt: 78½" x 78½"   ◆   **Finished block:** 10" x 10"

Materials

Yardage is based on 42"-wide fabric.

4 yards of cream fabric for blocks and sashing

36 assorted squares, 10" x 10", for blocks

⅔ yard of blue floral for border

⅜ yard of blue print for sashing squares

¾ yard of multicolored print for binding

7 yards of fabric for backing*

84" x 84" piece of batting

If your backing fabric measures a true 42" wide after trimming off the selvages, you'll need only 4¾ yards.

Cutting

All measurements include ¼"-wide seam allowances.

From the cream fabric, cut:
9 strips, 5" x 42"; cut into 72 squares, 5" x 5"
34 strips, 2½" x 42"; cut into:
    84 rectangles, 2½" x 10½"
    180 squares, 2½" x 2½"

From *each* of the assorted 10" squares, cut:*
2 squares, 5" x 5" (72 total)
8 squares, 2½" x 2½" (288 total)

From the blue print, cut:
4 strips, 2½" x 42"; crosscut into 49 squares,
    2½" x 2½"

From the blue floral, cut:
8 strips, 2½" x 42"

From the multicolored print, cut:
9 strips, 2½" x 42"

Refer to cutting diagram below.

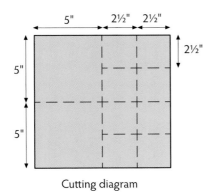

Cutting diagram

Making the Blocks

For each block, you'll need the following pieces:

    From cream: two 5" squares and five 2½" squares

    From three *different* assorted squares: two matching 5" squares, four matching 2½" squares, and four matching 2½" squares

1 Mark a diagonal line on the wrong side of a cream 5" square. Layer the marked square with an assorted 5" square, right sides together, and stitch ¼" from each side of the marked line. Cut the squares apart on the line to make two half-square-triangle units. Press the seam allowances toward the darker triangle. Trim the units to measure 4½" x 4½". Repeat to make four matching half-square-triangle units.

Make 4.

2 Draw a diagonal line on the wrong side of four matching assorted 2½" squares. Place a square on the cream corner of a half-square-triangle unit, right sides together. Sew on the marked line. Trim the excess corner fabric leaving a ¼" seam allowance. Press the seam allowances toward the resulting triangle. Make four matching units.

3 Sew a cream 2½" square to an assorted 2½" square. Press the seam allowances toward the darker square. Make four matching units.

Make 4.

4 Lay out the units from steps 2 and 3 in three rows as shown. Place the remaining cream 2½" square in the center of the block. Join the pieces in each row. Press the seam allowances in the directions indicated by the arrows.

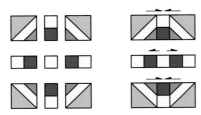

5 Join the rows and press the seam allowances toward the center. Repeat the process to make 36 blocks total.

Make 36.

Assembling the Quilt Top

1 Sew six blocks and seven cream rectangles together, alternating them as shown. Press the seam allowances toward the cream rectangles. Make six block rows.

Make 6.

2 Sew six cream rectangles and seven blue squares together, alternating them as shown. Press the seam allowances toward the cream rectangles. Make seven sashing rows.

Make 7.

3 Referring to the quilt assembly diagram above right and the quilt photo on page 126, lay out the block rows and sashing rows in a pleasing arrangement. Join the rows and press the seam allowances toward the sashing rows.

4 Sew the blue-floral strips together in pairs to make four long strips. Measure the length of the quilt top. Trim two of the strips to this length and sew them to the sides of the quilt top. Press the seam allowances toward the border. Measure the width of the quilt top, including the borders just added, and trim the two remaining strips to this measurement. Sew these strips to the top and bottom of the quilt top; press the seam allowances toward the strips.

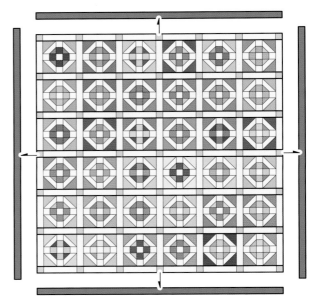

Quilt assembly

Finishing the Quilt

For help with any of the finishing steps, go to ShopMartingale.com/HowtoQuilt for free downloadable information.

1 Layer, baste, and quilt your quilt, or take it to your favorite long-arm machine quilter for finishing.

2 Using the multicolored 2½"-wide strips, make and attach binding.

Confetti Crossings

Two simple blocks combine for big impact in this quilt top. The number of half-square-triangle units needed may seem like a lot at first, but once they're made, the blocks come together quickly.

"Confetti Crossings," designed and pieced by Amy Ellis, machine quilted by Natalia Bonner.

Finished quilt: 93" x 93"   ◆   **Finished block: 12" x 12"**

Materials

Yardage is based on 42"-wide fabric.

4⅞ yards of cream print for blocks and border

3¼ yards of brown print for blocks

¼ yard *each* of 16 assorted prints for blocks

¾ yard of light-blue print for binding

7 yards of fabric for backing

99" x 99" piece of batting

Cutting

All measurements include ¼"-wide seam allowances.

From the cream print, cut:
13 strips, 8" x 42"; crosscut into 50 squares, 8" x 8"
12 strips, 4½" x 42"

From the brown print, cut:
13 strips, 8" x 42"; crosscut into 50 squares, 8" x 8"

From *each* of the 16 assorted prints, cut:
2 strips, 3½" x 42" (32 total)

From the light-blue print, cut:
10 strips, 2½" x 42"

Making the Blocks

Making 400 half-square-triangle units is no small feat, but the results are worth it. Put on some music and enjoy the process.

1 Draw lines from corner to corner along both diagonals on the wrong side of each cream-print square.

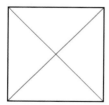

2 Pin a marked cream square to a brown-print square, right sides together. Sew ¼" from each side of both lines; make 50.

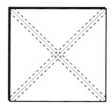

Make 50.

3 Cut each sewn square in half vertically and horizontally to make four smaller squares. Then cut on each diagonal line to create eight half-square-triangle units per set (400 total). Press the seam allowances toward the cream fabric in half the units and toward the brown fabric in the remaining units.

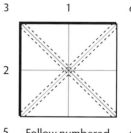

Follow numbered cutting lines to separate the units.

Make 200 of each.

4 Arrange 16 half-square-triangle units to make a block; make 25 blocks. Pay careful attention to the direction of the seam allowances. Chain stitch the units in pairs, and then into rows. Press the seam allowances in alternate directions from row to row. Pin and sew the rows together to complete the blocks. Press the seam allowances in one direction. Trim and square the blocks to 12½" x 12½".

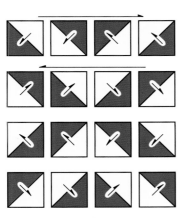

Arrows indicate seam
allowance direction.

5 Sew the assorted 3½" strips into eight strip sets of four fabrics each. Press the seam allowances in one direction. Cut 96 segments, 3½" wide, from the strip sets.

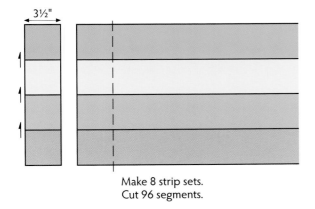

Make 8 strip sets.
Cut 96 segments.

6 Nesting the seam allowances, pin and sew four segments together to make a patchwork block; make 24. Press the seam allowances in one direction. Trim and square the blocks to 12½" x 12½".

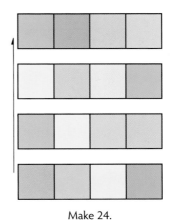

Make 24.

Assembling the Quilt Top

1 Lay out seven rows of seven blocks each, alternating the blocks as shown. Pin and sew the blocks together in rows, pressing the seam allowances in alternate directions from row to row.

2 Pin and sew the rows together to complete the quilt top. Press the seam allowances in one direction.

Quilt assembly

3 Join three cream 4½" strips with diagonal seams. Repeat to make four long pieced strips, one for each side of the quilt. Trim the seam allowances ¼" beyond the seamlines and press them open.

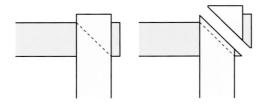

4 Measure through the center of the quilt top from top to bottom and cut two border strips to this length. Sew the borders to the quilt sides. Measure the quilt top, including the side borders, from side to side through the center and cut the remaining border strips to this length. Sew the borders to the top and bottom edges of the quilt.

Throw-Quilt Option

For a throw quilt, make 20 blocks (10 of each) for a quilt that measures 56" x 68".

Materials
2⅜ yards of cream print for blocks and borders
1¼ yards of brown print for blocks
¼ yard or 1 fat quarter (18" x 21") *each* of 16 assorted prints for blocks
⅝ yard of light-blue print for binding
3½ yards of fabric for backing
62" x 74" piece of batting

Finishing the Quilt

For help with any of the finishing steps, go to ShopMartingale.com/HowtoQuilt for free downloadable information.

1 Layer, baste, and quilt your quilt, or take it to your favorite long-arm machine quilter for finishing.

2 Using the light-blue 2½"-wide strips, make and attach binding.

Town Square

The folded-corner rectangle units on the outer edges of the blocks in this quilt appear to form a triangle, creating the illusion that the squares are floating on top.

"Town Square," designed and made by Kim Brackett

Finished quilt: 63½" x 63½"   ◆   **Finished block:** 6" x 6"

▶ Materials

Yardage is based on 42"-wide fabric.

24 strips, 2½" x 42", of assorted dark prints in reds, blues, browns, and greens for blocks and sashing

1⅔ yards of cream print for blocks and sashing

1⅔ yards of large-scale floral for outer border and binding

⅓ yard of red print for inner border

4¼ yards of fabric for backing

67½" x 67½" piece of batting

▶ Cutting

All measurements include ¼"-wide seam allowances.

From *each* of 12 assorted dark-print strips, cut:
2 rectangles, 2½" x 6½" (24 total)
3 rectangles, 2½" x 4½" (36 total)
4 squares, 2½" x 2½" (48 total)

From *each* of the remaining 12 assorted dark-print strips, cut:
1 rectangle, 2½" x 6½" (12 total)
3 rectangles, 2½" x 4½" (36 total)
6 squares, 2½" x 2½" (72 total)

From the remainder of 1 dark-print strip, cut:
1 square, 2½" x 2½" (If you don't have a leftover strip that is long enough to cut this square, use a scrap from either of your border prints.)

From the cream print, cut:
21 strips, 2½" x 42"; crosscut into:
    84 rectangles, 2½" x 6½"
    108 squares, 2½" x 2½"

From the red print, cut:
6 strips, 1½" x 42"

From the large-scale floral, cut:
6 strips, 6" x 42"
7 strips, 2½" x 42"

Making the Blocks

1 Using one dark and one cream 2½" square, make a half-square-triangle unit. Press the seam allowances toward the dark triangle. Make 36.

Make 36.

2 Select a dark 2½" square and a matching 2½" x 4½" rectangle. Sew the square to the cream side of a half-square-triangle unit from step 1. Press the seam allowances toward the square. Add the matching rectangle to the top of the unit. Press the seam allowances toward the rectangle. Repeat with the remaining units from step 1.

Make 36.

3 Select a dark 2½" x 4½" rectangle and a matching 2½" x 6½" rectangle. Make folded-corner units as shown using the rectangles and cream

Cutting from Scraps

If you prefer to use scraps, follow the instructions below, cutting the pieces in each set from the same fabric. See "Cutting" at left for instructions on cutting the borders and binding.

From assorted dark prints, cut:
36 squares, 2½" x 2½"
36 sets of:
    1 rectangle, 2½" x 4½"
    1 square, 2½" x 2½"
36 sets of:
    1 rectangle, 2½" x 6½"
    1 rectangle, 2½" x 4½"
49 squares, 2½" x 2½"

From assorted cream prints, cut:
108 squares, 2½" x 2½"
84 rectangles, 2½" x 6½"

2½" squares. Press the seam allowances toward the cream triangles. Make 36 matching pairs.

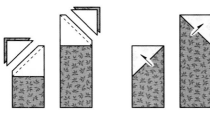

Make 36
matching pairs.

4 Working with matching pairs of units from step 3, sew the 2½" x 4½" folded-corner unit to the side of a unit from step 2. Press the seam allowances toward the folded-corner unit. Sew the remaining folded-corner unit to the top. Press the seam allowances toward the folded-corner unit you just added. Make 36 blocks.

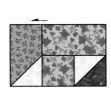 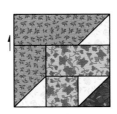

Make 36.

Assembling the Quilt Top

1 Arrange the blocks, cream 2½" x 6½" rectangles, and remaining dark 2½" squares as shown. Sew the units together in horizontal rows, pressing the seam allowances as shown. Sew the rows together. Press the seam allowances in one direction.

2 Add the red 1½"-wide inner-border strips to the sides, and then to the top and bottom of the quilt.

3 Add the floral 6"-wide outer-border strips in the same manner to complete the quilt top.

Finishing the Quilt

For help with any of the finishing steps, go to ShopMartingale.com/HowtoQuilt for free downloadable information.

1 Layer, baste, and quilt your quilt, or take it to your favorite long-arm machine quilter for finishing.

2 Using the floral 2½"-wide strips, make and attach binding.

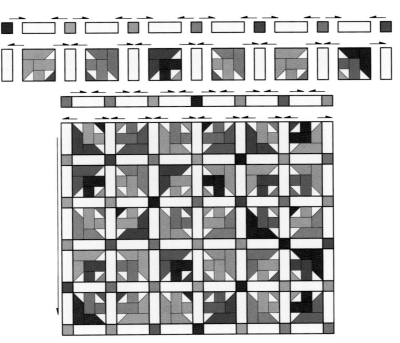

Quilt assembly

Traveling Star

This cozy lap-quilt design uses two coordinating blocks to make a secondary design. Deanne chose reds, greens, and blues, but feel free to substitute your favorite three-color combination.

"Traveling Star," designed and pieced by Deanne Eisenman, quilted by Annette Ashbach of The Quiltmaker's Nest

Finished quilt: 74" x 74"   ◆   **Finished block:** 12" x 12"

Materials

Yardage is based on 42"-wide fabric. Fat quarters measure 18" x 21".

11 fat quarters of assorted tan fabrics for blocks

10 fat quarters of assorted green fabrics for blocks

7 fat quarters of assorted red fabrics for blocks

4 fat quarters of assorted blue fabrics for blocks

1 yard of tan fabric for inner border

½ yard of red fabric for middle border

7 yards of blue fabric for outer border

5 yards of red print for binding

4½ yards of fabric for backing

82" x 82" piece of batting

Cutting

All measurements include ¼"-wide seam allowances. Cut strips across the width of the fabric. This quilt is made from two different blocks, and the cutting instructions are listed separately for each block. To make block assembly easier, be sure to label each piece with the piece and block number.

Cutting for Block 1

From the assorted tan fat quarters, cut a *total* of:
13 squares, 4½" x 4½" (A1)
104 squares, 2½" x 2½" (C1)
52 squares, 27" x 27" (G1)

From the assorted red fat quarters, cut a *total* of:
104 rectangles, 2½" x 4½" (B1)
104 squares, 2½" x 2½" (E1)

From the assorted green fat quarters, cut a *total* of:
52 squares, 27" x 27" (F1)
104 squares, 2½" x 2½" (D1)

Cutting for Block 2

From the assorted tan fat quarters, cut a *total* of:
6 squares, 5¼" x 5¼"; cut into quarters diagonally to yield 24 triangles (A2)
48 squares, 4½" x 4½" (E2)

From the assorted green fat quarters, cut a *total* of:
6 squares, 5¼" x 5¼"; cut into quarters diagonally to yield 24 triangles (B2)
192 squares, 2½" x 2½" (D2)

From the assorted blue fat quarters, cut a *total* of:
96 rectangles, 2½" x 4½" (C2)

Cutting for Borders and Binding

From the tan border fabric, cut:
4 strips, 3½" x 33½"
4 strips, 3½" x 30½"

From the red border fabric, cut:
4 strips, 1½" x 34½"
4 strips, 1½" x 33½"

From the blue border fabric, cut:
4 strips, 3¼" x 37¼"
4 strips, 3¼" x 34½"

From the red binding print, cut:
8 strips, 2" x 42"

Making Block 1

After sewing each seam, press the seam allowances in the direction indicated by the arrows (or press them open if you prefer).

1 To make the flying-geese units, draw a diagonal line from corner to corner on the wrong side of each tan C1 square. Use the marked squares and 52 of the red B1 rectangles to make 52 red/tan flying-geese units.

Make 52.

2 Repeat step 1 using the remaining red B1 rectangles and the green D1 squares to make 52 red/green flying-geese units.

Make 52.

3 To make the triangle squares, draw a diagonal line from corner to corner on the wrong side of each tan G1 square. Pair a G1 square with a green F1 square, right sides together. Sew ¼" from each side of the drawn line. Cut the squares apart to make two triangle squares, each measuring 2½" x 2½". Make a total of 104 triangle squares.

Make 104.

4 Join a triangle square from step 3 to each end of a red/green flying-geese unit from step 2 as shown. Make 26 of these rows.

Make 26.

5 Join a red E1 square to each end of a row from step 4 to complete row 1. Make 26 rows.

Row 1.
Make 26.

6 Join a red E1 square to each end of a red/tan flying-geese unit from step 1 as shown. Make 26 of these rows.

Make 26.

7 Join a triangle square from step 3 to each end of a row from step 6 to complete row 2. Make 26 rows.

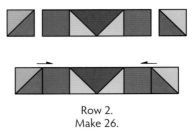

Row 2.
Make 26.

8 Join red/tan flying-geese units to opposite sides of a tan A1 square as shown. Then join red/green flying-geese units to each end of the row to complete row 3. Make 13 rows.

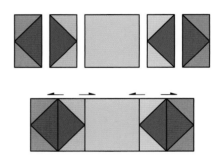

Row 3.
Make 13.

9 Lay out two of row 1, two of row 2, and one row 3 as shown. Sew the rows together to complete block 1. The block should measure 12½" x 12½". Make 13 blocks.

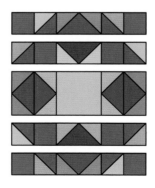

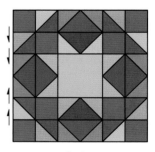

Block 1.
Make 13.

Making Block 2

1 Join a tan A2 triangle to a green B2 triangle as shown. Make 24 tan/green units.

Make 24.

2 Join two units from step 1 as shown to make a square unit. The unit should measure 4½" x 4½". Make 12 units.

Make 12.

3 Draw a diagonal line from corner to corner on the wrong side of each green D2 square. Use the marked squares and the blue C2 rectangles to make 96 blue/green flying-geese units as shown.

Make 96.

4 Join two flying-geese units from step 3 as shown. The unit should measure 4½" x 4½". Make 48 of these units.

Make 48.

5 Join tan E2 squares to opposite sides of the unit from step 4 to make row 1. Make 24 rows.

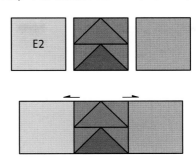

Row 1.
Make 24.

6 Join units from step 4 to opposite sides of a unit from step 2 to make row 2. Make 12 rows.

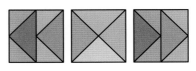
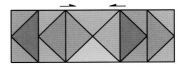

Row 2.
Make 12.

7 Lay out two of row 1 and one row 2 as shown. Sew the rows together to complete block 2. The block should measure 12½" x 12½". Make 12 blocks.

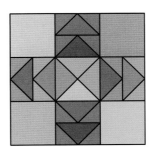 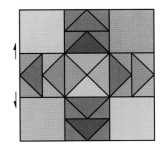

Block 2.
Make 12.

Assembling the Quilt Top

1 Lay out three of block 1 and two of block 2, alternating them as shown. Sew the blocks together to make row A. Press the seam allowances toward block 2 (or press them open). Make three rows.

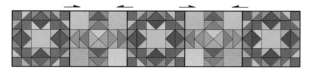

Row A.
Make 3.

2 Lay out three of block 2 and two of block 1, alternating them as shown. Sew the blocks together to make row B. Press the seam allowances toward block 2 (or press them open). Make two rows.

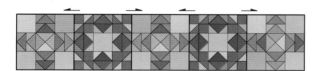

Row B.
Make 2.

3 Lay out the A and B rows, alternating them as shown. Sew the rows together and press the seam allowances in one direction (or press them open). The quilt top should measure 60½" x 60½".

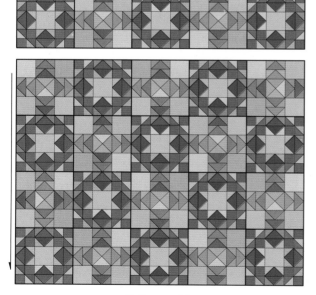

Quilt assembly

Adding the Borders

1 Join the tan 3½" x 30½" strips in pairs along the short ends to make two 60½"-long strips. Sew the strips to the sides of the quilt top.

2 Join the tan 3½" x 33½" strips in pairs along the short ends to make two 66½"-long strips. Sew the strips to the top and bottom of the quilt top.

3 Repeat step 1 using the red 1½" x 33½" strips to make two 66½"-long strips. Repeat step 2 using the red 1½" x 34½" strips to make two 68½"-long strips. Sew the strips to the sides, and then to the top and bottom of the quilt top.

4 Repeat step 1 using the blue 3¼" x 34½" strips to make two 68½"-long strips. Repeat step 2 using the blue 3¼" x 37¼" strips to make two 74"-long strips. Sew the strips to the sides, and then to the top and bottom of the quilt top.

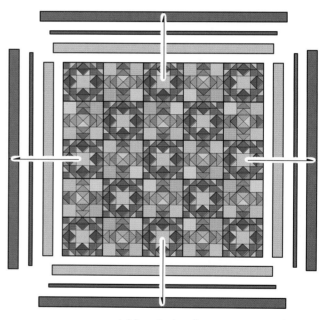

Adding the borders

Finishing the Quilt

For help with any of the finishing steps, go to ShopMartingale.com/HowtoQuilt for free downloadable information.

1 Layer, baste, and quilt your quilt, or take it to your favorite long-arm machine quilter for finishing.

2 Using the red 2"-wide strips, make and attach binding.

Vertigo

This fun, eye-catching quilt is made from two basic Nine Patch blocks, but it's hard to see where one block ends and the next one begins. If this color combination doesn't work for you, try one that does. You can't go wrong!

"Vertigo," designed and pieced by Julie Popa, quilted by Paula Murray

Finished quilt: 66½" x 75½" ◆ Finished Blocks 1 and 2: 9½" x 12½" ◆ Finished Blocks 3 and 4: 9½" x 9½"

▶ Materials

Yardage is based on 42"-wide fabric.

2¼ yards *total* of assorted black prints and red prints for blocks

2 yards *total* of assorted white prints for blocks

1⅝ yards of red print for border

⅓ yard of white print #1 for blocks

¼ yard *each* of white print #4 and black prints #2 and #3 for blocks

⅛ yard *each* of white prints #2 and #3 and black prints #1 and #4 for blocks

⅔ yard of black print #5 for binding

5¼ yards of fabric for backing

76" x 86" piece of batting

▶ Cutting

All measurements include ¼"-wide seam allowances. Cut all strips across the width of the fabric.

From white print #1, cut:
2 strips, 1½" x 42"
24 rectangles, 1½" x 5"

From black print #1, cut:
1 strip, 3" x 42"

From white print #2, cut:
1 strip, 3" x 42"

From black print #2, cut:
2 strips, 1½" x 42"
18 rectangles, 1½" x 5"

From the assorted black prints and red prints, cut a *total* of:
24 rectangles, 4" x 5"
5 strips, 6" x 18"
8 strips, 4" x 18"
12 rectangles, 3" x 5"
8 strips, 3" x 18"
3 strips, 5" x 18"

From the assorted white prints, cut a *total* of:
18 rectangles, 4" x 5"
10 strips, 4" x 18"
4 strips, 6" x 18"
16 rectangles, 3" x 5"
4 strips, 5" x 18"
6 strips, 3" x 18"

From white print #3, cut:
1 strip, 3" x 42"

From black print #3, cut:
2 strips, 1½" x 42"
16 rectangles, 1½" x 5"

From white print #4, cut:
2 strips, 1½" x 42"
12 rectangles, 1½" x 5"

From black print #4, cut:
1 strip, 3" x 42"

From the red print for border, cut:
8 strips, 6½" x 42"

From black print #5, cut:
8 strips, 2½" x 42"

Making Blocks 1 and 2

1 Sew a 1½" x 42" white print #1 strip to each long edge of the 3" x 42" black print #1 strip to make strip set A. Press the seam allowances toward the black strip. Crosscut the strip set into 12 segments, 4" wide. Sew a 1½" x 42" black print #2 strip to each long edge of the 3" x 42" white print #2 strip to make strip set B. Press the seam allowances toward the black strips. Crosscut the strip set into nine segments, 4" wide.

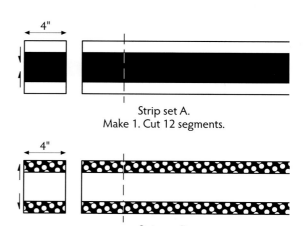

4"

Strip set A.
Make 1. Cut 12 segments.

4"

Strip set B.
Make 1. Cut 9 segments.

2 Add 1½" x 5" white print #1 rectangles to the sides of each strip set A segment as shown to make unit A. Press the seam allowances toward the just-added rectangles. Make 12. In the same manner, join 1½" x 5" black print #2 rectangles to the sides of each strip set B segment to make unit B. Press the seam allowances toward the just-added rectangles. Make nine.

Unit A.
Make 12.

Unit B.
Make 9.

3 Sew 4" x 5" assorted red or black rectangles to the sides of each A unit. Press the seam allowances toward the rectangles. In the same manner, join 4" x 5" assorted white rectangles to the sides of each B unit. Press the seam allowances toward the B units.

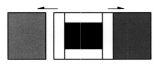 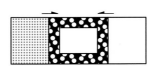

Make 12. Make 9.

4 Sew a 4" x 18" assorted white strip to each long edge of a 6" x 18" assorted black or red strip to make strip set C. Make five. Press the seam allowances toward the red or black strips. Crosscut the strip sets into 24 segments, 3" wide. Sew a 4" x 18" assorted red or black strip to each long edge of a 6" x 18" assorted white strip to make strip set D. Make four. Press the seam allowances toward the

red or black strips. Crosscut the strip sets into 18 segments, 3" wide.

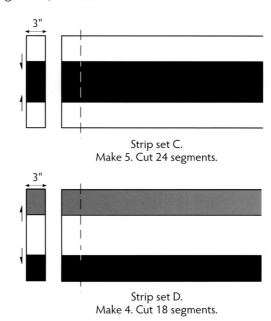

Strip set C.
Make 5. Cut 24 segments.

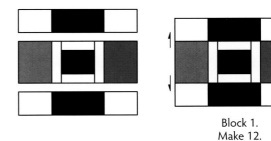

Strip set D.
Make 4. Cut 18 segments.

5 Add strip set C segments to the top and bottom of each A unit from step 3 to complete block 1. Make 12. Join strip set D segments to the top and bottom of each B unit from step 3 to complete block 2. Make nine. Press the seam allowances toward the strip-set segments.

Block 1.
Make 12.

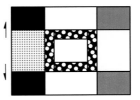

Block 2.
Make 9.

Making Blocks 3 and 4

1 Sew a 1½" x 42" black print #3 strip to each long edge of the 3" x 42" white print #3 strip to make strip set E. Press the seam allowances toward

the black strips. Crosscut the strip set into eight segments, 3" wide.

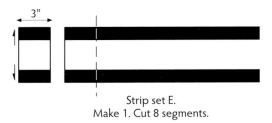

Strip set E.
Make 1. Cut 8 segments.

2 Sew a 1½" x 42" white print #4 strip to each long edge of the 3" x 42" black print #4 strip to make strip set F. Press the seam allowances toward the black strip. Crosscut the strip set into six segments, 3" wide.

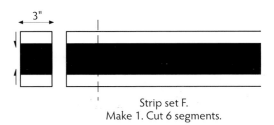

Strip set F.
Make 1. Cut 6 segments.

3 Add 1½" x 5" black print #3 rectangles to the top and bottom of each strip set E segment as shown to make unit C. Make eight. In the same manner, join 1½" x 5" white print #4 rectangles to the top and bottom of each strip set F segment to make unit D. Make six.

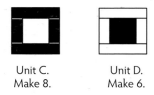

Unit C.   Unit D.
Make 8.   Make 6.

4 Sew 3" x 5" assorted white rectangles to the sides of each C unit. Press the seam allowances toward the C units. In the same manner, join 3" x 5" assorted black or red rectangles to the sides of each D unit. Press the seam allowances toward the rectangles.

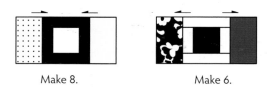

Make 8.   Make 6.

5 Sew a 3" x 18" assorted black or red strip to each long edge of a 5" x 18" assorted white

strip to make strip set G. Make four. Press the seam allowances toward the red or black strips. Crosscut the strip sets into 16 segments, 3" wide.

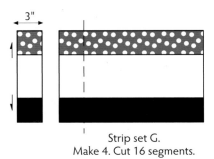

Strip set G.
Make 4. Cut 16 segments.

6 Sew a 3" x 18" assorted white strip to each long edge of a 5" x 18" assorted black or red strip to make strip set H. Make three. Press the seam allowances toward the red or black strips. Crosscut the strip sets into 12 segments, 3" wide.

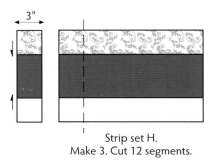

Strip set H.
Make 3. Cut 12 segments.

7 Add strip set G segments to the top and bottom of each C unit from step 4 to complete block 3. Make eight. Join strip set H segments to the top and bottom of each D unit from step 4 to complete block 4. Make six. Press seam allowances toward the C and D units.

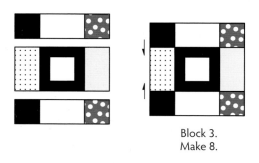

Block 3.
Make 8.

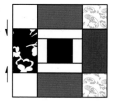

Block 4.
Make 6.

Assembling the Quilt Top

1 Arrange the blocks into seven horizontal rows as shown below. Be careful to position the blocks correctly within the rows. Rotate the blocks as needed to distribute the colors and create a pleasing layout. Sew the blocks into rows. Press the seam allowances in opposite directions from row to row. Sew the rows together. Press the seam allowances in one direction.

2 Sew the red-print border strips together end to end and press the seam allowances to one side. Measure the length of the quilt top through the center. Cut two borders to this length and add them to the sides of the quilt top. Measure the width of the quilt top through the center. Cut the remaining borders to this measurement and add them to the top and bottom of the quilt.

Finishing the Quilt

For help with any of the finishing steps, go to ShopMartingale.com/HowtoQuilt for free downloadable information.

1 Layer, baste, and quilt your quilt, or take it to your favorite long-arm machine quilter for finishing.

2 Using the 2½"-wide strips of black print #5, make and attach binding.

Quilt assembly

Checkerboard Stars

This quilt presents a great opportunity to play with many colors. You'll be using a total of 28 fat quarters. Have fun with the color combinations! Since the quilt design consists of just one block, set on point, the color is what makes this quilt sing.

"Checkerboard Stars," designed and pieced by Deanne Eisenman, quilted by Mindy Prohaski of Quilting on Cameo

Finished quilt: 65⅜" x 65⅜"   ◆   **Finished block:** 11⅞" x 11⅞"

▶ Materials

Yardage is based on 42"-wide fabric. Fat quarters are 18" x 21".

12 fat quarters of assorted light fabrics for blocks and border corner squares

10 fat quarters of assorted dark fabrics for blocks and border corner squares

6 fat quarters of assorted medium fabrics for blocks

13 yards of light fabric for border

½ yard of dark fabric for binding

4½ yards of fabric for backing

74" x 74" piece of batting

▶ Cutting

All measurements include ¼"-wide seam allowances. Cut strips across the width of the fabric. When cutting your fabrics, keep the pieces for blocks 1 and 2 separate.

Cutting for Block 1

From 8 of the assorted light fat quarters, cut a *total* of:
52 rectangles, 2½" x 4½" (C)
104 squares, 2½" x 2½" (B)

From the assorted medium fat quarters, cut a *total* of:
13 squares, 4½" x 4½" (A)

From 5 of the assorted dark fat quarters, cut a *total* of:
104 squares, 2½" x 2½" (D)

Cutting for Block 2

From 8 of the assorted light fat quarters, cut a *total* of:
12 squares, 4½" x 4½" (A)
96 squares, 2½" x 2½" (D)

From the assorted medium fat quarters, cut a *total* of:
48 rectangles, 2½" x 4½" (C)
48 squares, 2½" x 2½" (E)

From 5 of the assorted dark fat quarters, cut a *total* of:
48 squares, 2½" x 2½" (B)

Cutting for Setting Triangles

From 4 of the assorted light fat quarters, cut a *total* of:
24 squares, 65" x 65"; cut in half diagonally to yield 48 triangles

From 5 of the assorted dark fat quarters, cut a *total* of:
26 squares, 65" x 65"; cut in half diagonally to yield 52 triangles

Cutting for Borders and Binding

From the light border fabric, cut:
8 strips, 4½" x 42"

From the remaining assorted dark fabrics, cut a *total* of:
4 squares, 4½" x 4½"

From the remaining assorted light fabrics, cut a *total* of:
16 squares, 2½" x 2½"

From the dark binding fabric, cut:
7 strips, 2" x 42"

Before You Cut

Before you begin cutting, select four light fat quarters and five dark fat quarters for setting triangles. These triangles are used to set the Star blocks on point.

In block 1 the pieces are labeled A through D. In block 2 they are labeled A through E. When cutting a particular piece, you'll want to cut the amount needed from various fat quarters to achieve the desired scrappy look. For example, you would not want to cut all of the A pieces from the same fat quarter. Careful planning will help you determine how many of each piece to cut from a specific fat quarter. A handy tip is to draw the quilt top on graph paper and then use colored pencils to attain the desired color placement. Be sure to label all your pieces with the block number and letter!

Making Block 1

After sewing each seam, press the seam allowances in the direction indicated by the arrows (or press them open if you prefer).

1 Use the folded-corner technique as shown to make the units. Draw a diagonal line from corner to corner on the wrong side of 52 of the light B squares. Place a marked square on the upper-right corner of a medium A square as shown, right sides together. Sew along the line and trim the excess fabric, leaving a ¼" seam allowance.

2 Repeat step 1, adding marked squares to the remaining three corners of the A square to make a center unit. The unit should measure 4½" square. Make 13 units.

Make 13.

3 Again using the folded-corner technique, join two dark D squares to one light C rectangle to make a flying-geese unit as shown. Make 52 units.

Make 52.

4 Join light B squares to opposite ends of a flying-geese unit from step 3 to make a row. Make 26.

Make 26.

5 Join flying-geese units from step 3 to opposite sides of a center unit from step 2 as shown to make a row. Make 13.

     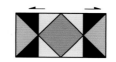

Make 13.

6 Lay out two rows from step 4 and one row from step 5 as shown. Join the rows to complete the block. The block should measure 8½" square. Make 13 blocks.

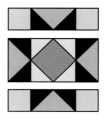 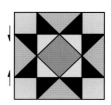

Make 13.

Making Block 2

Once again, use the folded-corner technique to make the units. After sewing each seam, press the seam allowances in the direction indicated by the arrows (or press them open).

1 Draw a diagonal line from corner to corner on the wrong side of the dark B squares. Using the marked squares and the light A squares, repeat steps 1 and 2 of "Making Block 1" to make 12 center units.

Make 12.

2 Join two light D squares to one medium C rectangle to make a flying-geese unit as shown. Make 48 units.

Make 48.

3 Join medium E squares to opposite ends of a flying-geese unit from step 2 to make a row. Make 24.

Make 24.

4 Join flying-geese units from step 2 to opposite sides of a center unit from step 1 to make a row. Make 12.

 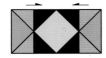

Make 12.

5 Lay out two rows from step 3 and one row from step 4 as shown. Join the rows to complete the block. The block should measure 8½" square. Make 12 blocks.

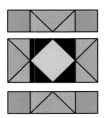 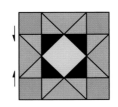

Make 12.

Adding the Setting Triangles

After sewing each seam, press the seam allowances in the direction indicated by the arrows (or press them open).

1 Join dark half-square triangles to opposite sides of each block 1, making sure the triangles are centered along the sides of the block. The ends of the triangles will extend beyond the block a little; do not trim off these ends after sewing. Take care when pressing the bias edges of the triangles, as they stretch easily.

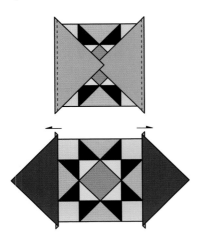

2 Repeat step 1, sewing dark triangles to the remaining two sides of each block 1. Make 13.

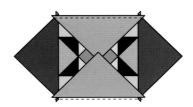

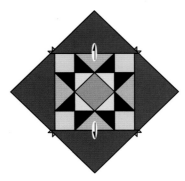

Make 13.

3 Repeat steps 1 and 2, sewing light half-square triangles to each block 2. Make 12.

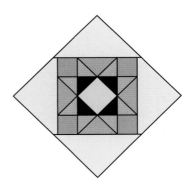

Make 12.

4 Trim and square up the blocks, making sure to leave ¼" beyond the points of the Star blocks for seam allowance. The blocks should all be the same size.

Assembling the Quilt Top

1 Lay out three of block 1 and two of block 2, alternating them as shown. Join the blocks to make a row. Press the seam allowances in one direction (or press them open). Make three of these rows.

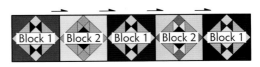

Make 3.

2 Lay out three of block 2 and two of block 1, alternating them as shown. Join the blocks to make a row. Press the seam allowances in one direction (or press them open). Make two of these rows.

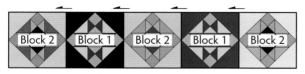

Make 2.

3 Lay out the rows, alternating them as shown. Join the rows and press the seam allowances in one direction (or press them open).

Quilt assembly

Adding the Borders

1 Draw a diagonal line from corner to corner on the wrong side of the light 2½" border squares. Using the marked squares and the dark 4½" border squares, repeat steps 1 and 2 of "Making Block 1" to make four corner units. Each unit should measure 4½" square.

Make 4.

2 Measure the length and width of your quilt top; it should measure 57⅜". Trim four of the light border strips to measure 29" long. Trim the remaining four light border strips to 28⅞". Join a 29"-long strip and a 28⅞"-long strip along the short ends to make a 57⅜"-long strip. Make four of these border strips.

3 Join border strips to opposite sides of the quilt top. Join a corner unit from step 1 to each end of the two remaining border strips. Sew the strips to the top and bottom of the quilt top. Press the seam allowances toward the strips.

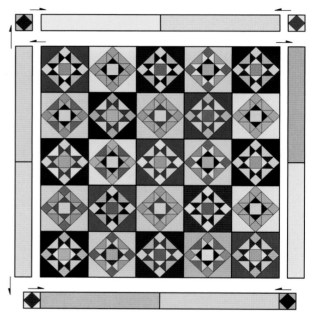

Adding the borders

Finishing the Quilt

For help with any of the finishing steps, go to ShopMartingale.com/HowtoQuilt for free downloadable information.

1 Layer, baste, and quilt your quilt, or take it to your favorite long-arm machine quilter for finishing.

2 Using the dark 2"-wide strips, make and attach binding.

Hot Cross

Carrie likes the challenge of choosing a block and then figuring out what size to cut the pieces and still fit everything into a 10" square of fabric. She calls this her "MacGyver" process. The finished blocks reminded Carrie of the wonderful rolls you find everywhere at Easter.

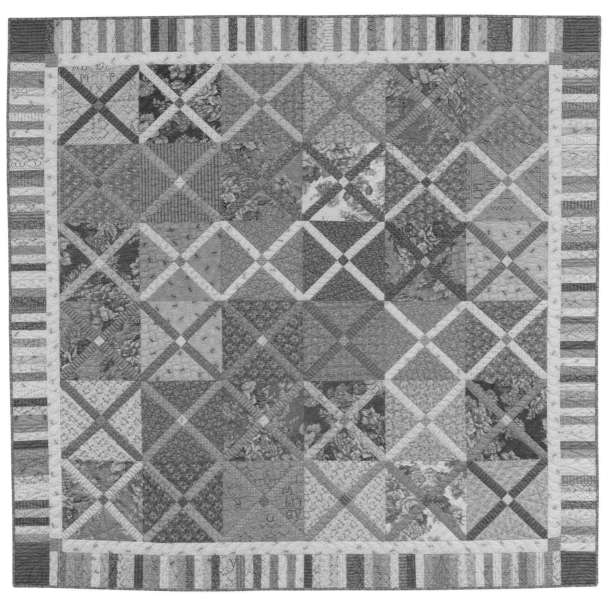

"Hot Cross," designed by Carrie Nelson, pieced by Sue Maitre, quilted by Diane Tricka

Finished quilt: 69½" x 69½"   ◆   **Finished block:** 9½" x 9½"

▶ Materials

Yardage is based on 42"-wide fabric.

36 assorted squares, 10" x 10", for blocks (Carrie used Layer Cakes.)

46 assorted squares, 10" x 10", for blocks and pieced outer border (Carrie used Layer Cakes.)

½ yard of cream print for inner border

⅝ yard of fabric for binding

4½ yards of fabric for backing

75" x 75" piece of batting

▶ Cutting

All measurements include ¼"-wide seam allowances.

From *each* of the 36 assorted squares for blocks:
1 square, 10" x 10"; cut into quarters diagonally to yield 4 triangles (144 total)

From *each* of 36 assorted squares for blocks and outer border, cut:
1 strip, 1½" x 10" (36 total), from the *crosswise* grain
6 strips, 1½" x 8", from the *lengthwise* grain; crosscut 1 of the strips into:
    1 strip, 1½" x 5" (36 total)
    1 square, 1½" x 1½" (36 total)

From 1 assorted square for blocks and outer border, cut:
1 strip, 2" x 10"; crosscut into 4 inner-border squares, 2" x 2"
5 border strips, 1½" x 10"

From 1 assorted square for blocks and outer border, cut:
4 outer-border squares, 5" x 5"

From *each* of the remaining 8 assorted squares for blocks and outer border, cut:
6 border strips, 1½" x 10" (48 total)

From the inner-border fabric, cut:
6 strips, 2" x 42"

From the binding fabric, cut:
2"-wide bias strips to make 290" of bias binding

Making the Blocks

For each block, you will need the following pieces:
    Four matching triangles
    Four matching 1½" x 8" strips
    One 1½" square

Use a scant ¼"-wide seam allowance throughout. After sewing each seam, press the seam allowances as indicated by the arrows.

1 Lay out the pieces for each block as shown. Sew the pieces together in diagonal rows, and then sew the rows together to complete the block. Make a total of 36 blocks.

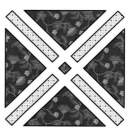

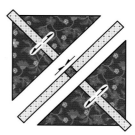

Make 36.

2 Position a 12½" square ruler with a 45° line on top of a block, centering the 45° line in the middle of the narrow strip. Align the 5" lines on the ruler horizontally and vertically with the points of

the small center square and the 10" marks with the center of the narrow strips as shown. Trim two sides of the block. Turn the block, realign the ruler, and trim the remaining sides. Each block should measure 10" square.

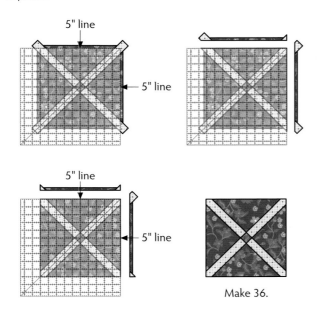

Make 36.

Assembling the Quilt Top

1 Lay out the blocks in six rows of six blocks each as shown in the quilt assembly diagram on page 154. Sew the blocks together in rows and press the seam allowances in opposite directions from row to row (or press them open).

2 Sew the rows together and press the seam allowances in one direction (or press them open). The quilt top should measure 57½" x 57½".

Adding the Borders

1 Piece the 2"-wide inner-border strips together end to end. From the strips, cut four strips, 57½" long.

2 Sew two inner-border strips to the sides of the quilt top and press the seam allowances toward the borders.

3 Sew a 2" square to each end of the two remaining inner-border strips and press. Sew these borders to the top and bottom of the quilt top and press the seam allowances toward the border.

4 Sort the 1½"-wide strips as follows:
89 strips, 1½" x 10" (5 are extra)
36 strips, 1½" x 8"
36 strips, 1½" x 5"

5 Cut the 1½" x 10" strips in half to make 168 strips measuring 1½" x 5". Trim the 8" strips to measure 1½" x 5". Sort the strips anew into four sets of 60 strips each, keeping as much variety as possible in each group.

6 Sew the strips in one set together as shown and press the seam allowances in one direction (or press them open). The pieced strip should measure 5" x 60½". Repeat to make a total of four pieced outer-border strips.

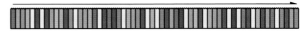

Make 4.

7 Sew two outer-border strips to the sides of the quilt top. If you used Layer Cakes, keep the pinked edges on the outside. Press the seam allowances toward the outer border.

8 Sew a 5" outer-border square to each end of the two remaining outer-border strips and press. Sew these borders to the top and bottom of the quilt top and press the seam allowances toward the outer border.

Finishing the Quilt

For help with any of the finishing steps, go to ShopMartingale.com/HowtoQuilt for free downloadable information.

1 Layer, baste, and quilt your quilt, or take it to your favorite long-arm machine quilter for finishing.

2 Using the 2"-wide bias strips, make and attach binding.

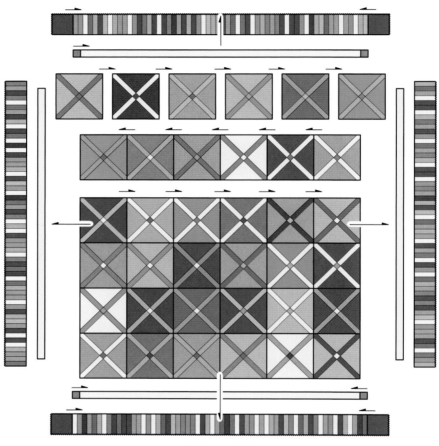

Quilt assembly

Feed Sacks

You don't have to be afraid of set-in pieces. While the center white squares look like they're set in, these blocks are assembled with partial seams and couldn't be any simpler.

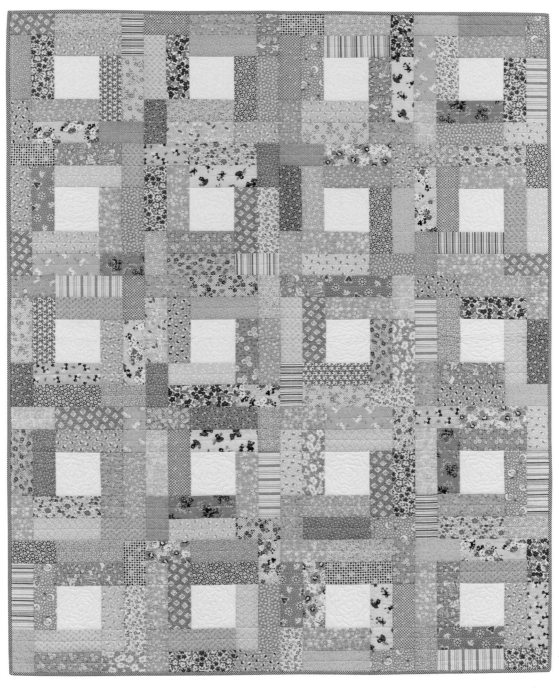

"Feed Sacks," designed and made by Kim Brackett
Finished quilt: 48½" x 60½" ◆ **Finished block:** 12" x 12"

▶ Materials

Yardage is based on 42"-wide fabric.

½ yard of white solid for blocks

40 strips, 2½" x at least 36", of assorted 1930s reproduction prints for blocks

⅓ yard of red print for binding

3½ yards of fabric for backing

52½" x 64½" piece of batting

▶ Cutting

All measurements include ¼"-wide seam allowances.

From *each* of the 40 assorted 1930s reproduction print strips, cut:
4 rectangles, 2½" x 6½" (160 total)
2 rectangles, 2½" x 4½" (80 total)

From the white solid, cut:
3 strips, 4½" x 42"; crosscut into 20 squares, 4½" x 4½"

From the red print, cut:
6 strips, 2½" x 42"

Cutting from Scraps

If you prefer to use scraps, follow the instructions below. See "Cutting" above for instructions on cutting the binding.

From assorted prints, cut:
160 rectangles, 2½" x 6½"
80 rectangles, 2½" x 4½"

From white solid, cut:
20 squares, 4½" x 4½"

Making the Blocks

1 Sew two 2½" x 6½" rectangles together. Press the seam allowances toward the rectangle on the right. Sew a 2½" x 4½" rectangle to the top of the unit as shown. Press the seam allowances toward the 4½" rectangle. Make 80 units.

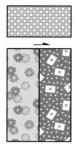

Make 80.

2 Sew a white 4½" square to a unit from step 1, sewing a partial seam beginning at the outer edge and sewing about halfway as shown. Backstitch to secure the partial seam. Press the partial seam allowances away from the white center square.

3 Join three more units to the white square in the order shown. Press the seam allowances away from the white center square. After the last unit is attached, finish sewing the partial seam to complete the block. Make 20 blocks.

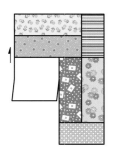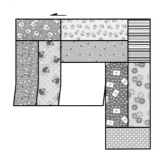

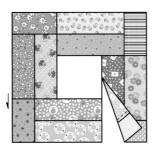

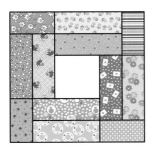

Make 20.

Assembling the Quilt Top

1 Arrange the blocks in five horizontal rows of four blocks each.

2 Sew the blocks together in rows, pressing the seam allowances in opposite directions from row to row. Sew the rows together. Press the seam allowances in one direction.

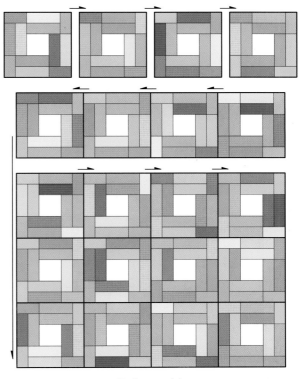

Quilt assembly

Finishing the Quilt

For help with any of the finishing steps, go to ShopMartingale.com/HowtoQuilt for free downloadable information.

1 Layer, baste, and quilt your quilt, or take it to your favorite long-arm machine quilter for finishing.

2 Using the red 2½"-wide strips, make and attach binding.

Pieces of Eight

If you're a fan of pirate movies, you're probably familiar with pieces of eight. A "piece of eight," *or* peso de ocho, *is a Spanish silver dollar. Vickie devised a quilt design with nine blocks that form interlocking eights. This block is a jewel made with just squares and half-square-triangle units.*

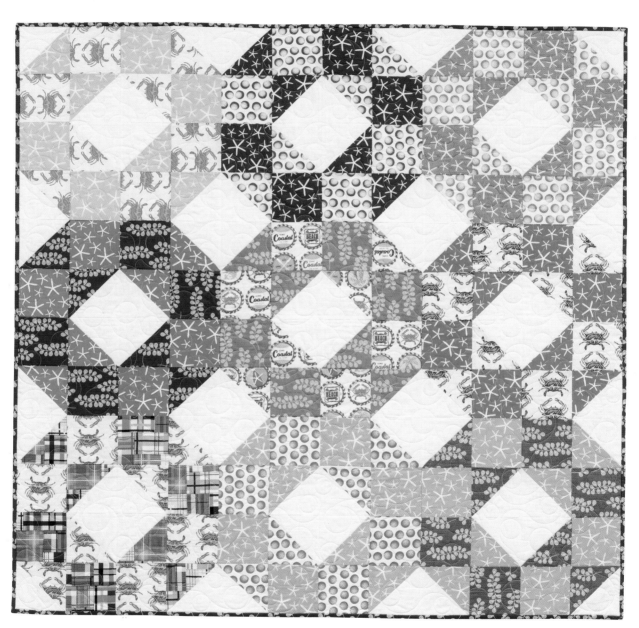

"Pieces of Eight," designed and pieced by Vickie Eapen, machine quilted by Al Kuthe

Finished quilt: 54½" x 54½"   ◆   **Finished block:** 18" x 18"

Materials

Yardage is based on 42"-wide fabric.

¼ yard or 1 fat quarter *each* of 18 assorted prints
for blocks

1⅛ yards of light solid for blocks

½ yard of blue print for binding

3⅓ yards of fabric for backing

60" x 60" piece of batting

Cutting

All measurements include ¼"-wide seam allowances.

From the light solid, cut:
6 strips, 5½" x 42"; crosscut into 36 squares,
5½" x 5½"

From *each* of the 18 assorted prints, cut:
4 squares, 5" x 5" (72 total)
2 squares, 5½" x 5½" (36 total)

From the blue print, cut:
6 strips, 2¼" x 42"

Making the Blocks

1 Mark a diagonal line on the wrong side of each
light 5½" square. Layer each light square with a
print 5½" square, right sides together. Sew ¼" from
each side of the drawn line, cut the units apart, and
press the seam allowances toward the print fabric.
Make two half-square-triangle units from each pair
(18 sets of four matching units total). Trim each unit
to 5" x 5".

Make 18 sets of 4.

2 Select two different sets of four matching units
from step 1 along with their matching 5" squares.
Arrange the pieces into four horizontal rows as
shown. Sew the pieces in each row together. Press
the seam allowances in opposite directions from
row to row. Sew the rows together. Press the seam
allowances in one direction. The completed block

should measure 18½" x 18½". Repeat to make a total
of nine blocks.

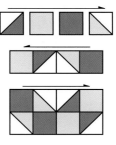
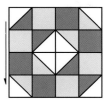

Make 9.

Assembling the Quilt Top

1 Arrange the blocks into three horizontal rows of
three blocks each, rotating the blocks so that the
seam allowances nest together.

2 Sew the blocks in each row together. Press the
seam allowances in opposite directions from
row to row. Sew the rows together. Press the seam
allowances in one direction.

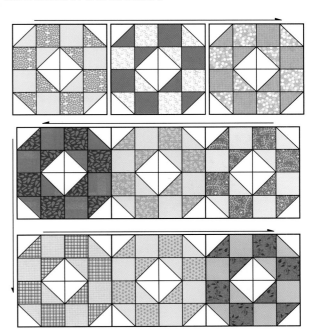

Quilt assembly

Finishing the Quilt

For help with any of the finishing steps, go to
ShopMartingale.com/HowtoQuilt for free
downloadable information.

1 Layer, baste, and quilt your quilt, or take it to your
favorite long-arm machine quilter for finishing.

2 Using the blue 2¼"-wide strips, make and attach
binding.

Not Manly Enough

Robin originally made this quilt for a friend's condo, but the colors weren't "manly enough" for him. That was OK! This quilt goes together so quickly that she simply made him another quilt in all neutrals and kept this version for herself.

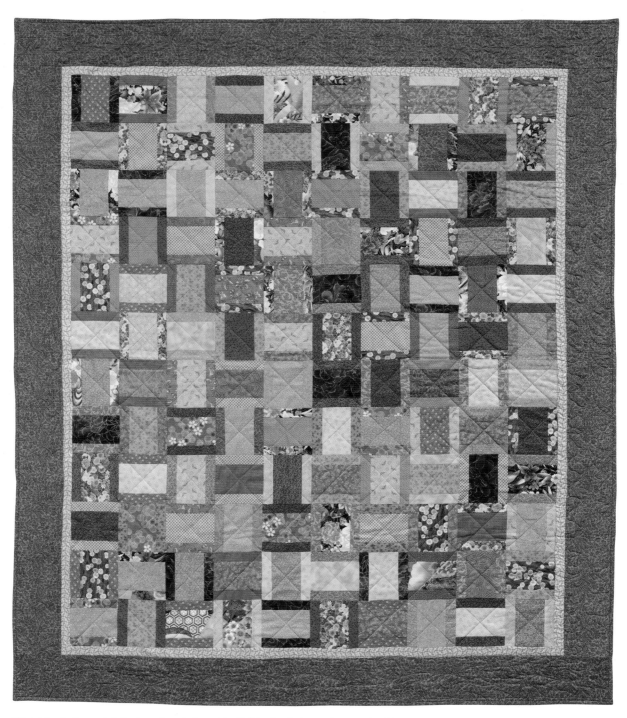

"Not Manly Enough," designed and pieced by Robin Strobel, machine quilted by Karen Burns of Compulsive Quilting

Finished quilt: 62½" x 72½"   ◆   **Finished block:** 5" x 5"

Materials

Yardage is based on 42"-wide fabric. Fat quarters are 18" x 21".

18 fat quarters of assorted tan and brown prints for blocks

6 fat quarters of assorted turquoise prints for blocks

1¾ yards of dark-turquoise print for outer border and binding

⅜ yard of tan print for inner border

3¾ yards of fabric for backing

68" x 78" piece of batting

Cutting

All measurements include ¼"-wide seam allowances.

From *each* of the 24 fat quarters, cut:
5 rectangles, 3½" x 5½" (120 total)
10 rectangles, 1½" x 5½" (240 total)*

From the tan print, cut:
6 strips, 1½" x 42"

From the dark-turquoise print, cut:
7 strips, 5½" x 42"
7 strips, 2½" x 42"

Keep rectangles of the same fabric together.

Making the Blocks

Randomly sew matching 1½" x 5½" rectangles to both long sides of a 3½" x 5½" contrasting rectangle. Press the seam allowances toward the darker fabric. Make 120 blocks.

Make 120.

Assembling the Quilt Top

1 Arrange the blocks in 12 rows of 10 blocks per row, alternating the direction of each block as shown in the quilt assembly diagram at right.

2 Sew the blocks together in rows. Press the seam allowances in opposite directions from row to row. Sew the rows together. Press the seam allowances in one direction.

Adding the Borders

1 Piece the 1½" tan-print strips end to end to make one long strip. From this, cut two strips, 60½" long, and sew them to the sides of the quilt top. From the remaining pieced strip, cut two strips, 52½" long, and sew them to the top and bottom of the quilt. Press the seam allowances toward the borders.

2 Piece the 5½" dark-turquoise strips end to end to make one long strip. From this strip, cut four strips, 62½" long, and sew them to the quilt top for the outer border. Press.

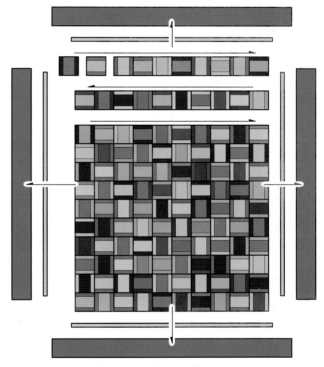

Quilt assembly

Finishing the Quilt

For help with any of the finishing steps, go to ShopMartingale.com/HowtoQuilt for free downloadable information.

1 Layer, baste, and quilt your quilt, or take it to your favorite long-arm machine quilter for finishing.

2 Using the dark-turquoise 2½"-wide strips, make and attach binding.

Rainbow Cakes

This bright, fun design provides an opportunity to dig through your scraps and put together a scrapbook quilt with assorted bits from other quilts you've made. If you don't have enough scraps, use precuts, such as fat quarters, fat eighths, 2½"-wide strips, and 10" squares.

"Rainbow Cakes," designed and made by Elizabeth Dackson

Finished quilt: 66½" x 87½"   ◆   **Finished block:** 14" x 12"

Materials

Yardage is based on 42"-wide fabric.

2⅞ yards of light-gray solid for block, sashing, and border

⅝ yard *each* of assorted pink, red, orange, yellow, green, blue, and purple scraps (4⅜ yards total) for blocks

⅔ yard of black-and-white print for binding

5⅓ yards of fabric for backing

75" x 96" piece of batting

Cutting

All measurements include ¼"-wide seam allowances. In the quilt shown, Elizabeth worked with scraps and cut rectangles of varying widths for each "layer" of the cake blocks. For the sake of simplicity, however, these cutting instructions will result in uniformly sized rectangles. Feel free to be as creative with sizes as you like; just make sure that the bottom layer measures 6½"x14½", the middle layer measures 4½"x10½", and the top layer measures 2½"x6½".

From *each* of the assorted pink, red, orange, yellow, green, blue, and purple scraps, cut:
24 rectangles, 2½" x 6½" (168 total)
24 rectangles, 2" x 4½" (168 total)
24 rectangles, 1⅜" x 2½" (168 total)

From the light-gray solid, cut:
12 strips, 2½" x 42"; crosscut into 96 rectangles, 2½" x 4½"
15 strips, 3" x 42"; crosscut 6 strips into 18 strips, 3" x 12½"
8 strips, 2" x 42"

From the black-and-white print, cut:
8 strips, 2½" x 42"

Making the Blocks

Use a scant ¼" seam allowance and press seam allowances open after sewing each seam.

1 For the bottom layer of the cake block, sew one 2½" x 6½" rectangle of each color together in rainbow order: pink, red, orange, yellow, green, blue, and purple. Measure, and trim to 6½" x 14½" if necessary.

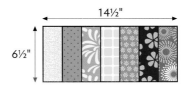

2 For the middle layer, sew one 2" x 4½" rectangle of each color together in the same order: pink, red, orange, yellow, green, blue, and purple. Trim to 4½" x 10½". Sew a gray 2½" x 4½" rectangle to each end of the unit as shown.

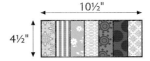 

If Bigger Is Better

If your scrap box is overflowing, then a king-size quilt could be the solution! You'll need to make 48 blocks, set 6 x 8, for a 99½" x 116½" finished size.

Materials
5⅝ yards of light-gray solid for blocks and sashing
1¼ yards *total* of assorted pink scraps for blocks
1¼ yards *total* of assorted red scraps for blocks
1¼ yards *total* of assorted orange scraps for blocks
1¼ yards *total* of assorted yellow scraps for blocks
1¼ yards *total* of assorted green scraps for blocks
1¼ yards *total* of assorted blue scraps for blocks
1¼ yards *total* of assorted purple scraps for blocks
1 yard of black-and-white print for binding
9¼ yards of fabric for backing
108" x 124" piece of batting

3 For the top layer, sew one 1⅜" x 2½" rectangle of each color together in the same order: pink, red, orange, yellow, green, blue, and purple. Trim to 2½" x 6½". Sew a gray 2½" x 4½" rectangle to each end of the unit as shown.

4 Sew the bottom and middle layers together. Then add the top layer, aligning the raw edges, and press.

5 Repeat steps 1–4 to make a total of 24 blocks.

Make 24.

Assembling the Quilt Top

1 Arrange your blocks into six rows of four blocks each in an order that is pleasing to your eye. Rotating every other block adds a sense of movement to the quilt. Once you're happy with the layout, add the gray 3" x 12½" sashing pieces between the blocks in each row. Sew the pieces together into rows, pressing seam allowances open as you go.

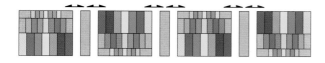

2 Sew the remaining gray 3" x 42" strips together end to end to make one long strip. Cut into five sashing strips, 64" long.

3 Sew the rows together with the sashing strips, first sewing them in pairs and then sewing the pairs together. Press.

4 Sew the gray 2" x 42" strips together to make one long strip. Cut two border strips, 2" x 85". Sew these to the sides of the quilt top. Press. Cut two border strips, 2" x 66½", and sew these to the top and bottom of the quilt top. Press.

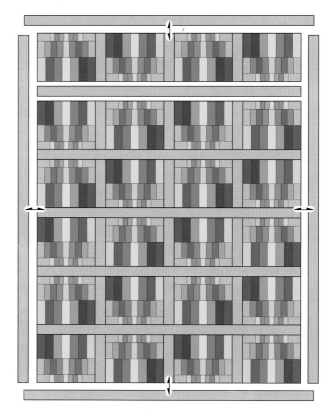

Quilt assembly

Finishing the Quilt

For help with any of the finishing steps, go to ShopMartingale.com/HowtoQuilt for free downloadable information.

1 Piece the backing together using a vertical seam. Layer, baste, and quilt your quilt, or take it to your favorite long-arm machine quilter for finishing.

2 Using the black-and-white 2½"-wide strips, make and attach binding.

Lunch Box Social

Fun-to-stitch patchwork blocks, myriad prints, and striped sashing-strip accents come together seamlessly in this cheerful little table topper. Lay it on a table, add a simple centerpiece, and enjoy a dollop of instant warmth and charm.

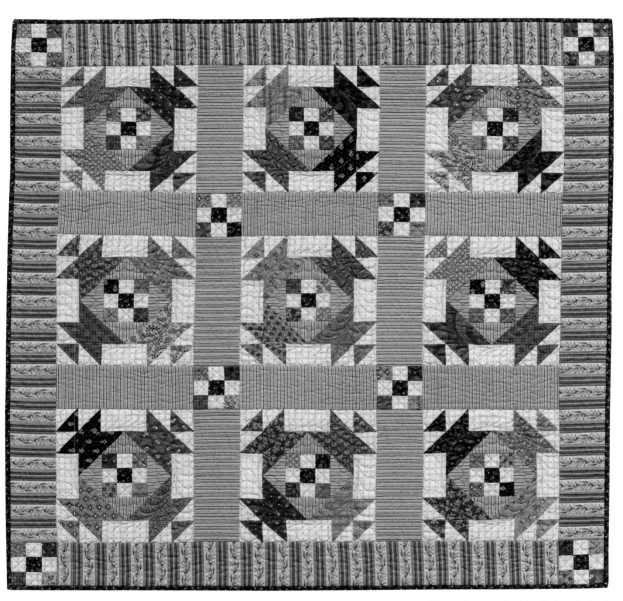

"Lunch Box Social," designed by Kim Diehl, pieced by Barbara Walsh and Kim Diehl, machine quilted by Deborah Poole

Finished quilt: 39½" x 39½" ◆ **Finished block:** 9" x 9"

Materials

Yardage is based on 42"-wide fabric. A chubby sixteenth is 9" x 11".

18 chubby sixteenths of assorted prints for blocks and nine-patch units

⅞ yard of tan print for blocks

⅔ yard of small-scale medium-hued stripe or print for blocks and sashing strips

½ yard of dark-blue print (or a complementary color of your choosing) for nine-patch unit center squares and binding

½ yard of large-scale stripe or print in a complementary color for border

2⅞ yards of fabric for backing*

45" x 45" piece of batting

If you don't prewash your fabric and it has a selvage-to-selvage measurement of at least 44", you can reduce this amount to 1¼ yards.

Cutting

All measurements include ¼"-wide seam allowances. Cut strips across the width of the fabric in the order given unless otherwise indicated.

From the tan print, cut:
4 strips, 1½" x 42"; crosscut *2 of the strips* into 34 squares, 1½" x 1½"
4 strips, 2⅜" x 42"; crosscut into 54 squares, 2⅜" x 2⅜". Cut in half diagonally to yield 108 triangles.
4 strips, 2" x 42"; crosscut into 36 rectangles, 2" x 3½"

From the dark-blue print, cut:
1 strip, 1½" x 42"
5 strips, 2½" x 42"

From *each* of the 18 assorted print chubby sixteenths, cut:
1 strip, 3½" x 11"; crosscut into:
    2 squares, 3½" x 3½" (combined total of 36)
    4 squares, 1½" x 1½" (combined total of 72)
1 strip, 2⅜" x 11"; crosscut into 3 squares, 2⅜" x 2⅜". Cut in half diagonally to yield 6 triangles (combined total of 108).
Keep the pieces organized by print.

From the small-scale medium-hued stripe or print, cut:
5 strips, 2" x 42"; crosscut into:
    18 rectangles, 2" x 3½"
    18 rectangles, 2" x 6½"
3 strips, 3½" x 42"; crosscut into 12 rectangles, 3½" x 9½"

From the large-scale stripe or print, cut:
4 strips, 3½" x 33½"

Making the Nine-Patch Units

1 Join a tan 1½" x 42" strip to each long side of the dark-blue 1½" x 42" strip to make a strip set. Press the seam allowances toward the dark-blue strip. Crosscut the strip set into 17 segments, 1½" wide.

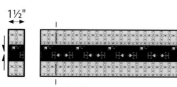

1½"

Make 1 strip set.
Cut 17 segments.

2 Join assorted-print 1½" squares to opposite sides of a tan 1½" square. Press the seam allowances toward the assorted-print squares. Repeat for a total of 34 pieced units measuring 1½" x 3½", including seam allowances. Please note that you'll have four unused assorted-print squares; these have been included for added variety as you piece your nine-patch units.

Make 34.

3 Lay out two pieced units from step 2 and one strip-set unit from step 1 into three horizontal rows as shown. Join the rows. Press the seam allowances away from the middle row. Repeat for a total of 17 pieced nine-patch units measuring 3½" square, including seam allowances.

Make 17.

Making the Half-Square-Triangle Units

Stitch each assorted-print triangle to a tan triangle along the long diagonal edges. Press the seam allowances toward the assorted-print triangle. Trim away the dog-ear points. Repeat for a total of 108 pieced half-square-triangle units measuring 2" x 2", including seam allowances. For greater ease in piecing the blocks, keep these units organized by print.

Make 108.

Making the Blocks

1 Join small-scale stripe 2" x 3½" rectangles to the right and left sides of a pieced nine-patch unit. Press the seam allowances away from the nine-patch unit. Join small-scale stripe 2" x 6½" rectangles to the remaining sides of the nine-patch unit. Press the seam allowances away from the nine-patch unit. Repeat for a total of nine pieced center units. Reserve the remaining nine-patch units for later use.

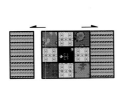 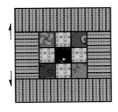

Make 9.

2 Use a pencil and an acrylic ruler to draw a diagonal line from corner to corner on the wrong side of each assorted-print 3½" square.

3 Layer marked squares on two opposite corners of a pieced center unit. Stitch on the drawn line, open the pieces, press, and trim. In the same manner, add marked squares to the remaining corners of the center unit. Repeat for a total of nine block center units measuring 6½" square, including seam allowances.

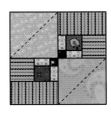 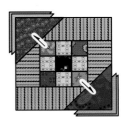

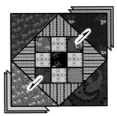

Make 9.

4 Lay out a center unit from step 3, 12 half-square-triangle units (three each of the four colors that match the pieced center unit corners), and four tan 2" x 3½" rectangles as shown. Join the half-square-triangles and tan rectangles on each side of the center unit. Press the seam allowances toward the rectangles. Join these units to the sides of the center unit to make the middle row. Press the seam allowances away from the center unit. Join the pieces in the top and bottom rows. Press the seam allowances toward the rectangles. Join the rows. Press the seam allowances away from the

middle row. Repeat for a total of nine pieced blocks measuring 9½" square, including seam allowances.

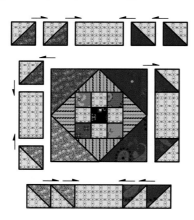

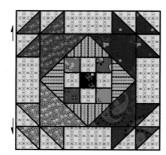

Make 9.

Assembling the Quilt Top

1 Lay out three pieced blocks and two small-scale stripe 3½" x 9½" rectangles in alternating positions. Join the pieces. Press the seam allowances toward the rectangles. Repeat for a total of three block rows measuring 9½" x 33½", including seam allowances.

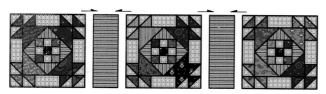

Make 3.

2 Lay out three small-scale stripe 3½" x 9½" rectangles and two reserved nine-patch units in alternating positions. Join the pieces. Press the seam allowances toward the rectangles. Repeat for a total of two pieced sashing rows measuring 3½" x 33½", including seam allowances.

Make 2.

3 Using the quilt photo on page 165 as a guide, alternately lay out the pieced block rows and the pieced sashing rows to form the quilt center. Join the rows. Press the seam allowances toward the sashing rows.

4 Join large-scale stripe 3½" x 33½" strips to the right and left sides of the quilt center. Press the seam allowances toward the large-scale stripe strips.

5 Join a reserved nine-patch unit to each end of the remaining two large-scale stripe strips. Press the seam allowances away from the nine-patch units. Join these pieced strips to the remaining sides of the quilt center. Press the seam allowances toward the newly added pieced strips. The pieced quilt top should now measure 39½" square, including seam allowances.

Finishing the Quilt

For help with any of the finishing steps, go to ShopMartingale.com/HowtoQuilt for free downloadable information.

1 Layer, baste, and quilt your quilt, or take it to your favorite long-arm machine quilter for finishing.

2 Using the dark-blue 2½"-wide strips, make and attach binding.

Hearty Blend

This quilt will steal your heart away. The design is created with the basic and versatile Shaded Four Patch block. Don't you agree this would be a great quilt to give as a wedding or anniversary gift?

"Hearty Blend," designed and made by Cathy Wierzbicki

Finished quilt: 67" x 75" ◆ **Finished block: 4" x 4"**

Materials

Yardage is based on 42"-wide fabric.

3 yards *total* of assorted reds for blocks and sashing squares

2⅜ yards of dark-red fabric for border

2 yards of light-pink print for sashing strips

1½ yards *total* of assorted lights for block backgrounds

¾ yard of fabric for binding

4¾ yards of fabric for backing

71" x 79" piece of batting

Cutting

All measurements include ¼"-wide seam allowances. Cut all pieces across the fabric width unless otherwise indicated.

From the assorted lights, cut:
180 squares, 2⅞" x 2⅞"; cut in half diagonally to yield 360 triangles

From the assorted reds, cut:
188 squares, 2½" x 2½"
90 squares, 4⅞" x 4⅞"; cut in half diagonally to yield 180 triangles

From the light-pink print, cut on the *lengthwise* grain:
6 rectangles, 2½" x 16½"
4 strips, 2½" x 60½"

From the dark-red fabric, cut on the *lengthwise* grain:
2 strips, 6" x 56½"
2 strips, 6" x 75½"

From the binding fabric, cut:
8 strips, 2½" x 42"

Making the Blocks

1 Stitch light half-square triangles to two adjacent sides of each red 2½" square as shown to make a pieced triangle. Press the seam allowances toward the square.

2 Sew a red half-square triangle to each pieced triangle to complete the blocks. Press the seam allowances toward the red triangle. Make 180.

Make 180.

Assembling the Quilt Top

1 Stitch four blocks together as shown to make row A. Make 24 rows. Stitch four blocks together as shown to make row B. Make 21 rows.

Row A
Make 24.

Row B
Make 21.

2 Stitch together eight of row A and seven of row B, alternating rows. Begin and end with row A. Make three vertical panels.

Row A

Row B

Make 3.

3 Refer to the quilt assembly diagram below to alternately stitch the light-pink 2½" x 60½" strips and panels together, beginning and ending with a strip. Press the seam allowances toward the strips.

4 Stitch four red 2½" squares and three light-pink 2½" x 16½" rectangles together in alternating positions, beginning and ending with a square. Make two sashing strips.

Make 2.

5 Stitch the pieced sashing strips to the top and bottom edges of the quilt top.

6 Stitch the dark-red 6" x 56½" strips to the top and bottom edges of the quilt top. Stitch the 6" x 75½" strips to the quilt sides. Press the seam allowances toward the strips.

Finishing the Quilt

For help with any of the finishing steps, go to ShopMartingale.com/HowtoQuilt for free downloadable information.

1 Layer, baste, and quilt your quilt, or take it to your favorite long-arm machine quilter for finishing.

2 Using the 2½"-wide strips, make and attach the binding.

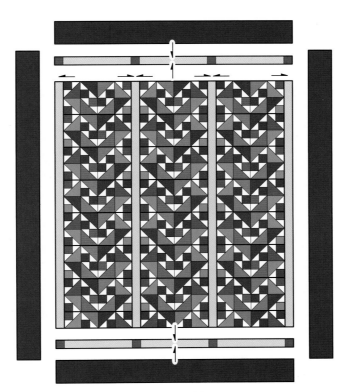

Quilt assembly

Patchwork Weave

This quilt is great in any color group you'd like to work with. The Mosaic block centers are offset by grid work, and the overall effect is sure to wow its recipient. Use precut strips or coveted fabrics from your stash for the block centers, and create this stunner in no time! This square block will leave everyone wondering, "How'd you do that?"

"Patchwork Weave," designed and pieced by Amy Ellis, machine quilted by Natalia Bonner

Finished quilt: 60" x 72"   ◆   **Finished block:** 12" x 12"

Materials

Yardage is based on 42"-wide fabric.

3⅛ yards of cream solid for blocks

1⅝ yards of dark-gray print for blocks

24 strips, 2½" x 42", of assorted prints for blocks

⅝ yard of blue tone on tone for binding

4½ yards of fabric for backing

66" x 78" piece of batting

Cutting

All measurements include ¼"-wide seam allowances.

From the cream solid, cut:

6 strips, 2" x 42"

7 strips, 7½" x 42"; crosscut 4 of the strips into 60 rectangles, 2½" x 7½"

1 strip, 12½" x 42"; crosscut into 11 rectangles, 2" x 12½"

6 strips, 4" x 42"

From the dark-gray print, cut:

3 strips, 12½" x 42"; crosscut into 60 rectangles, 1½" x 12½"

9 strips, 1½" x 42"

From the blue tone on tone, cut:

7 strips, 2½" x 42"

Pressing Matters

Amy recommends pressing the strip-set seam allowances open. With so many seams in a small area, the block is flatter and more comfortable with open seam allowances.

To ensure matching seams at intersections, use lots of fine, sharp pins that won't distort the fabric. Place a pin on each side of the seam allowances after matching the seam itself to prevent slippage while sewing the cross seam.

If you prefer, press the seam allowances to one side. It may be necessary to reverse their direction and re-press some seam allowances so they nest properly (lie in opposite directions) at each seam intersection.

Making the Blocks

1 For the block centers, sew together four assorted 2½"-wide strips to create a strip set; make six. Press the seam allowances open to reduce bulk. Cut the strip sets into 150 segments, 1½" wide.

1½"

Make 6 strip sets. Cut 150 segments.

2 Separate the strip-set segments into groups of five, choosing segments for maximum variety in each group. Matching seams, piece each group together to make a block center. Press the seam allowances in one direction. Trim to 5½" x 8½". Make 30.

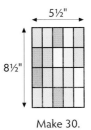

5½"

8½"

Make 30.

3 Sew a white 4"-wide strip to each side of a gray 1½"-wide strip; make three strip sets. Press the seam allowances toward the gray strips. Cut the strip sets into 60 segments, 1½" wide.

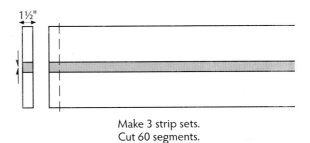

1½"

Make 3 strip sets.
Cut 60 segments.

4 Sew a gray 1½"-wide strip to each side of a white 7½"-wide strip; press the seam allowances toward the white strips. Sew a white 2"-wide strip to each gray strip; press the seam allowances toward the white fabric. Make three strip sets. Cut the strip sets into 49 segments, 2" wide.

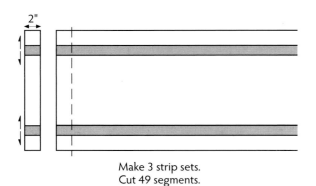

Make 3 strip sets.
Cut 49 segments.

5 Sew a 1½"-wide segment from step 3 to each long side of a Mosaic block center. Press the seam allowances outward; make 30.

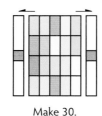

Make 30.

6 Sew cream 2½" x 7½" rectangles to the top and bottom of each block. Press the seam allowances toward the cream rectangles; make 30.

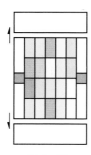

Make 30.

7 Sew gray 1½" x 12½" rectangles to the long sides of the blocks. Press the seam allowances toward the gray rectangles. Add 2" x 12½" segments (cut in step 4) to both long edges of 19 blocks. Press the seam allowances toward the gray rectangles.

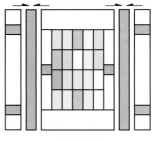

Make 19.

8 Sew a 2"-wide segment from step 4 to one long edge of each remaining block. Attach a cream 2" x 12½" rectangle to the opposite long edge; make 11.

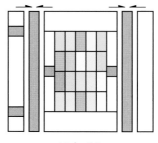

Make 11.

9 Trim and square the blocks to 12½" x 12½".

Identical Variation

If you'd rather make all your blocks the same, there's enough fabric in your strip sets to accomplish that. Simply don't cut the cream 2" x 12½" rectangles listed in the cutting instructions, and increase the number of segments cut in step 4 to 60.

Assembling the Quilt Top

1 Arrange the blocks in six rows of five blocks each, placing the 11 blocks with a solid cream edge around the perimeter of the quilt top.

2 Sew the blocks together into rows, pressing the seam allowances in opposite directions from row to row. Sew the rows together, and press the seam allowances in one direction.

Finishing the Quilt

For help with any of the finishing steps, go to ShopMartingale.com/HowtoQuilt for free downloadable information.

1 Layer, baste, and quilt your quilt, or take it to your favorite long-arm machine quilter for finishing.

2 Using the blue tone-on-tone 2½"-wide strips, make and attach binding.

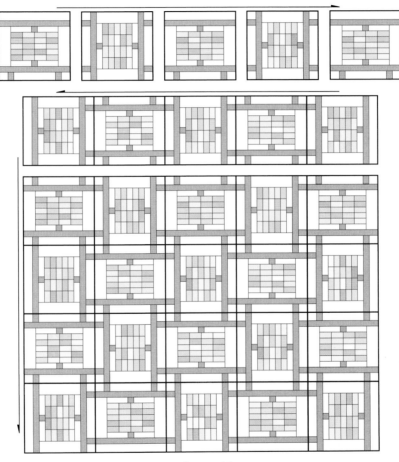

Quilt assembly

Reflections

Kate never tires of red and aqua, no matter how many times she uses them together. This quilt's black-print background really makes the colors pop.

"Reflections," designed and made by Kate Henderson
Finished quilt: 66¼" x 78"

▶ Materials

Yardage is based on 42"-wide fabric.

40 strips, 2½" x 42", of assorted red and aqua prints for blocks

3⅝ yards of black print for background and binding

4¼ yards of fabric for backing

73" x 84" piece of batting

45°-triangle ruler at least 8½" tall (such as the Large Kaleido-Ruler by Marti Michell) *OR* Template plastic

▶ Cutting

All measurements include ¼"-wide seam allowances.

From the black print, cut:
8 strips, 8½" x 42"
22 strips, 2½" x 42"

Making the Rows

1 Organize the assorted red and aqua strips into 10 strip sets of four strips each. Sew the strips in each set together along their long edges. Press the seam allowances open.

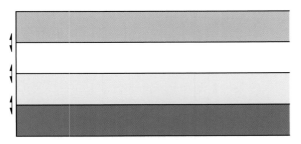

Make 10 strip sets.

2 Place the prepared template on one strip set, aligning the blunted point with one long raw edge of the fabric and the base of the triangle with the opposite raw edge. Trace along the template's angled edges and cut. Rotate the template 180° and position it next to the angled cut edge, making sure the top and bottom of the triangle align with the fabric edges. Cut a second triangle. Repeat to cut eight triangles from each strip set (80 total).

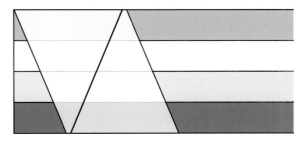

Cut 8 from each, 80 total.

3 Remove the selvages from a black 8½" x 42" strip and fold the strip in half, matching the raw edges. Position the template on a folded strip, aligning the top and bottom edges as before, and positioning the guideline along the cut ends of the strip. Cut along the angled edge of the template to make two half triangles. Continue cutting the fabric strip to make four pairs of full triangles, rotating the template 180° each time. Unfold the remainder of the strip and cut one more triangle. Repeat with the other black 8½" x 42" strips. You will have 16 half triangles (eight pairs) and 72 full triangles.

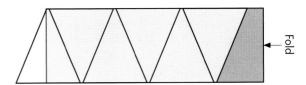

Fold

Cutting Triangles

To make the quilt without using a specialty ruler, trace the pattern on page 179 onto template plastic and cut it out. Be sure to trace the guideline near the center of the triangle onto the template. Lay the template on the assembled strip sets or strips as directed, mark the angled lines onto the fabric, and cut along the lines. Use scissors, or lay a rotary-cutting ruler along the line and cut with a rotary cutter.

To use the Large Kaleido-Ruler, position the blunted tip of the ruler's 45° triangle on one raw edge of the fabric, with the 8½" line on the opposite raw edge. Cut along the angled edges of the ruler. When cutting the half triangles, align the dotted line to the left of the ruler's center with the ends of the fabric strip.

4 Arrange 10 strip-set triangles and nine black triangles into a row. Add a half triangle at each end and sew the triangles together. Press all the seam allowances open. Make eight.

Make 8 rows.

Assembling the Quilt Top

1 Sew two black 2½" x 42" strips together end to end. Press the seam allowances open. Cut seven sashing strips, 66¾" long.

2 Arrange the triangle rows and sashing strips as shown. Sew the rows and sashing strips together. Press the seam allowances toward the sashing strips.

Finishing the Quilt

For help with any of the finishing steps, go to ShopMartingale.com/HowtoQuilt for free downloadable information.

1 Layer, baste, and quilt your quilt, or take it to your favorite long-arm machine quilter for finishing.

2 Using the black 2½"-wide strips, make and attach binding.

Quilt assembly

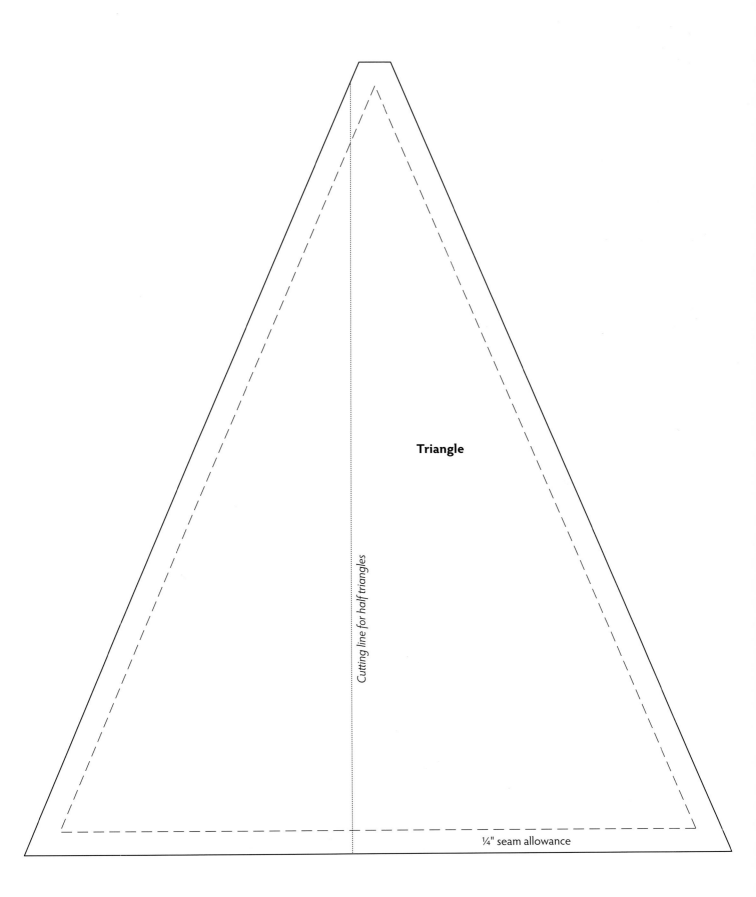

Triangle

Cutting line for half triangles

¼" seam allowance

Bull's Eye

The quest for a quilt pattern with a masculine feel was the inspiration for this design. This block goes together best if you foundation piece everything except the center four-patch unit. After foundation piecing the units, trim them to size, remove the foundation paper, and assemble the block traditionally.

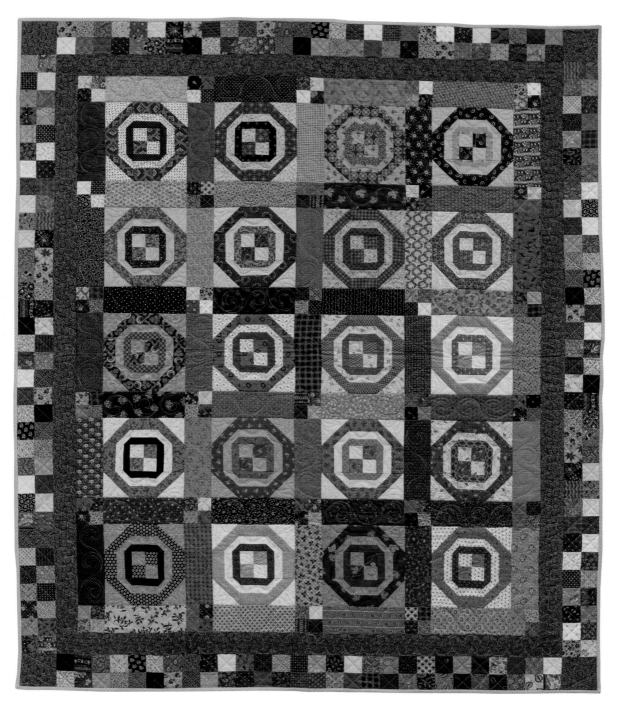

"Bull's Eye," designed and pieced by Nancy Allen, custom machine quilted by Valerie Gines

Finished quilt: 64½" x 76½" ◆ **Finished block:** 9" x 9"

▶ Materials

Yardage is based on 42"-wide fabric.

4½ yards *total* of assorted medium and dark scraps for blocks, sashing, four-patch cornerstones, and checkerboard outer border

2⅝ yards *total* of various light fabrics for block backgrounds, sashing, four-patch cornerstones, and checkerboard outer border

⅞ yard of brown print for inner border and corner squares

⅔ yard of fabric for binding

4¾ yards of fabric for backing

73" x 85" piece of batting

Foundation paper for paper piecing

▶ Cutting

All measurements include ¼"-wide seam allowances.

From the medium and dark scraps, cut:
60 squares, 2" x 2"
124 squares, 2½" x 2½"
49 rectangles, 3½" x 9½"

From 1 medium or dark scrap, cut *for each block*:
Piece A4: 2 squares, 2" x 2"; cut in half diagonally to yield 4 triangles (80 total)*
Piece B1: 4 rectangles, 1¾" x 4" (80 total)*

From a second medium or dark scrap, cut *for each block*:
Piece A2: 4 rectangles, 2" x 6" (80 total)*
Piece B3: 4 rectangles, 2½" x 4" (80 total)*
2 squares, 2" x 2" (40 total)

From the light fabrics, cut:
60 squares, 2" x 2"
124 squares, 2½" x 2½"

From 1 light fabric, cut *for each block*:
Piece A1: 2 squares, 4½" x 4½"; cut in half diagonally to yield 4 triangles (80 total)*
Piece A3: 4 rectangles, 1½" x 4" (80 total)*
Piece B2: 4 rectangles, 2" x 4" (80 total)*
2 squares, 2" x 2" (40 total)

From the brown print, cut:
6 strips, 3" x 42"
4 squares, 4½" x 4½"

From the binding fabric, cut:
8 strips, 2¼" x 42"

These pieces are for foundation piecing and do not have to be cut as precisely as for traditional piecing.

Making the Blocks

1 Make 80 copies each of foundation patterns A and B on page 183.

2 Using pieces A1–A4, foundation piece pattern A. Begin with light background piece A1. Place it right side up on the unmarked side of pattern A, covering the space numbered 1 and extending ¼" beyond the diagonal line. Hold the pattern up to the light to make sure that the space is covered. Place a medium or dark A2 piece on top of piece A1, right sides together and ensuring the raw edges are aligned with the diagonal of piece A1. Pin in place. Turn the piece over and sew on the marked line. Trim the seam allowances to ¼" and press toward piece A2. Add pieces A3 and A4 in the same manner. Trim the finished unit to size and remove the paper. Make four units. For more information on foundation piecing, visit ShopMartingale.com/HowtoQuilt.

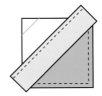

Make 4.

3 Using pieces B1–B3, foundation piece pattern B, beginning with a medium or dark piece B1 and a light background piece B2. Press the seam allowances toward the piece just added. Trim the finished unit to size and remove the paper. Make four units.

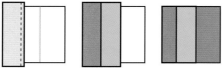

Make 4.

4 Make a four-patch unit using two light 2" squares and two medium or dark 2" squares. Press the seam allowances as shown.

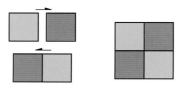

Make 1.

5 Lay out the units for the block as shown and sew them into rows; press the seam allowances as shown. Sew the rows together and press the seam allowances open.

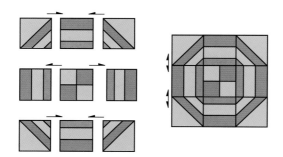

6 Repeat steps 2–5 to make a total of 20 blocks.

Assembling the Quilt Top

1 Lay out the blocks in five rows of four blocks each. When you're happy with the arrangement, add five 3½" x 9½" sashing rectangles to each row. Sew the blocks and sashing rectangles together. Press all seam allowances toward the sashing rectangles.

Make 5 rows.

2 Mix and match the 60 medium and dark and 60 light 2" squares into sets of four until you have 30 sets. Sew into four-patch units and spin the seam allowances. Make 30 four-patch units.

3 Sew five four-patch units from step 2 together with four 3½" x 9½" sashing rectangles as shown to make a sashing row. Press all seam allowances toward the sashing rectangles. Repeat to make six sashing rows.

Make 6.

4 Join the sashing rows and block rows, referring to the quilt assembly diagram on page 183. Press the seam allowances toward the sashing rows. The quilt center should now measure 38½" x 62½".

Adding the Borders

Refer to the quilt assembly diagram as you add the borders. If you need more information on adding borders, visit ShopMartingale.com/HowtoQuilt.

1 Sew six brown-print 3" x 42" strips together end to end and press the seam allowances open. Cut two strips, 63½" long, and two strips, 56½" long.

2 Sew the longer border strips to the sides of the quilt; press the seam allowances toward the borders. Sew the shorter border strips to the top and bottom of the quilt. Press the seam allowances toward the borders. The quilt should now measure 56½" x 68½".

3 Mix and match the 248 assorted light, medium, and dark 2½" squares and sew them into two-patch units; press the seam allowances toward the darker fabric. Sew 34 two-patch units together to make a side border strip. Press all seam allowances in the same direction. Make two.

Make 2.

4 Sew the strips from step 3 to the left and right sides of the quilt center. Press the seam allowances toward the brown inner border.

5 Sew 28 two-patch units together to make a strip; press all seam allowances in the same direction. Make two. Add a brown-print 4½" square to each end of both border strips. Press the seam allowances toward the squares.

Make 2.

6 Sew the strips from step 5 to the top and bottom of the quilt center. Press the seam allowances toward the brown inner border. Stay stitch around the outside of your quilt, about ⅛" from the edge. The quilt center should now measure 64½" x 76½".

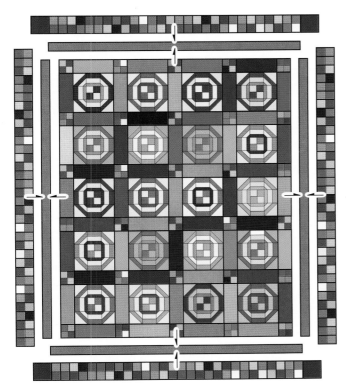

Quilt assembly

Finishing the Quilt

For help with any of the finishing steps, go to ShopMartingale.com/HowtoQuilt for free downloadable information.

1 Layer, baste, and quilt your quilt, or take it to your favorite long-arm machine quilter for finishing.

2 Using the 2¼"-wide strips, make and attach binding.

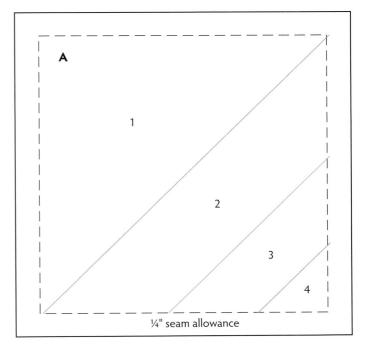

¼" seam allowance

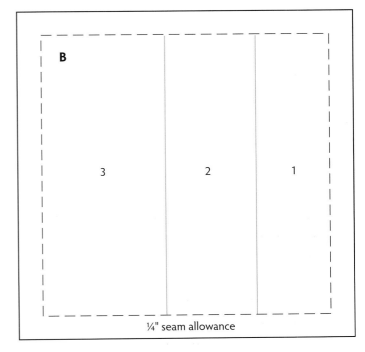

¼" seam allowance

Karen's Puzzle

Most women in the 1800s *could not afford large pieces of fabric. When they had saved enough scraps, they sorted them into light and dark values and pieced them into quilts. In keeping with this era, this quilt has no solid borders. Instead, the block design was continued to finish off the dark stars on the sides of the quilt.*

"Karen's Puzzle," designed by Robin Strobel, pieced by Karen Soltys, quilted by Pam Clarke

Finished quilt: 51½" x 63½" ◆ **Finished block:** 12" x 12"

Materials

Yardage is based on 42"-wide fabric.

¼ yard *each* of 20 different light prints for blocks*

¼ yard *each* of 20 different dark prints for blocks*

½ yard *total* of fabric for binding

3¼ yards of fabric for backing

56" x 68" piece of batting

Fat eighths (9" x 21") or fat quarters (18" x 21") work well here. If you use fat eighths, you will need additional fabric for the binding. If you use fat quarters, cut the excess fabric into squares and rectangles. To be thrifty like our ancestors, sew those extra pieces together for the quilt back.

Cutting

All measurements include ¼"-wide seam allowances. Cut strips across the width of the fabric unless indicated otherwise.

From *each* light print, cut:
5 squares, 3⅞" x 3⅞" (100 total)
10 squares, 2" x 2" (200 total)
2 squares, 3½" x 3½" (40 total)

From *each* dark print, cut:
5 squares, 3⅞" x 3⅞" (100 total)
10 squares, 2" x 2" (200 total)
2 squares, 3½" x 3½" (40 total)

From *each* of 12 different prints (remainders of above), cut:
1 strip, 2½" x 21" (12 total; optional, for a scrappy binding)

Making the Units

Each dark star is made from four identical half-square-triangle units and a center square of the same dark fabric. Each four-patch unit is made from any combination of light and dark fabrics. The four-patch units are not a problem, but a traditional Indiana Puzzle block contains one whole and three partial dark stars. (Only when the blocks are placed together do the other stars become apparent.) With this type of block, it can be confusing to attempt a scrappy quilt and ensure the correct fabric placement in the blocks. In this case, it is actually easier to spread out all the units on a work wall before you sew the units together. Make certain that the dark stars all use the same light and dark fabrics, and then sew the units into rows. Finally, sew the rows together.

Although you won't be sewing an actual block together, if you were, each block would be made using the following units:

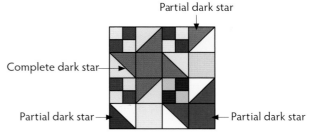

Traditional Indiana
Puzzle Block

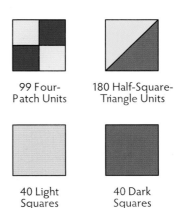

99 Four-
Patch Units

180 Half-Square-
Triangle Units

40 Light
Squares

40 Dark
Squares

1 You will need to make four identical half-square-triangle units for each dark star, as well as a couple of extras to finish the pattern at the edges of the quilt. First, keep the sets of five 3⅞" light squares together. Divide the sets of five 3⅞" dark squares into two sets of two squares each and a single remaining square. To make the half-square-triangle units, mark a diagonal line on the wrong side of each 3⅞" light square. Layer one of these squares with a dark 3⅞" square, right sides together. Stitch ¼" from each side of the marked line. Cut apart on the line and press toward the dark fabric. Repeat, using the same two fabrics to make four identical half-square-triangle units. Using the same light fabric, pair it with two squares of a different dark fabric and make four more half-square-triangle units. Pair the fifth 3⅞" square of the light fabric with still another different 3⅞" dark square and make two half-square-triangle units. Repeat these steps with all the remaining 3⅞" squares. Make 40 sets of four identical half-square-triangle units and 20 sets of two identical units (200 total).

Make 40 sets of 4 identical units and 20 sets of 2 identical units.

2 To make the four-patch units, stitch a 2" light square to a 2" dark square, right sides together. Press toward the dark fabric. Repeat with two more squares of the same fabrics, and sew together as shown. Press. Repeat with the remaining 2" light and dark squares. Make 100.

Make 100.

3 Arrange the half-square-triangle units, four-patch units, and 3½" squares into rows. (You will have some half-square-triangle units and one four-patch unit left over.) Arrange the four half-square-triangle units and matching dark square that form each dark star, leaving gaps for the four-patch units and light squares. Then place the light squares on the work wall, and play the game of musical squares—trying to keep the same light fabric from touching itself. Finally, add the four-patch units, once again trying to keep the fabrics nicely mixed, and also being very careful to position the light and dark squares correctly. The tip of each dark star should touch a dark square. Step back and squint at the quilt. Your eye should want to move across the surface, and not get fixated at one area. If all you can do is stare at one spot, think about

Fat-Eighth Cutting Layout

Depending on whether you're using traditional quarter-yard cuts, fat quarters, or fat eighths, you'll cut your fabric in different ways. If you use fat eighths, cut carefully following the cutting diagram. There is little room for error, but if you make one and don't have enough fabric, just add another print! This is a scrap quilt—more is better.

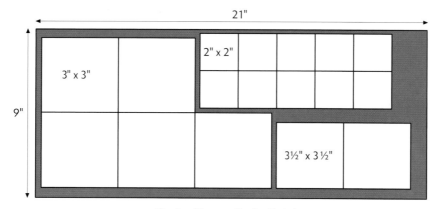

Cutting Diagram for Fat Eighth

what catches your eye and rearrange the fabrics to break up the pattern. You may want to take the time to attach a small piece of masking tape with a number and letter indicating the row and placement on the upper-left corner of each unit. For example, the first row of units would be marked 1a, 1b, 1c, etc., up to 1q. Sew the units into rows and press seam allowances away from the half-square-triangle units. Sew the rows together.

Finishing the Quilt

For help with any of the finishing steps, go to ShopMartingale.com/HowtoQuilt for free downloadable information.

1 Layer, baste, and quilt your quilt, or take it to your favorite long-arm machine quilter for finishing.

2 Using the 2½"-wide strips, make and attach binding.

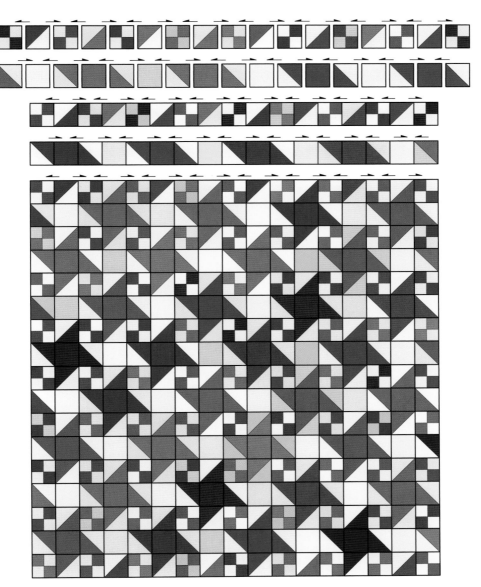

Quilt assembly

Diamond Dust

This quilt was designed for 2½"-wide strips of fabric. The instructions here are for cutting your own, but you could easily use a precut assortment. Separate the strips into lights and darks, and then sew them into strip sets. You'll be dazzling yourself with beautiful diamonds in no time at all.

"Diamond Dust," designed and pieced by Cathy Wierzbicki, machine quilted by Bonnie Gibbs

Finished quilt: 64½" x 80½"   ◆   **Finished block:** 8" x 16"

Materials

Yardage is based on 42"-wide fabric.

5 yards *total* of assorted light fabrics for blocks and border

5 yards *total* of assorted dark or medium fabrics for blocks and border

1 yard of accent or contrast fabric for border

2 yards of fabric for binding

5 yards of fabric for backing

69" x 85" piece of batting

See-through template plastic

Cutting

All measurements include ¼"-wide seam allowances.

From the assorted light fabrics, cut a *total* of:
66 strips, 2½" x 42"

From the assorted dark or medium fabrics, cut a *total* of:
66 strips, 2½" x 42"

From the accent or contrast fabric, cut:
12 strips, 2½" x 42"

From the binding fabric, cut:
8 strips, 2¼" x 42"

Making the Blocks

After sewing each seam, press seam allowances in the directions indicated by the arrows.

1 Make templates for the small and large rectangles using the patterns on page 191. Be sure to include all of the markings. You will be using both sides of these templates to cut your blocks, so flip each template over and mark the reverse side with an *R*.

2 Alternately join two light strips and two dark or medium strips along the long edges to make a strip set. Repeat to make a total of 24 strip sets.

3 Position the large rectangle template on a strip set so that the markings on the template correspond with the fabrics and seamlines. Carefully cut around the perimeter of the template with a rotary cutter. (If you're uncomfortable using the rotary cutter along the edge of the template plastic, trace around the plastic with a sharp pencil or fabric marker, remove the template, and then use your ruler

and rotary cutter to cut on the marked lines.) Cut two rectangles in one direction; then turn the template to the reverse side and cut two more rectangles, making sure the markings correspond with the fabrics. Repeat with the remaining strip sets. Each strip set will yield two right-slanting and two left-slanting units—enough to make one Diamond block. Save your large scraps to use later when cutting the border units.

Make 24 strip sets.
Cut 2 left-slanting and 2 right-slanting
rectangles from each strip set.

Cut 48.   Cut 48.

4 Sew four different rectangles from step 3 together. Repeat to make a total of 24 Diamond blocks.

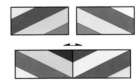   

Make 24.

Making the Border Strips

1 Sew together one light strip and one dark or medium strip along the long edges to make a strip set. Repeat to make a total of 15 strip sets. You will have strips left over to make more strip sets if needed. The actual quantity of strip sets needed will depend on how many units you can cut from the leftovers of the Diamond blocks.

2 Position the small rectangle template on a strip set so that the markings on the template correspond with the fabrics and seamlines. Using the same cutting method as for the Diamond blocks, cut out four left-slanting rectangles, and then reverse the

template and cut out four right-slanting rectangles. Cut a total of 72 left-slanting rectangles and 72 right-slanting rectangles using the remaining strip sets and the leftover pieces from the Diamond block strip sets. Make more strip sets if needed to yield the required amount.

Make 15 to 18 strip sets.
Cut a total of 72 left-slanting and
72 right-slanting rectangles.

Cut 72.   Cut 72.

3 Sew a left-slanting and a different right-slanting rectangle from step 2 together to make a pieced triangle. Make a total of 56 pieced triangles.

Make 56.

4 Sew together 12 pieced triangles each for the top and bottom borders, reversing the direction of the triangles at the midpoint of the strip so that all of the points face toward the strip center. In the same manner, sew together 16 triangles each for the side borders. Join the accent or contrast 2½" x 42" strips end to end using diagonal seams. From the pieced strip, cut four strips, 2½" x 48½", and four strips, 2½" x 64½". Sew the 48½"-long strips to the long sides of the top and bottom borders and the 64½"-long strips to the long sides of the side borders.

Top/bottom border.
Make 2.

Side border.
Make 2.

5 From the remaining rectangles from step 2, join four left-slanting rectangles and four right-slanting rectangles to make a corner unit. Repeat to make a total of four units. Sew a unit to each end of the top and bottom borders. You may notice that the corner units in the quilt shown are made differently; the method described here is easier and slightly more scrappy.

Make 4.

Assembling the Quilt Top

1 Refer to the quilt assembly diagram below to arrange the Diamond blocks into eight rows of three blocks each. Rearrange the blocks if necessary until you are pleased with the position of the fabrics and colors. Sew the blocks in each row together, and then sew the rows together.

2 Sew the side borders to the quilt top, and then add the top and bottom borders.

Quilt assembly

Finishing the Quilt

For help with any of the finishing steps, go to ShopMartingale.com/HowtoQuilt for free downloadable information.

1 Layer, baste, and quilt your quilt, or take it to your favorite long-arm machine quilter for finishing.

2 Using the 2¼"-wide strips, make and attach binding.

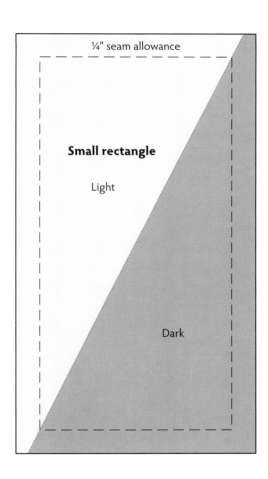

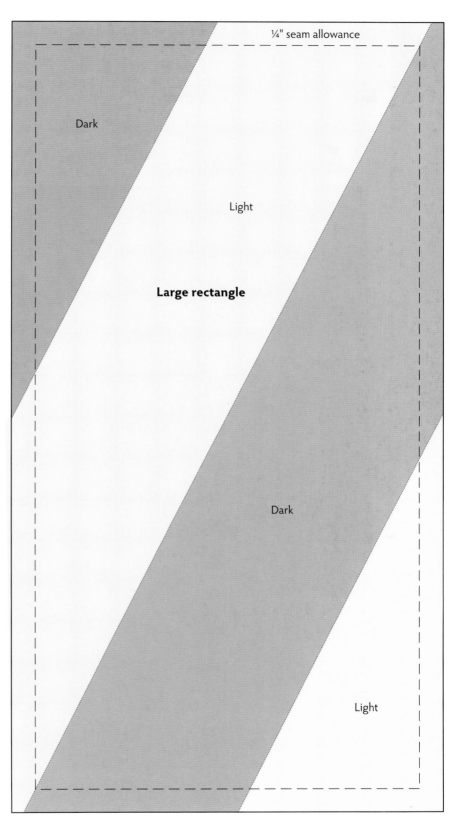

Japanese Stars and Pinwheels

Sally had been keeping a small collection of Asian fabrics in her stash for a long time. But until this quilt, she'd never made an entire project with them. Sally supplemented the fabrics from her stash with fat quarters, Jelly Rolls, and other pieces she found while shopping at the American Quilter's Society show in Paducah, Kentucky.

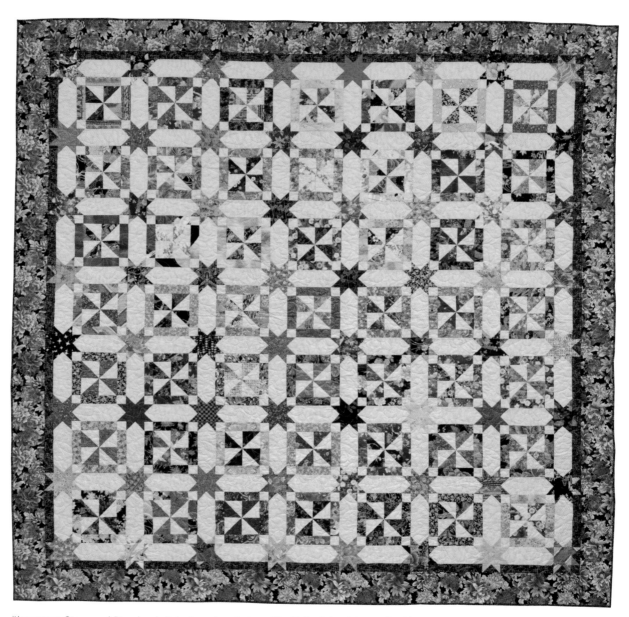

"Japanese Stars and Pinwheels," designed and pieced by Sally Schneider, quilted by Leona VanLeeuwen
Finished quilt: 101½" x 101½" ◆ **Finished block: 9" x 9"**

Materials

Yardage is based on 42"-wide fabric.

5 yards of cream fabric for background and sashing

3 yards *total* of assorted dark fabrics for blocks and sashing squares*

3¼ yards *total* of assorted medium fabrics for blocks and sashing squares*

1 yard of gray print for inner border

2 yards of floral for outer border

⅞ yard of fabric for binding

9½ yards of fabric for backing

106" x 106" piece of batting

The yardages given for assorted darks and mediums are estimates based on using darks for the Pinwheel block center and mediums for the block borders. As with any scrap quilt, varying the value placement makes the quilt more interesting, so feel free to play with that aspect of the quilt design. As long as there is some contrast between the pinwheels and the block border, and with the background, the values will work in any position.

Cutting

All measurements include ¼"-wide seam allowances.

From the cream fabric, cut:
13 strips, 3½" x 42"; crosscut into 98 rectangles, 3½" x 4½"
10 strips, 2" x 42"; crosscut into 196 squares, 2" x 2"
11 strips, 9½" x 42"; crosscut into 112 rectangles, 3½" x 9½"

From *each* of 49 dark fabrics, cut:
2 rectangles, 3½" x 4½" (98 total)

From *each* of 64 dark and medium fabrics, cut:
1 square, 3½" x 3½" (64 total)
1 strip, 2" x 18"; crosscut into 8 squares, 2" x 2" (512 total)

From *each* of 49 medium fabrics, cut:
1 strip, 2" x 28"; crosscut into 4 rectangles, 2" x 6½" (196 total)

From the inner-border fabric, cut:
2 strips, 3½" x 42"; crosscut into 32 rectangles, 2" x 3½"
2 strips, 9½" x 42"; crosscut into 28 rectangles, 2" x 9½"
1 strip, 2" x 10"; crosscut into 4 squares, 2" x 2"

From the outer-border fabric, cut:
11 strips, 6" x 42"

From the binding fabric, cut:
11 strips, 2¼" x 42"

Making the Blocks

Directions are for making one block. For each block, you'll need two 3½" x 4½" background rectangles, two matching dark 3½" x 4½" rectangles, four matching medium-value 2" x 6½" rectangles, and four 2" background squares.

1 Use Sally's special technique for making half-square-triangle units. Mark the wrong side of two 3½" x 4½" background rectangles using a square ruler with a 45° line through the center. Align the diagonal line of the ruler with the short side of the rectangle. Draw a diagonal line from the corner of the rectangle to the long side. Rotate the rectangle and repeat from the opposite corner. You will have two parallel lines ½" apart. Place each marked rectangle right sides together with a dark 3½" x 4½" rectangle. Sew on the drawn lines, and then cut between them.

Press the seam allowances toward the dark fabric. Repeat to make four half-square-triangle units.

Make 4.

Direction Counts

Be sure that you sew all the pinwheels "whirling" in the same direction. It's very easy to get some of them backward.

2 Arrange the four half-square-triangle units as shown to form a pinwheel. Sew the units together into rows. Join the rows, pressing the seam allowances in the directions indicated.

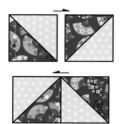
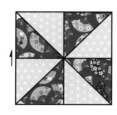

3 Sew medium-value 2" x 6½" rectangles to two opposite sides of the pinwheel. Press the seam allowances toward the rectangles.

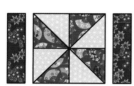

4 Add a 2" background square to each end of the two remaining medium-value rectangles. Press the seam allowances toward the rectangle.

Make 2.

5 Sew the units from step 4 to the two remaining edges of the pinwheel unit. Press the seam allowances away from the block center. Make 49 blocks.

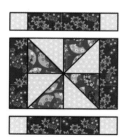
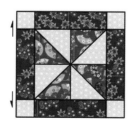

Make 49.

Making the Sashing Strips and Inner Border

1 Arrange the blocks and 3½" x 9½" background sashing strips as desired. For the sashing stars, select one 3½" dark or medium square for the star center (cornerstone) and eight matching 2" squares for the star points. Place the cornerstones in the desired position in your layout and pin or place the squares around each cornerstone, at the ends of the sashing strips.

2 Working with just one sashing strip at a time and using the folded-corner technique as shown, sew diagonally across the squares and trim the excess, leaving a ¼" seam allowance. Press the seam allowances in the directions indicated.

3 Replace the sashing strip in your arrangement. Repeat until all are completed. It's important to work with just one sashing strip at a time and replace it when you are finished with it, because it's very easy to get them mixed up.

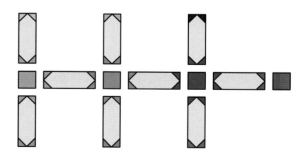

Matching or Not?

The squares used for the folded corners can match the cornerstone or they can be different, but all eight squares should be the same fabric.

4 For the outer edges of the quilt top, arrange inner-border 2" x 3½" rectangles where the cornerstones meet the outside edge. Using the folded-corner technique again, add the matching dark or medium 2" squares to both ends of the rectangle to complete the star points. Replace the unit on your design wall.

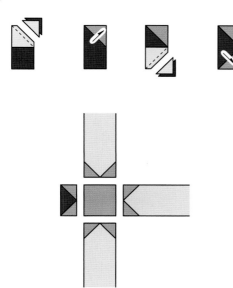

5 Arrange the inner-border 2" x 9½" strips around the edges of the quilt, adding the inner-border 2" squares at the corners.

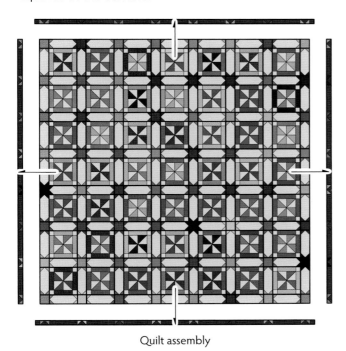

Quilt assembly

Assembling the Quilt Top

1 Sew the blocks, sashing strips, and cornerstones together in rows, referring to the quilt assembly diagram below left. Press the seam allowances toward the blocks.

2 Join the rows, pressing the seam allowances toward the blocks.

Adding the Outer Border

1 Sew the outer-border strips together end to end to make one long strip. Measure the quilt through the center from top to bottom and cut two strips to that length.

2 Sew the trimmed border strips to the sides of the quilt top. Press the seam allowances toward the outer border.

3 Measure the quilt through the center from side to side, including the borders just added. Cut two strips that length.

4 Sew the trimmed border strips to the top and bottom of the quilt top. Press the seam allowances toward the outer border.

Finishing the Quilt

For help with any of the finishing steps, go to ShopMartingale.com/HowtoQuilt for free downloadable information.

1 Layer, baste, and quilt your quilt, or take it to your favorite long-arm machine quilter for finishing.

2 Using the 2¼"-wide strips, make and attach binding.

Pie in the Sky

Gather your favorite prints and colors and play matchmaker to your heart's content as you blend them into this pleasing patchwork bed quilt. So incredibly simple to sew, yet devastatingly complex in appearance, this quilt is one you'll want to dream under night after night.

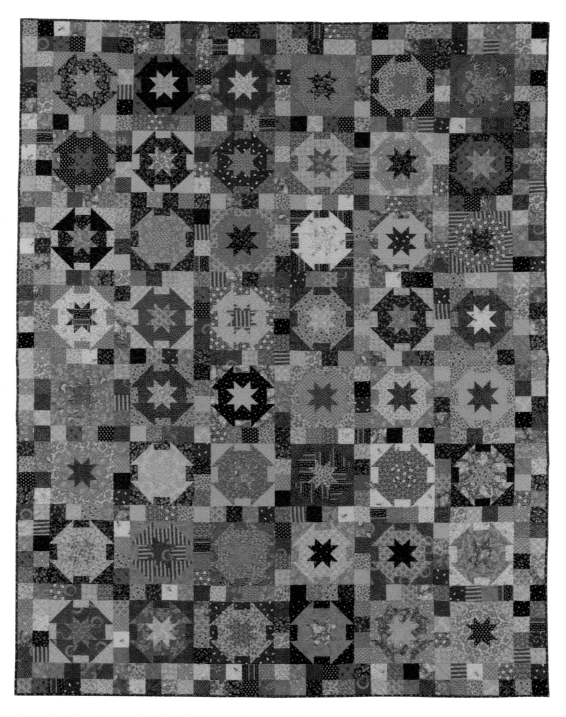

"Pie in the Sky," designed by Kim Diehl, pieced by Deb Behrend and Kim Diehl, machine quilted by Deborah Poole
Finished quilt: 66½" x 86½"   ◆   **Finished block:** 8" x 8"

▶ Materials

Yardage is based on 42"-wide fabric. Fat quarters are 18" x 21".

The number of assorted prints used for this quilt can be reduced by purchasing half-yard cuts of 24 assorted prints, and then cutting along the center fold of each half-yard piece to yield 2 fat quarters, for a total of 48.

48 fat quarters of assorted prints for blocks, sashing, and border

⅔ yard of dark print for binding

5¼ yards of fabric for backing

72" x 92" rectangle of batting

▶ Cutting

All measurements include ¼"-wide seam allowances. Cut pieces across the width of the fabric unless otherwise indicated.

From the length of *each* of the 48 fat quarters, cut:

2 strips, 1½" x 21"; crosscut 1 strip into 8 squares, 1½" x 1½" (384 total)

3 strips, 2½" x 21"; crosscut 2 strips into 16 squares, 2½" x 2½" (768 total)

1 strip, 3⅞" x 21"; crosscut into 4 squares, 3⅞" x 3⅞". Cut in half diagonally to yield 8 triangles (384 total).

From the dark print, cut:

8 strips, 2½" x 42"

Easily Organize Fat Quarters for Cutting and Sewing

Pressing the fat quarters flat and carefully layering them into stacks of six prints greatly speeds up the cutting process. Once the patchwork pieces are cut, separate them as specified in "Organizing the Patchwork Pieces" and keep them grouped by print.

Organizing the Patchwork Pieces

Separate the patchwork pieces cut from *each* fat quarter into the following sets, grouping them by print.

Background Sets

1 strip, 1½" x 22"
4 triangles

Churn Dash Sets

1 strip, 2½" x 22"
4 triangles

Star Sets

8 squares, 1½" x 1½"
1 square, 2½" x 2½"

Sashing/Border Sets

15 squares, 2½" x 2½".*

*If you layered your fat quarters for cutting as suggested in the tip below left, just group together your layered sets of sashing/border squares; the individual prints can be separated later, if desired, when you stitch your patchwork.

Making the Blocks

Sew all pieces with right sides together unless otherwise noted.

1 Select a set of block background pieces cut from one print and a set of Churn Dash pieces cut from a second print. Join the 1½" x 22" and 2½" x 22" strips along one long edge to make a strip set. Press the seam allowances toward the wide Churn Dash strip. Crosscut the strip set into four segments, 2½" wide.

Make 1 strip set.
Cut 4 segments.

2 Join a background triangle to a Churn Dash triangle, stitching along the long raw edges. Press the seam allowances toward the Churn Dash triangles. Trim away the dog-ear points. Repeat for a total of four half-square-triangle units.

Make 4.

3 Select a set of star pieces cut from a third print. Use a pencil to draw a diagonal line on the wrong side of each 1½" square. Layer a prepared square over one corner of a strip-set segment from step 1,

placing it on the wide Churn Dash print. Stitch the pair together exactly on the drawn line. Repeat for a total of four pieced units. Press, and then trim the excess corner fabric. In the same manner, sew, press, and trim the remaining 1½" prepared squares, placing them in mirror-image positions to form four pieced star-point units.

Make 4.

4 Lay out the half-square-triangle units, the 2½" square, and the pieced star-point units as shown to form a block. Join the pieces in each horizontal row. Press the seam allowances of the top and bottom rows toward the outer large triangle units. Press the seam allowances of the middle row toward the center square. Join the rows. Press the seam allowances toward the middle row.

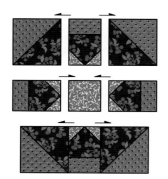 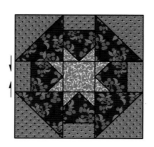

5 Repeat steps 1–4 for a total of 48 blocks measuring 8½" square, including seam allowances.

Making the Sashing and Border Strips

1 Select 33 assorted-print 2½" squares. Join the squares to make a row. Press the seam allowances in one direction. Repeat for a total of 11 rows. To give you added flexibility as you piece your blocks, there are a handful of extra squares.

Make 11 rows.

2 Select two rows from step 1. Reverse the direction of one row to allow the seam allowances to nest together. Join the two rows. Press the center seam allowances to one side. Repeat for a total of two double rows for the top and bottom borders. The remaining rows are for the horizontal sashing.

Make 2 double rows.

3 Select four assorted-print 2½" squares. Join the squares to make a strip. Press the seam allowances in one direction. Repeat for a total of 72 vertical sashing strips.

Make 72.

Assembling the Quilt Top

1 Select six blocks and nine vertical sashing strips. Lay out the pieces as shown to make a horizontal block row. Press the seam allowances away from the blocks. Repeat for a total of eight block rows.

Make 8 rows.

2 Referring to the quilt photo on page 196, lay out the top and bottom border rows, the block rows, and the horizontal sashing rows to form the quilt top. Join the rows. Press the seam allowances away from the block rows. The pieced quilt top should now measure 66½" x 86½", including seam allowances.

Finishing the Quilt

For help with any of the finishing steps, go to ShopMartingale.com/HowtoQuilt for free downloadable information.

1 Layer, baste, and quilt your quilt, or take it to your favorite long-arm machine quilter for finishing.

2 Using the dark-print 2½"-wide strips, make and attach binding.

Tessellation

This is a great quilt to build from your stash. You can use a wide variety of fabrics: Liberty, William Morris, 1930s reproductions, brights, earth tones, or a mixture of scraps. They all work. You only need one strip from each fabric, so it won't make a dent in your collection.

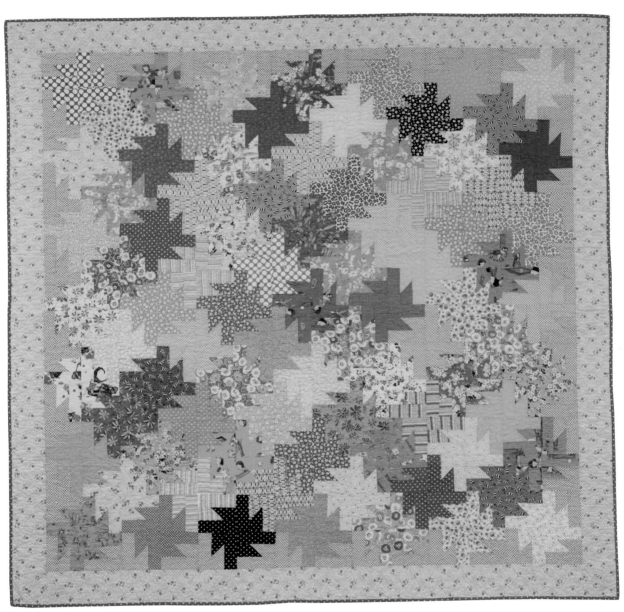

"Tessellation," designed and made by Sandy Klop

Finished quilt: 71½" x 71½" ◆ **Finished block:** 9" x 9"

Materials

Yardage is based on 42"-wide fabric.

85 strips, 2" x 42", of assorted fabrics for blocks and pieced inner border

2¼ yards of light-blue print for outer border

⅞ yard of light-blue polka dot for pieced inner border

⅝ yard of fabric for binding

4¼ yards of fabric for backing

76" x 76" piece of batting

Cutting

All measurements include ¼"-wide seam allowances.

From *each* of the 85 assorted fabric strips, cut:
4 rectangles, 2" x 5" (340 total)
4 rectangles, 2" x 3½" (340 total)

From the light-blue polka dot, cut:
13 strips, 2" x 42"; cut into 52 rectangles, 2" x 5", and 52 rectangles, 2" x 3½"

From the light-blue print, cut on the *lengthwise* grain:
4 strips, 4½" x 76"

From the binding fabric, cut:
8 strips, 2¼" x 42"

Making the Pinwheel Blocks

1 To make the first Pinwheel block, select a main fabric (you will use the whole stack) as well as four different corner fabrics. For the four corners you will need only one piece of each size. Set the rest of the corner pieces aside for now.

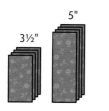 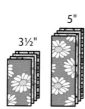

Main fabric   Corner fabrics

2 Sew the eight 2" x 3½" rectangles together on the diagonal, pairing the main fabric with each corner fabric. Press toward the main fabric.

Sew 3½" pieces on the diagonal.   Trim.

3 With the main fabric on top and right sides together, sew the four 2" x 5" main fabric rectangles along the right side of the diagonal pairs. Press toward the main fabric.

4 Sew four 2" x 5" corner pieces to the left side of each unit from step 3, matching corner colors.

Organizing Hint

Layer each 2" x 3½" rectangle on top of a matching 2" x 5" rectangle and place them in a large box such as a pizza box. This will make it easier to select fabrics as you need them.

5 Sew the four sections together with the main fabric, creating a pinwheel shape.

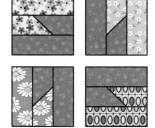

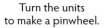
Turn the units to make a pinwheel.

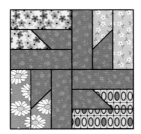
Finished block

6 For the next Pinwheel block, choose a different main fabric (pinwheel color). Match two corners (one of each size) with the previous block and select two new corners. Remember to set the remaining corners aside. Don't put them back with the full sets.

7 Work across the row until you have a row of five blocks. You can sew the pinwheels together as you complete each block.

8 For the second row, choose a new main fabric and match the two corners from above; also select two new corners.

9 For the next block, choose a new main fabric, match three adjacent corners, and select one new corner. Complete the row and sew it to the first row.

10 Complete three more rows and sew to the rows above.

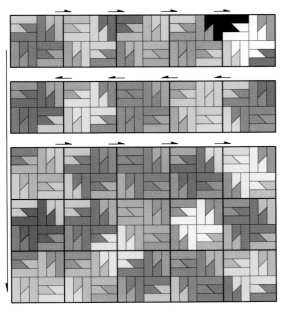
Quilt assembly

Making the Border Pinwheel Blocks

1 For the top border, select a new main fabric and match the two inside corners to the first row of the quilt. Use the blue polka-dot fabric for the two outside corners.

2 Continue to make the top border row and then the bottom. Make the side borders, continuing around the quilt until the 20 border blocks for the sides are completed and ready to sew to the quilt.

3 Make each of the four corner blocks with a new main fabric. Match one inside corner to the quilt and use the blue polka-dot fabric for the other three corners.

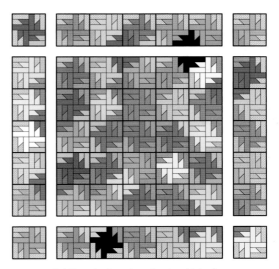
Adding the border pinwheel blocks

Adding the Mitered Border

1 Mark the center of a 4½" x 76" light-blue outer-border strip and the center of a quilt side. Pin the border to the side, matching center points. Begin and end sewing ¼" from the ends of the quilt top. Repeat for all four borders.

2 Fold the quilt wrong sides together at one corner and align the raw edges of the quilt. The borders should be right sides together. Pin to hold in place.

3 Position a ruler so that the 45° angle line is on the stitching line of the border and the ¼" mark is exactly at the end of the stitching line. Cut the diagonal edge of the borders and then stitch a ¼" seam. Press the seam allowances open. Repeat for the remaining three corners.

Finishing the Quilt

For help with any of the finishing steps, go to ShopMartingale.com/HowtoQuilt for free downloadable information.

1 Layer, baste, and quilt your quilt, or take it to your favorite long-arm machine quilter for finishing.

2 Using the 2¼"-wide strips, make and attach binding.

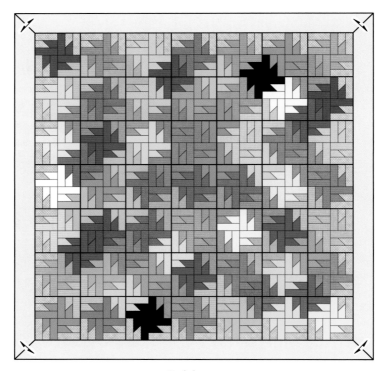

Quilt layout

Carefree

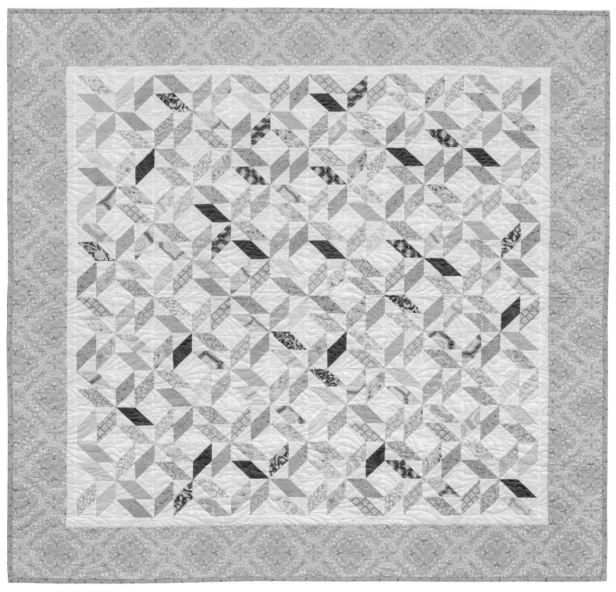

Piecing the blocks for this quilt in a random, scrappy fashion creates a design that's spirited and carefree.

"Carefree," designed and pieced by Gerri Robinson, machine quilted by Rebecca Segura

Finished quilt: 62½" x 62½"   ◆   **Finished block:** 8" x 8"

Materials

Yardage is based on 42"-wide fabric.

36 strips, 2½" x 42", of assorted bright fabrics for blocks

3 yards of white solid for block backgrounds and inner border

2 yards of orange print for outer border

⅝ yard of teal print for binding

4¼ yards of fabric for backing

72" x 72" piece of batting

Cutting

All measurements include ¼"-wide seam allowances.

From *each* of the 36 strips of bright fabric, cut:
8 rectangles, 2½" x 4½" (288 total)

From the white solid, cut:
576 squares, 2½" x 2½"
5 strips, 1½" x 42"

From the orange print, cut on the *lengthwise* grain:
2 strips, 6½" x 54"
2 strips, 6½" x 66"

From the teal print, cut:
7 strips, 2½" x 42"

Making the Blocks

1 Sew two white 2½" squares and one bright 2½" x 4½" rectangle together as shown to make a rectangular unit. Make a total of 288 units.

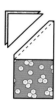

Make 288.

2 Randomly sew two units from step 1 together to make a 4½" square. Press the seam allowances in one direction. Make a total of 144 units.

3 Randomly sew four units from step 2 together to make a block. Press the seam allowances in the directions indicated. The block should measure 8½" square. Make a total of 36 blocks.

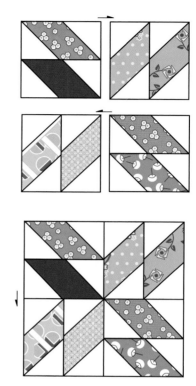

Make 36.

Assembling the Quilt Top

1 Refer to the quilt assembly diagram to arrange the blocks into six rows of six blocks each.

2 Sew the blocks together into rows and press the seam allowances in opposite directions from row to row. Sew the rows together and press the seam allowances in one direction.

Adding the Borders

1 Join the white 1½"-wide strips end to end. Measure and cut the inner-border strips, and then sew them to the quilt top. Press the seam allowances toward the border.

2 Repeat to add the orange 6½"-wide outer-border strips. Press the seam allowances toward the outer border.

Finishing the Quilt

For help with any of the finishing steps, go to ShopMartingale.com/HowtoQuilt for free downloadable information.

1 Layer, baste, and quilt your quilt, or take it to your favorite long-arm machine quilter for finishing.

2 Using the teal 2½"-wide strips, make and attach binding.

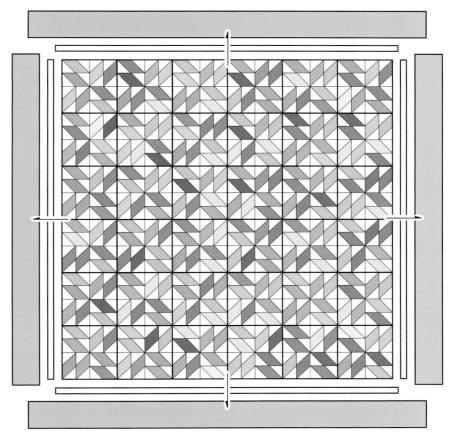

Quilt assembly

Whirling Fans

Fan blocks and fan quilts are among Nancy's favorite designs, so when she came across this Double Fan block designed by Alice Brooks, she was smitten. This design is ideal for charm squares or for using up lots of little scraps.

"Whirling Fans," designed and pieced by Nancy Mahoney, machine quilted by Nan Moore

Finished quilt: 59½" x 67½"   ◆   **Finished block:** 8" x 8"

▶ Materials

Yardage is based on 42"-wide fabric.

4¼ yards of cream solid for blocks and borders

120 squares, 5" x 5", *OR* 1⅞ yards *total* of assorted 1930s reproduction prints for Fan blocks

1 yard of green 1930s reproduction print for Fan blocks

26 squares, 6" x 6", *OR* 1 yard *total* of assorted 1930s reproduction prints for Broken Dishes blocks

½ yard of fabric for binding

3¾ yards of fabric for backing

65" x 73" piece of batting

Template plastic

▶ Cutting

All measurements include ¼"-wide seam allowances. Make templates for pieces A–D using the patterns on page 210.

From the cream solid, cut:
8 strips, 8½" x 42"; crosscut into 30 squares, 8½" x 8½"
5 strips, 5¾" x 42"; crosscut into 26 squares, 5¾" x 5¾"
7 strips, 4" x 42"
5 strips, 2½" x 42"

From *each* of the 5" squares, cut:
1 of template A (120 total)
1 of template B (120 total)

From the green print, cut:
30 of template C
30 of template D

From *each* of the 6" squares, cut:
1 square, 5¾" x 5¾" (26 total)

From the binding fabric, cut:
7 strips, 2" x 42"

Making the Fan Blocks

1 Sew together four A pieces as shown. Sew together four B pieces as shown. Press the seam allowances open to reduce bulk. Make 30 large fan units and 30 small fan units.

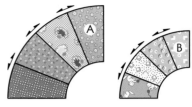

Make 30 of each.

2 Fold the seam allowances along the curved top edge of each fan unit to the wrong side and press in place to make a finished edge. It doesn't matter if the seam allowances are not a uniform width, but you do want a smooth finished curve.

Smooth Curves

An easy way to achieve a smooth curved edge on the fan units is to make a template using heat-resistant plastic. To do this, trace four large fan blades (A) side by side onto a piece of paper. You don't need the seam allowance between the blades or along the curved edge, but trace a ¼" seam allowance along the side edges and inside curve. Use the traced pattern to make a plastic template for the large fan unit. Mark the center seamline for placement guidance. Repeat to make a plastic template for the small fan unit. Place the plastic template on the wrong side of the fan unit and press the seam allowance over the edge of the template.

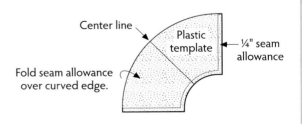

Center line

Plastic template

¼" seam allowance

Fold seam allowance over curved edge.

3 Fold an 8½" cream square in half diagonally and lightly finger-press to create a center line. Place a large fan unit in one corner, matching the center seamline with the creased line, and then place a small fan unit in the opposite corner. Using your favorite appliqué technique, prepare 30 green C pieces and 30 green D pieces. Place a C piece along the base of the large fan unit and a D piece along the base of the small fan unit. Appliqué the pieces in place along the curved edges. Note that the sides of the fans will be sewn into the block seam. Make 30 Double Fan blocks. Gently press and then trim each block to 8½" x 8½" as needed.

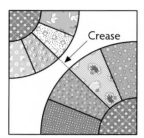

Crease

Make 30.

Making the Broken Dishes Blocks

1 Draw intersecting diagonal lines from corner to corner on the wrong side of a 5¾" cream square. Layer the marked square right sides together with a 5¾" print square. Stitch a scant ¼" from each side of both drawn lines.

2 Cut the squares apart horizontally and vertically as shown to yield four 2⅞" squares. Then cut the squares apart on the drawn lines to yield eight triangle squares, each 2⅞" square.

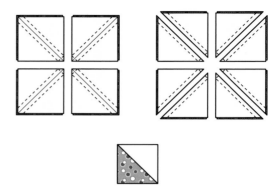

3 Lay out four triangle squares in a four-patch arrangement as shown. Sew the squares together in rows, and then sew the rows together. To reduce bulk in the center of the block and create opposing seams, use a seam ripper to remove one or two stitches from the seam allowance. Gently reposition the seam allowances to evenly distribute the fabric, and press the seam allowances in opposite directions. Make 52 Broken Dishes blocks.

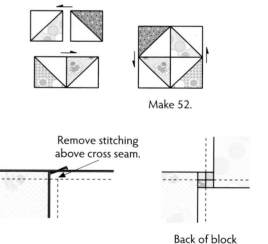

Make 52.

Remove stitching above cross seam.

Back of block

Assembling the Quilt Top

1 Lay out six rows of five blocks each as shown in the quilt assembly diagram below right.

2 Sew the blocks together in rows, pressing the seam allowances in opposite directions from row to row. Sew the rows together and press the seam allowances in one direction.

Adding the Borders

1 Sew the 2½"-wide cream inner-border strips together end to end. From this strip, cut two 48½"-long strips and sew them to opposite sides of the quilt top. Then cut two 44½"-long strips and sew them to the top and bottom of the quilt top. Press the seam allowances toward the border. The quilt top should measure 44½" x 52½" for the Broken Dishes border to fit properly.

2 Lay out 13 Broken Dishes blocks as shown. Sew the blocks together to make a side border. Repeat to make a second side border. Lay out 13 blocks as shown and sew them together to make the top border. Repeat to make the bottom border. Note that the blocks in the side borders are oriented differently than those in the top and bottom borders. Press the seam allowances as indicated by the arrows.

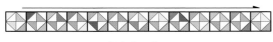

Side border.
Make 2.

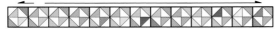

Top/bottom border.
Make 2.

3 Sew the border strips from step 2 to the sides, and then to the top and bottom of the quilt top. Press the seam allowances toward the cream inner border.

4 Sew the 4"-wide cream outer-border strips together end to end. Measure the length of the quilt top; it should be 60½". Trim two cream strips to this length and sew them to the sides of the quilt top. Press the seam allowances toward the outer border. Measure the width of the quilt top; it should be 59½". Trim two cream strips to this length and sew them to the top and bottom of the quilt in the same manner. Press the seam allowances toward the outer border.

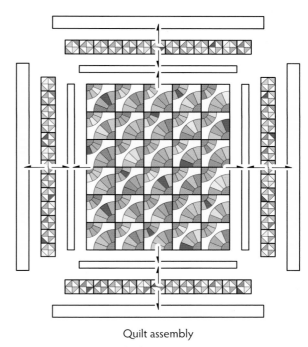

Quilt assembly

Finishing the Quilt

For help with any of the finishing steps, go to ShopMartingale.com/HowtoQuilt for free downloadable information.

1 Layer, baste, and quilt your quilt, or take it to your favorite long-arm machine quilter for finishing.

2 Using the 2"-wide strips, make and attach binding.

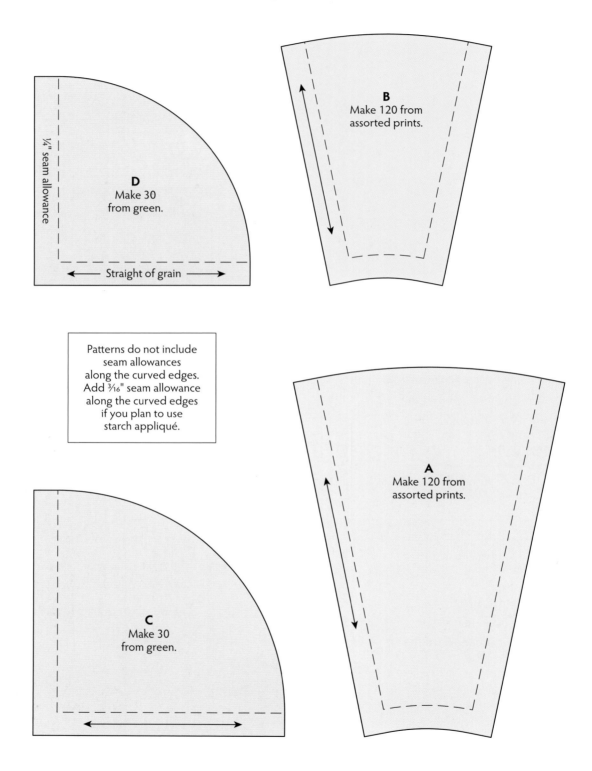

D
Make 30
from green.

¼" seam allowance

Straight of grain

B
Make 120 from
assorted prints.

Patterns do not include
seam allowances
along the curved edges.
Add ³⁄₁₆" seam allowance
along the curved edges
if you plan to use
starch appliqué.

C
Make 30
from green.

A
Make 120 from
assorted prints.

Geese in Flight

This quilt can be made from an assortment of fabric scraps or just a variety of batiks. If you like one-color scrap quilts, you can use strips from your blue stash, green stash, or whatever color you choose. Each 4½" x 42" strip will make 16 "geese."

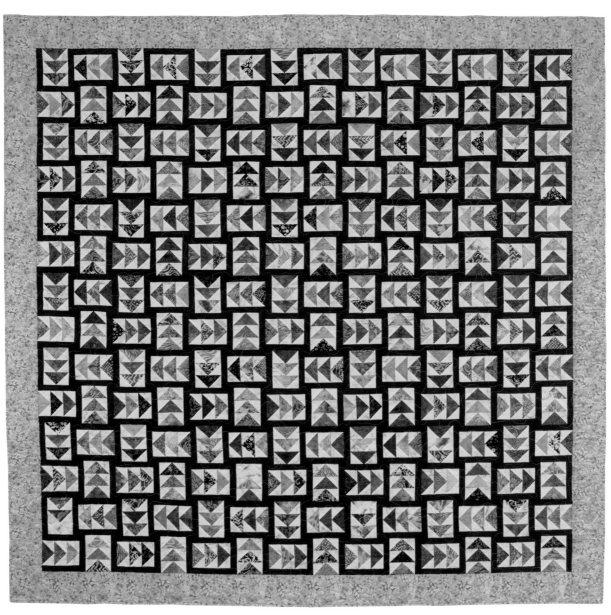

"Geese in Flight," designed and made by Jo Parrott
Finished quilt: 96½" x 96½"   ◆   Finished block: 12" x 12"

Materials

Yardage is based on 42"-wide fabric.

5¾ yards of light fabric for block backgrounds

5 yards *total* of assorted prints and/or batiks for blocks

3¼ yards of dark print for sashing

2⅞ yards of fabric for border and binding

9¼ yards of fabric for backing*

102" x 102" piece of batting

*If your backing fabric is 108" wide, you'll need only 3 yards.

Cutting

All measurements include ¼"-wide seam allowances. Cut all strips across the width of fabric (selvage to selvage). When using scraps, the strips can be cut crosswise or lengthwise to get the longest cut.

From the light fabric for block backgrounds, cut:
74 strips, 2½" x 42"; crosscut into 1176 squares, 2½" x 2½"

From the assorted prints and/or batiks, cut a *total* of:
37 strips, 4½" x 42"; crosscut into 588 rectangles, 2½" x 4½"

From the dark print for sashing, cut:
16 strips, 6½" x 42"; crosscut into 392 rectangles, 1½" x 6½"

From the fabric for border and binding, cut:
10 strips, 6½" x 42"
10 strips, 2¼" x 42"

Bonus Half-Square Triangles

If you want to make use of the extra corner fabric, stitch a second seam ½" from the first seam as shown. Cut between the two stitching lines. You'll have the rectangle and triangle unit, plus a half-square triangle for another project.

Making the Blocks

Directions are for one block. Each block is assembled using 12 different scrap/batik 2½" x 4½" rectangles and 24 background 2½" squares. Repeat to make a total of 49 blocks.

1 Draw a diagonal line from corner to corner on the wrong side of the background squares. Place a marked square on one end of a scrap/batik rectangle, right sides together and raw edges aligned. Sew on the marked line and trim away the corner fabric, leaving a ¼"-wide seam allowance. Press the resulting triangle open.

2 Place a marked background square on the opposite end of the rectangle, positioning the square as shown. Sew, trim, and press in the same manner. Repeat to make a total of 12 flying-geese units.

Make 12.

3 Sew three flying-geese units together as shown. Press the seam allowances in one direction. Repeat to make a total of four units.

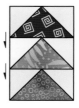

Make 4.

4 Sew 1½" x 6½" dark rectangles to opposite sides of each unit from step 3. Press the seam allowances toward the rectangles.

Make 4.

5 Lay out the units in a four-patch arrangement as shown. Sew the units together in rows, and then sew the rows together to complete a block. Press all seam allowances toward the sashing strips. Make a total of 49 blocks.

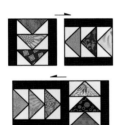
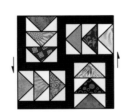

Assembling the Quilt Top

1 Lay out the blocks in seven rows of seven blocks each. Rearrange the blocks as desired until you are pleased with the arrangement.

2 Sew the blocks together into rows, pressing the seam allowances in opposite directions from row to row. Sew the rows together and press the seam allowances in one direction.

3 Using the 6½"-wide strips, add the border to your quilt top.

Finishing the Quilt

For help with any of the finishing steps, go to ShopMartingale.com/HowtoQuilt for free downloadable information.

1 Layer, baste, and quilt your quilt, or take it to your favorite long-arm machine quilter for finishing.

2 Using the 2¼"-wide strips, make and attach binding.

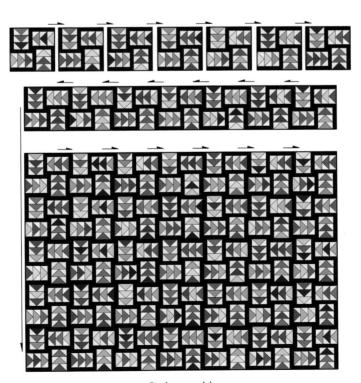

Quilt assembly

Rainbow Stash Buster

Like many quilters, Megan loves making stash-buster quilts. In this project, she used scraps of some of her favorite prints. But you don't have to make it in rainbow hues; make your quilt unique by using your favorite prints and colors.

"Rainbow Stash Buster," designed and pieced by Megan Jimenez, quilted by Wendy Castle

Finished quilt: 54½" x 54½"   ◆   **Finished block:** 13½" x 13½"

Materials

Yardage is based on 42"-wide fabric.

8 strips, 5½" x 42", of white fabric for blocks

7 strips, 5½" x 42", of assorted orange and yellow prints for blocks

6 strips, 5½" x 42", of assorted blue and green prints for blocks

4 strips, 5½" x 42", of assorted red and pink prints for blocks

3 strips, 5½" x 42", of assorted purple prints for blocks

½ yard of purple print for binding

3½ yards of fabric for backing

60" x 60" piece of batting

Cutting

All measurements include ¼"-wide seam allowances.

From the white strips, cut:
50 squares, 5½" x 5½"

From *each* of the orange and yellow strips, cut:
6 squares, 5½" x 5½" (42 total; 2 are extra)

From *each* of the blue and green strips, cut:
6 squares, 5½" x 5½" (36 total; 4 are extra)

From *each* of the red and pink strips, cut:
4 squares, 5½" x 5½" (16 total)

From *each* of the purple strips, cut:
2 squares, 5½" x 5½" (6 total)

From the purple print, cut:
6 strips, 2½" x 42"

Making the Blocks

1. Mark a diagonal line on the wrong side of a white square. Layer the marked square with an orange or yellow square, right sides together, and stitch ¼" from each side of the drawn line. Cut the squares apart on the line to make two half-square-triangle units. Press the seam allowances toward the darker triangle. Trim the units to measure 5" x 5". Make 40 units total.

Make 40.

2. Repeat step 1 to make the number of half-square-triangle units indicated for each color combination:

Pair orange or yellow squares with different orange or yellow squares to make 20 units.

Pair blue or green squares with white squares to make 32 units.

Pair blue or green squares with different blue or green squares to make 16 units.

Pair red or pink squares with white squares to make 16 units.

Pair red or pink squares with different red or pink squares to make 8 units.

Pair purple squares with white squares to make 12 units.

3. Referring to the quilt photo on page 214 and the block diagrams, lay out nine half-square-triangle units as shown. Sew the units together in rows. Press the seam allowances in the directions indicated by the arrows. Join the rows; press. Make the number of blocks indicated for each color combination.

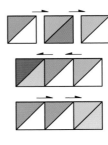 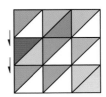

Block A.
Make 4.

 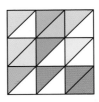

Block B.
Make 4.

Block C.
Make 8.

Assembling the Quilt Top

1 Lay out one A block, one B block, and two C blocks as shown. Sew the blocks together in pairs. Press the seam allowances in the directions indicated by the arrows. Sew the pairs together to make a quadrant. Press the seam allowances to one side. Repeat to make four quadrants total.

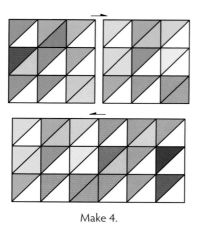

Make 4.

2 Lay out the quadrants from step 1 as shown. Sew the quadrants together in rows and then join the rows. Press the seam allowances in the directions indicated by the arrows.

Finishing the Quilt

For help with any of the finishing steps, go to ShopMartingale.com/HowtoQuilt for free downloadable information.

1 Layer, baste, and quilt your quilt, or take it to your favorite long-arm machine quilter for finishing.

2 Using the purple 2½"-wide strips, make and attach binding.

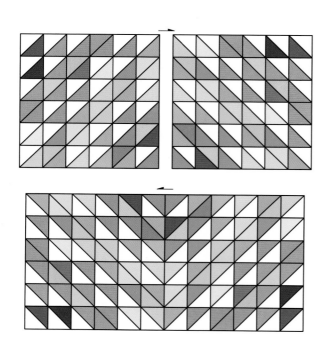

Quilt assembly

Hourglass

Although Kim used precut strips from two different fabric collections for this quilt, it's a perfect project for using a single bundle of precut strips. Just choose 26 strips that play well together, and combine them with a single background fabric. It will be striking, no matter what style of fabrics you use.

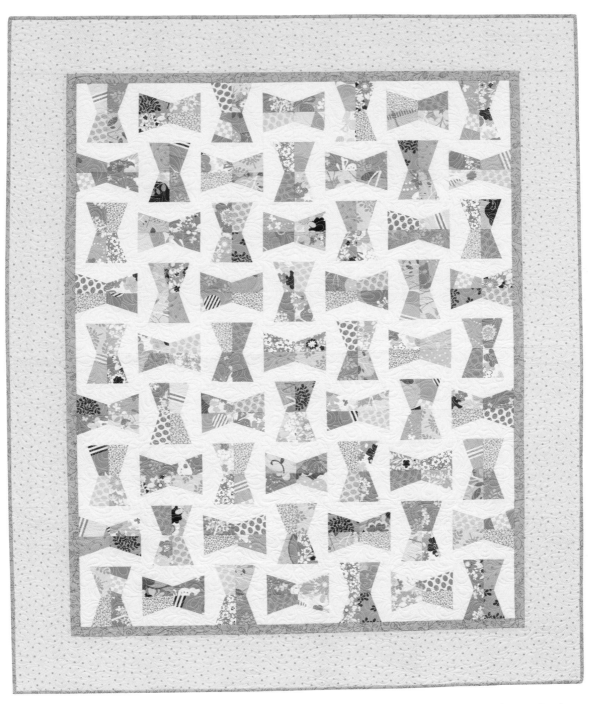

"Hourglass," designed and made by Kim Brackett
Finished quilt: 55½" x 67½" ◆ Finished block: 6" x 6"

▶ Materials

Yardage is based on 42"-wide fabric.

26 strips, 2½" x 42", of assorted dark prints for blocks

2 yards of white solid for blocks

1⅛ yards of yellow print for outer border

⅞ yard of green print for inner border and binding

4 yards of fabric for backing

60" x 72" piece of batting

▶ Cutting

All measurements include ¼"-wide seam allowances.

From the white solid, cut:
26 strips, 2½" x 42"

From the green print, cut:
5 strips, 1½" x 42"
7 strips, 2½" x 42"

From the yellow print, cut:
6 strips, 6" x 42"

Cutting from Scraps

If you prefer to use scraps, follow the instructions below. See "Cutting" above for instructions on cutting the borders and binding.

From assorted dark prints, cut:
252 rectangles, 2½" x 5"

From assorted light prints, cut:
252 rectangles, 2½" x 5"

To make individual units, sew together a dark rectangle and a light rectangle along the long edges. Press the seam allowances of half of the units toward the dark fabric (as for the A strip sets) and half of the units toward the white solid (as for the B strip sets). Follow the instructions for cutting and assembling the blocks beginning with step 3 of "Making the Blocks" on page 219.

Making the Blocks

The block units in this quilt will have bias edges. Be mindful of these edges when handling the blocks and quilt top so that they don't stretch out of shape. You may find it helpful to use spray starch on your strip sets after sewing the 2½" strips together in pairs. Once the block units are cut, press only the seam allowances; avoid touching the iron on the outside edges of the blocks.

1 Sew a white 2½" x 42" strip to the long edge of a dark 2½" x 42" strip. Before pressing the seam allowances, cut the strip set in half to yield two strip sets approximately 21" long.

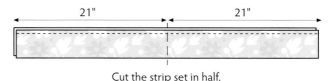

Cut the strip set in half.

2 Press the seam allowances of one of the 21" strip sets toward the dark strip. This is strip set A. Press the seam allowances of the other strip set toward the white strip. This is strip set B. Make a total of 26 A strip sets and 26 B strip sets.

Strip set A.
Make 26.

Strip set B.
Make 26.

3 Trace or photocopy the pattern on page 220 onto paper to make a cutting guide. Cut out the paper guide around the outside edges. It should be 3½" square. Tape the guide right side up to the bottom of a small square ruler, aligning the edges with the 3½" lines.

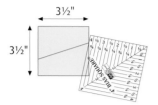

4 Using an A strip set (seam allowances pressed toward the dark strip) right side up, place the ruler on the strip set so the line in the middle of the guide follows the seamline on the strip set. Cut along the right and top edges of the ruler. Remove the piece from the strip set, rotate it, and trim the edges as shown, placing the previously cut edges along the edge of the guide. Cut along the right and top edges of the ruler. Cut five of these units from each A strip set to yield 130 A units.

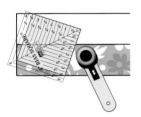 

Cut 130.

5 Using a B strip set (seam allowances pressed toward the white solid) wrong side up, place the ruler on the strip set so the line in the middle of the cutting guide follows the stitching line. Cut along the right and top edges of the ruler. Remove the piece from the strip set, rotate it, and trim the edges as shown, placing the previously cut edges along the edge of the guide. Cut along the right and top edges of the ruler. Cut five of these units from each B strip set to yield 130 B units.

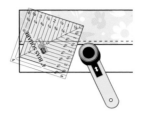 

Cut 130.

6 Sew an A unit to a B unit as shown. Press the seam allowances toward the B unit. Make 126. (You'll have four A units and four B units left over.)

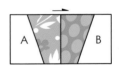

Make 126.

7 Sew together two units from step 6 as shown. Press the seam allowances in a clockwise direction. Make a total of 63 blocks.

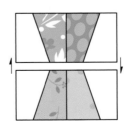 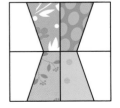

Make 63.

Assembling the Quilt Top

1 Arrange the blocks in nine horizontal rows of seven blocks each as shown, rotating every other block a quarter turn.

2 Sew the blocks together in rows, pressing the seam allowances in opposite directions from row to row. Join the rows. Press the seam allowances in one direction.

Adding the Borders

1 Add the green 1½"-wide strips to the quilt top for the inner border.

2 Add the yellow 6"-wide strips to the quilt top for the outer border.

Finishing the Quilt

For help with any of the finishing steps, go to ShopMartingale.com/HowtoQuilt for free downloadable information.

1 Layer, baste, and quilt your quilt, or take it to your favorite long-arm machine quilter for finishing.

2 Using the green 2½"-wide strips, make and attach binding.

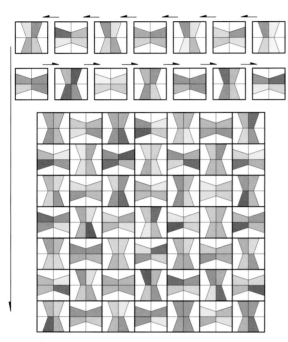

Quilt assembly

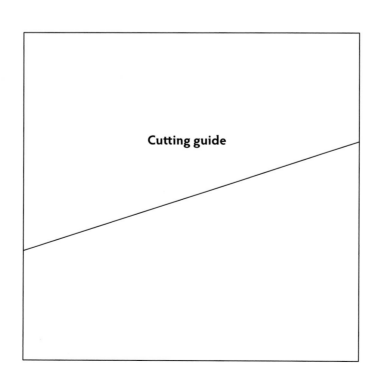

Cutting guide

Sunny Days

Fresh blue and yellow florals were the perfect choice for this quilt, which was inspired by a Judy Hopkins design, "Arctic Nights." This simple design comes together in a snap, especially if you use an assortment of precut 2½"-wide strips in your favorite cheerful palette.

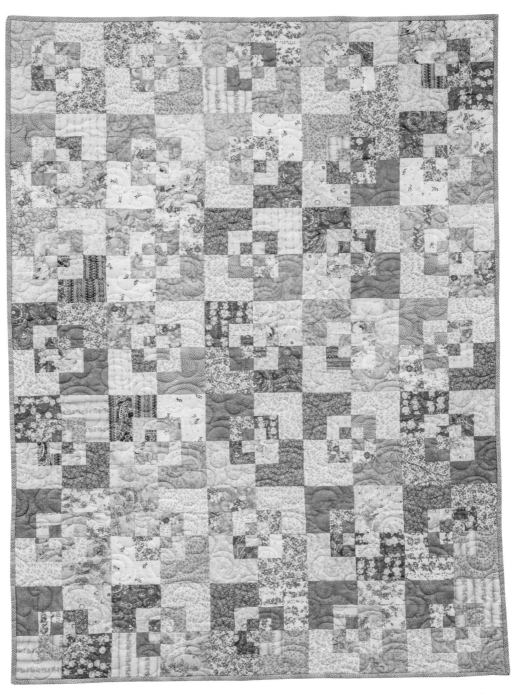

"Sunny Days," designed and pieced by Nancy J. Martin, quilted by Frankie Schmitt

Finished quilt: 40½" x 56½"   ◆   **Finished block:** 8" x 8"

Materials

Yardage is based on 42"-wide fabric.

24 strips, 2½" x 42", of yellow and light-blue prints for blocks

24 strips, 2½" x 42", of darker blue prints for blocks

½ yard of fabric for binding

2¾ yards of fabric for backing

48" x 64" piece of batting

Cutting

Measurement includes a ¼"-wide seam allowance.

From the binding fabric, cut:
2¼"-wide bias strips to make 202" of bias binding

Making the Blocks

1 Layer a 2½" x 42" light strip and a 2½" x 42" dark strip right sides together, aligning the long edges. Square up one end of this layered pair of strips and then cut:

    3 rectangles, 2½" x 4½" (A)

    3 squares, 2½" x 2½" (B)

    3 rectangles, 1½" x 2½" (C)

Set these pieces aside.

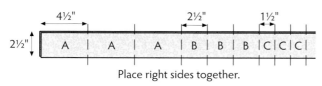

Place right sides together.

2 From the remaining length, trim the layered strips to 1½" by 11".

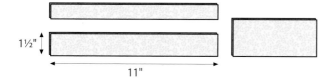

3 Sew the 1½" x 11" layered strips together along the long edges to make a strip set. From this strip set, cut a total of six segments, 1½" wide.

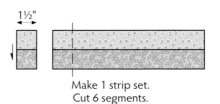

Make 1 strip set.
Cut 6 segments.

4 Join a strip-set segment from step 3 to each of the C rectangles from step 1 as shown, being careful to orient the strip-set segments in the correct direction for each combination. Make three of each combination. The units should measure 2½" x 2½" (raw edge to raw edge).

Make 3.   Make 3.

5 Join the B squares from step 1 to the units from step 4 as shown, being careful to add the correct light or dark square to the unit. Make three of each combination.

Make 3.   Make 3.

6 Stitch the A rectangles from step 1 to the units from step 5 as shown, being careful to add the correct light or dark rectangle. Make three dark units and three light units. The units should measure 4½" x 4½".

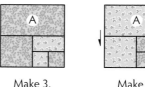

Make 3.   Make 3.

7 Repeat steps 1–6 with the remaining light and dark strips. When you have cut and stitched all 24 sets of strips, you will have 72 light units and 72 dark units.

8 Randomly mix and match two light and two dark units to make a block. Make 35 blocks as shown. You will have two light and two dark units left over. You may want to wait until you have laid out all the blocks before pressing the final seam allowances. Once the blocks are arranged, you can press the seam allowances so that they will butt together.

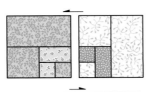

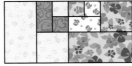

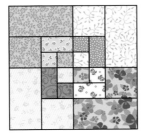

Make 35.

Assembling the Quilt Top

1 Arrange the blocks into seven horizontal rows of five blocks each. Note that the blocks are positioned with the darker blue fabrics at the upper left and lower right.

2 Sew the blocks into rows. Press the seam allowances in opposite directions from row to row. Sew the rows together. Press the seam allowances in one direction.

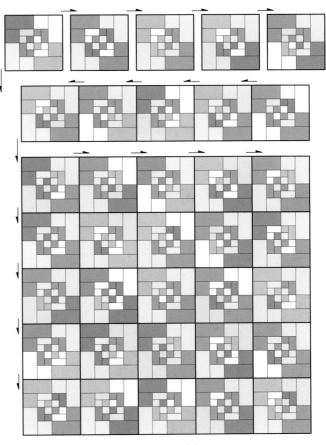

Quilt assembly

Finishing the Quilt

For help with any of the finishing steps, go to ShopMartingale.com/HowtoQuilt for free downloadable information.

1 Layer, baste, and quilt your quilt, or take it to your favorite long-arm machine quilter for finishing.

2 Using the 2¼"-wide bias strips, make and attach binding.

Confused Nine Patch

This quilt design features two different colorations of the simple Nine Patch block, alternating them with plain squares. Don't you just love the versatile Nine Patch? Try to use 35 different strips, 2½" x 42". Shop for what you don't have or swap with your friends if necessary.

"Confused Nine Patch," designed and made by Gayle Bong

Finished quilt: 82½" x 94½" ◆ **Finished A and B blocks: 6" x 6"** ◆ **Finished border block: 4" x 6"**

Materials

Yardage is based on 42"-wide fabric except where noted.

3 yards of dark-blue tone on tone for blocks, pieced first border, second border, and binding

3 yards *total* of assorted pastel fabrics for blocks and pieced third border

2⅛ yards of cream fabric for block backgrounds

2 yards of dark-blue print for fourth border

7½ yards of fabric for backing*

90" x 102" piece of batting

If your backing fabric is 108" wide, you'll need only 2½ yards.

Cutting

All measurements include ¼"-wide seam allowances. Please read all instructions before starting.

From the assorted pastels, cut:
72 strips, 2½" x 21"

From the cream fabric, cut:
9 strips, 2½" x 21"; crosscut *1* of the strips in half to make 2 strips, 2½" x 21"
4 strips, 6½" x 42"; crosscut into 20 squares, 6½" x 6½"
3 strips, 6½" x 42"; crosscut into 18 rectangles, 4½" x 6½"
4 squares, 4½" x 4½"

From the dark-blue tone on tone, cut:
20 strips, 2½" x 42"; crosscut *16* of the strips in half to make 32 strips, 2½" x 21" (1 is extra)
8 strips, 2½" x 42"
10 strips, 2¼" x 42"

From the dark-blue print, cut:
9 strips, 6½" x 42"

Making the A Blocks

After sewing each seam, press the seam allowances as indicated by the arrows.

1 Sew three pastel strips together along the long edges to make a strip set. Repeat to make a total of 19 strip sets, joining different prints in each set. Press the seam allowances in either direction. Crosscut the strip sets into 140 segments, 2½" wide.

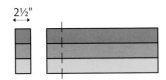

Make 19 strip sets. Cut 140 segments.

2 Sew three pastel segments together to make block A, rotating the segments or re-pressing the seam allowances so they alternate. Make 30 blocks. Set aside the remaining 50 segments for the pieced third border.

Block A.
Make 30.

Making the B Blocks and Border Blocks

1 Using the 2½" x 21" strips, sew a dark-blue tone-on-tone strip to each long edge of a pastel strip to make a strip set. Make 15 strip sets. Crosscut the strip sets into 120 segments, 2½" wide.

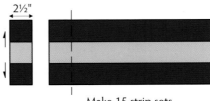

Make 15 strip sets.
Cut 120 segments.

2 Using the 2½" x 42" strips, sew a cream strip to each long edge of a dark-blue tone-on-tone strip to make a strip set. Make four strip sets. Make a half strip set in the same manner using the 2½" x 21" dark-blue and cream strips. Crosscut the strip sets into 71 segments, 2½" wide.

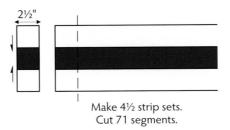

Make 4½ strip sets.
Cut 71 segments.

3 Sew segments from steps 1 and 2 together as shown to make 49 B blocks and 22 border blocks.

Block B.
Make 49.

Border block.
Make 22.

Assembling the Quilt Top

1 Alternately sew together five of block A and four of block B. Add a border block to each end of the row as shown to complete row 1. Make six rows.

Row 1.
Make 6.

2 Alternately sew together five of block B and four 6½" cream squares. Add a 4½" x 6½" cream rectangle to each end of the row to complete row 2. Make five rows.

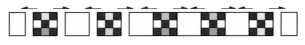

Row 2.
Make 5.

3 Alternately join five border blocks and four 4½" x 6½" cream rectangles. Add a 4½" cream square to each end of the row to complete the top pieced border row. Repeat to make the bottom pieced border row.

Top/bottom border row.
Make 2.

4 Alternately lay out rows 1 and 2, arranging them as necessary to distribute the color well. Sew the rows together. Attach the top and bottom pieced border rows.

5 Attach the 2½"-wide dark-blue tone-on-tone border strips to the quilt top. Add the borders to the sides first, and then to the top and bottom edges.

6 Using the pastel strip-set segments you set aside earlier, join 13 segments end to end to make a side border. Make two pieced borders. Sew these borders to the sides of the quilt top. Join 12 segments end to end to make the top pieced border. Remove one square from the strip. Repeat to make the bottom

pieced border. Sew these borders to the top and bottom of the quilt top.

Top/bottom border.
Make 2.

Side border.
Make 2.

7 Repeat step 5 to attach the 6½"-wide dark-blue strips to the quilt for the fourth border.

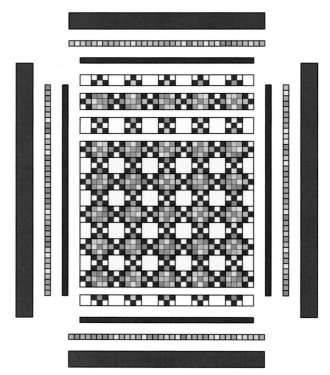

Quilt assembly

Finishing the Quilt

For help with any of the finishing steps, go to ShopMartingale.com/HowtoQuilt for free downloadable information.

1 Layer, baste, and quilt your quilt, or take it to your favorite long-arm machine quilter for finishing.

2 Using the 2¼"-wide tone-on-tone strips, make and attach binding.

Winter White

This design started with the name of a fabric collection, Glace. It was a Christmas collection and glacé is French for "ice," which naturally made Carrie think of ice cream. Actually, the white, red, and brown fabrics made her think of her absolute favorite ice cream—Winter White Chocolate from Baskin-Robbins, which is only available at Christmastime.

"Winter White," designed by Carrie Nelson, pieced by Lissa Alexander, machine quilted by Alicia Key

Finished quilt: 90½" x 90½"   ◆   Finished block: 8" x 8"

Materials

Yardage is based on 42"-wide fabric.

2¼ yards of background fabric for flying-geese units and inner border

1⅜ yards of floral for outer border

18 squares, 10" x 10", of assorted medium- or dark-blue fabrics for flying-geese units

46 squares, 10" x 10", of assorted medium-value fabrics for plain squares and inner-border squares

¾ yard of fabric for binding

8½ yards of fabric for backing

98" x 98" piece of batting

Cutting

All measurements include ¼"-wide seam allowances.

From the background fabric, cut:
9 strips, 4⅞" x 42"; crosscut into 72 squares, 4⅞" x 4⅞"
8 strips, 2½" x 42"

From *each* of the medium- or dark-blue squares, cut:
1 square, 9¼" x 9¼" (18 total)

From *each* of 45 medium-value squares, cut:
1 square, 8½" x 8½" (45 total)

From the remaining medium-value square, cut:
4 squares, 2½" x 2½"

From the floral, cut:
9 strips, 7½" x 42"

From the binding fabric, cut:
2"-wide bias strips to make 375" of bias binding

Corner Squares

Just because the cutting instructions say to cut four 2½" squares from one medium square, that doesn't mean you have to do it that way! To Carrie, cutting four squares means using four different fabrics. Do likewise if you wish.

Making the Blocks

Use a scant ¼"-wide seam allowance throughout. After sewing each seam, press the seam allowances in the direction indicated by the arrows (or press them open).

1 Use Carrie's special technique to make four matching flying-geese units at once. Mark a diagonal line on the wrong side of four 4⅞" background squares. With right sides together, place two marked squares on opposite corners of a 9¼" blue square. The points of the small squares will overlap just a bit and the drawn line will extend from corner to corner as shown.

2 Stitch a scant ¼" from each side of the drawn line. Cut the squares apart on the drawn line. Press the seam allowances toward the small triangles.

3 With right sides together, place the remaining marked squares on the corners of both pieces. Stitch a scant ¼" from each side of the drawn line. Cut apart on the drawn line. Press the seam allowances toward the small triangles. The units should measure 4½" x 8½". Make a total of 18 sets of four matching flying-geese units (72 total).

4 Join the flying-geese units in pairs as shown. The geese blocks should measure 8½" square. Make a total of nine sets of four matching geese units (36 total).

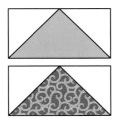 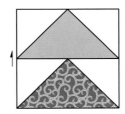

Make 36.

Assembling the Quilt Top

This quilt top is assembled in rows of geese units and medium squares. To keep pressing easy, press the seam allowances toward the medium squares whenever possible.

1 Lay out the 8½" medium squares and geese units in nine rows of nine squares/units each, making sure to rotate the geese units as shown in the quilt assembly diagram at right. Join the squares and geese units into rows. Press the seam allowances toward the plain squares or to one side (or press them open).

2 Join the rows to complete the quilt top. The quilt top should measure 72½" x 72½".

Adding the Borders

1 For the inner border, sew the 2½"-wide background strips together end to end. From the long strip, cut four 72½"-long strips. Sew two of the strips to opposite sides of the quilt top. Join 2½" medium squares to both ends of the two remaining border strips. Press the seam allowances toward the border strips. Sew these borders to the top and bottom of the quilt top and press the seam allowances toward the border.

2 For the outer border, join the 7½"-wide floral strips end to end. From the long strip, cut two 76½"-long strips for the side borders and two 85½"-long strips for the top and bottom borders.

3 Sew the borders to the sides, and then to the top and bottom edges of the quilt top. Press the seam allowances toward the outer border.

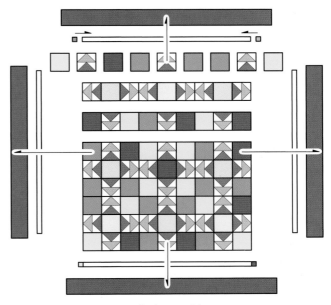

Quilt assembly

Finishing the Quilt

For help with any of the finishing steps, go to ShopMartingale.com/HowtoQuilt for free downloadable information.

1 Layer, baste, and quilt your quilt, or take it to your favorite long-arm machine quilter for finishing.

2 Using the 2"-wide bias strips, make and attach binding.

Martin's Pennies

Carol's father-in-law, Martin, had a collection of pennies and often shared them with his grandchildren. The stack of rectangles that she cut for this quilt brought back memories of her three children playing with his coins.

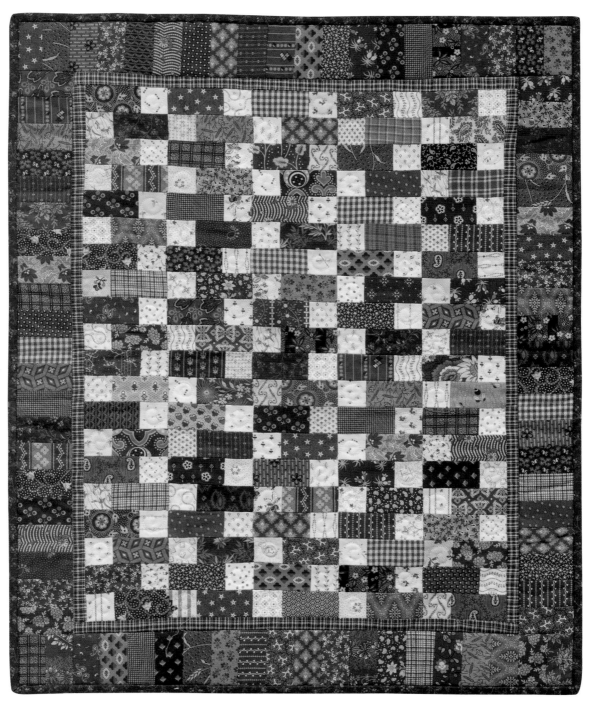

"Martin's Pennies," designed and made by Carol Hopkins
Finished quilt: 20½" x 25½"

▶ Materials

Yardage is based on 42"-wide fabric. Fat quarters are 18" x 21".

3 fat quarters *total* of assorted blue and brown scraps, at least 2" x 3", for coin rows and outer border

1 fat quarter *total* of assorted light scraps, at least 2" x 2", for coin rows

¼ yard of plaid for inner border

¼ yard of blue print for binding

1⅛ yards of fabric for backing

26" x 31" piece of batting

▶ Cutting

All measurements include ¼"-wide seam allowances.

From the assorted blue and brown scraps, cut a *total* of:
182 rectangles, 1½" x 2½"

From the assorted light scraps, cut a *total* of:
100 squares, 1½" x 1½"

From the plaid, cut:
4 strips, 1" x 42"

From the blue print, cut:
3 strips, 2" x 42"

Making the Rows

Sew together five blue or brown rectangles and five light squares, alternating them as shown, to make a coin row. Press the seam allowances open. Make 20 rows.

Make 20.

To Add Interest

Include plaids, checks, and striped fabrics to create a quilt that looks like it was just pulled out of an old trunk.

Assembling the Quilt Top

1 Lay out the coin rows in alternating directions so that odd-numbered rows begin with a rectangle and even-numbered rows begin with a square.

2 Sew the rows together and press the seam allowances open after adding each row.

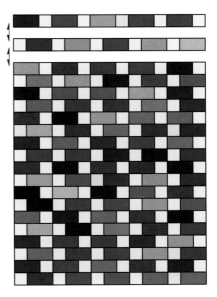

Adding the Borders

1 For the inner border, measure the length of the quilt top through the center and trim two plaid strips to this measurement. Sew the strips to the sides of the quilt and press the seam allowances toward the borders.

2 Measure the width of the quilt top through the center, including the just-added borders, and trim the two remaining plaid strips to this measurement. Sew the strips to the top and bottom of the quilt and press the seam allowances toward the borders.

3 For the outer border, sew 21 assorted blue and brown rectangles together side by side. Press the seam allowances open. Make two side border strips.

Make 2.

4 Sew 20 assorted blue and brown rectangles together side by side. Press the seam allowances open. Make two of these strips for the top and bottom of the quilt.

Make 2.

5 Sew the side border strips from step 3 to the left and right sides of the quilt. Press the seam allowances toward the pieced border. Sew the top and bottom border strips from step 4 to the top and bottom of the quilt. Press the seam allowances toward the pieced border.

Finishing the Quilt

For help with any of the finishing steps, go to ShopMartingale.com/HowtoQuilt for free downloadable information.

1 Layer, baste, and quilt your quilt, or take it to your favorite long-arm machine quilter for finishing.

2 Using the blue 2"-wide strips, make and attach binding.

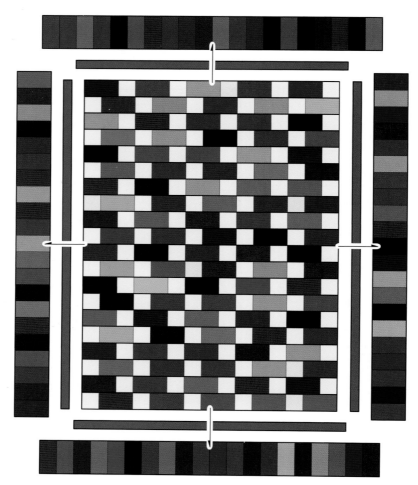

Adding the borders

Union Stars

Patriotism was high after the Civil War transformed America from a republic into a nation, and many women expressed their love for country by volunteering. This quilt was inspired by the women who faithfully organized and ministered to the men who fought to keep the union together.

"Union Stars," designed by Kathy Tracy, pieced by Jill Meszaros, machine quilted by Dawn Larsen

Finished quilt: 50½" x 64½"   ◆   **Finished block:** 12" x 12"

Materials

Yardage is based on 42"-wide fabric. Fat eighths are 9"x21".

1⅝ yards of red print for border

1⅓ yards *total* of assorted shirting prints for block backgrounds

1 fat eighth *each* of 5 different red prints for star points

½ yard of tan print for sashing

1 fat eighth *each* of 4 different medium-blue prints for star points

1 fat eighth *each* of 3 different dark-blue prints for star points

⅓ yard *total* of 6 different patriotic prints for star centers

⅛ yard of brown print for sashing squares

1 square, 6" x 6", *each* of 12 assorted red, blue, taupe, and gold prints for blocks

½ yard of dark-blue print for binding

3⅝ yards of fabric for backing

57" x 71" piece of batting

Cutting

All measurements include ¼"-wide seam allowances.

Cutting for 1 Block

From a patriotic print, cut:
1 square, 4½" x 4½"

From a shirting print, cut:
2 squares, 5¼" x 5¼"; cut into quarters diagonally to yield 8 triangles
4 squares, 2⅞" x 2⅞"; cut in half diagonally to yield 8 triangles
4 squares, 2½" x 2½"

From a red, dark-blue, or medium-blue print for star points, cut:
2 squares, 5¼" x 5¼"; cut into quarters diagonally to yield 8 triangles

From a contrasting red, dark-blue, or medium-blue print, cut:
4 squares, 2⅞" x 2⅞"; cut in half diagonally to yield 8 triangles

From a red, blue, taupe, or gold scrap, cut:
4 squares, 2½" x 2½"

Cutting for Sashing, Borders, and Binding

From the tan print, cut:
17 strips, 2½" x 12½"

From the brown print, cut:
6 squares, 2½" x 2½"

From the red print for outer border, cut on the *lengthwise* grain:
2 strips, 5½" x 54½"
2 strips, 5½" x 50½"

From the dark-blue print for binding, cut:
6 strips, 2½" x 42"

Making the Blocks

The instructions are written for making one block at a time using a variety of red, blue, gold, and light shirting prints. Some fabrics may be used more than once. In this quilt, there are five stars with red points, three stars with dark-blue points, and four stars with medium-blue points. All of the stars have contrasting secondary points in the background and a patriotic-print square in the center. Use the same shirting print throughout each block.

1 Choose eight matching red, dark-blue, or medium-blue 5¼" triangles for the main star points and eight shirting-print 5¼" triangles. Sew a light triangle to a dark triangle. Sew pairs of triangles together. Make eight units.

Make 8.

2 Sew two of the units together as shown to make an hourglass unit. Make four.

Make 4.

3 Choose the red or blue 2⅞" triangles for the secondary star points. Sew one triangle to a shirting-print 2⅞" triangle. Make eight.

Make 8.

4 Choose red, blue, gold, or taupe 2½" squares. Sew a square to a unit from step 3. Make four.

Make 4.

5 Sew the remaining units from step 3 to a shirting 2½" square. Make four.

Make 4.

6 Combine the units from step 4 with the units from step 5 as shown. Make four.

Make 4.

7 Arrange the units from step 6, the hourglass units from step 2, and a patriotic-print 4½" square into rows as shown. Sew the units into rows. Press. Sew the rows together to make the block.

8 Repeat steps 1–7 to make 12 blocks.

Make 12.

Assembling the Quilt Top

1 Sew three blocks together with two tan-print 2½" x 12½" sashing strips to make a row. Press the seam allowances toward the sashing. Make four rows.

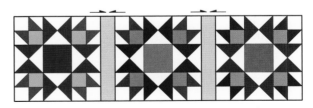

Make 4.

2 Sew three tan-print 2½" x 12½" sashing strips together with two brown 2½" squares to make a sashing row. Press the seam allowances toward the sashing strips. Make three rows.

Make 3.

3 Sew the rows of blocks and sashing together, pressing the seam allowances toward the sashing rows.

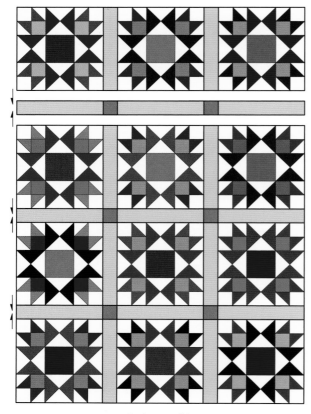

Quilt assembly

4 Sew the red-print 5½" x 54½" strips to the sides of the quilt. Press toward the border. Sew the 5½" x 50½" strips to the top and bottom of the quilt; press toward the border.

Adding the border

Finishing the Quilt

For help with any of the finishing steps, go to ShopMartingale.com/HowtoQuilt for free downloadable information.

1 Layer, baste, and quilt your quilt, or take it to your favorite long-arm machine quilter for finishing.

2 Using the dark-blue 2½"-wide strips, make and attach binding.

Cobblestones

Sometimes it's the simplest blocks that end up making the best quilting projects, as demonstrated by the cozy comfort of these Four Patch blocks, set on point in vertical rows. The addition of a linen-like background gives this project warmth and adds sophistication to the humble Four Patch blocks. Come and take a walk down a cobblestone path.

"Cobblestones," designed by Pat Wys, pieced by Marty Miller, quilted by Leisa Wiggley

Finished quilt: 60" x 77" ◆ **Finished block: 6" x 6"**

Materials

Yardage is based on 42"-wide fabric.

2⅞ yards of taupe solid for setting triangles

2½ yards *total* of assorted dark, medium, and light neutral prints for blocks

⅞ yard *total* of assorted fabrics for binding

3⅞ yards of fabric for backing

68" x 75" piece of batting

Cutting

All measurements include ¼"-wide seam allowances.

From the assorted neutral prints, cut a *total* of:
196 squares, 3½" x 3½"
176 squares, 2" x 2"

From the taupe solid, cut:
8 strips, 9¾" x 42"; crosscut into 31 squares, 9¾" x 9¾". Cut into quarters diagonally to yield 124 triangles.
2 strips, 5⅛" x 42"; crosscut into 8 squares, 5⅛" x 5⅛". Cut in half diagonally to yield 16 triangles.

From the assorted binding fabrics, cut:
2½"-wide bias strips to make 290" of bias binding

Dispersing Seams Evenly

When you have four seams intersecting in the center of a unit or block, it's a good idea to reduce the bulk by creating opposing seams where the seams come together. After the seam is sewn, use a seam ripper to remove two or three stitches from the seam allowance on both sides of the center seam as shown. Reposition both seam allowances to evenly distribute the fabric, and press the seam allowances in opposite directions so that the center lies flat. When you look at the wrong side of the block, the seam allowances should be going in one direction, either clockwise or counterclockwise around the center.

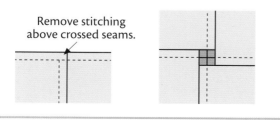

Remove stitching above crossed seams.

You Be the Judge!

Arrange your Four Patch and Combination Four Patch blocks as desired. Look at your blocks and consider the fabric arrangement and value of each block. See how it all looks when placed next to the background fabric. This should determine the placement of your blocks. Don't be afraid to put several Four Patch blocks with only one Combination Four Patch block in a row. Shake up the order with irregular arrangements of blocks. It will make a much more attractive and interesting quilt in the end.

Making the Blocks

1 Sew four assorted 3½" squares together to make a Four Patch block. See "Dispersing Seams Evenly" below left to pop the seam and flatten the center of the block. Make a total of 38 blocks.

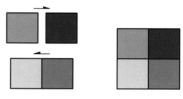

Make 38.

2 Repeat step 1 to make 44 small Four Patch blocks from assorted 2" squares.

3 Sew a Combination Four Patch block using two small blocks from step 2 and two 3½" squares. Make 22.

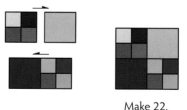

Make 22.

Assembling the Quilt Top

1 Arrange the blocks on point into seven vertical rows. There are nine blocks in rows 1, 3, 5, and 7 and eight blocks in rows 2, 4, and 6.

2 Sew taupe 9¾" triangles to the blocks as shown. Add taupe 5⅛" triangles to the rows with nine blocks as shown. Press the seam allowances toward the taupe triangles.

3 Sew the block rows together to complete the quilt top.

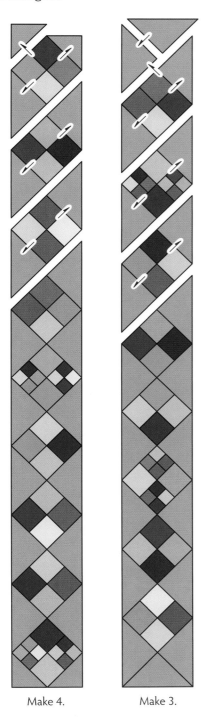

Make 4. Make 3.

Row 1   Row 2   Row 3   Row 4   Row 5   Row 6   Row 7

Quilt assembly

Finishing the Quilt

For help with any of the finishing steps, go to ShopMartingale.com/HowtoQuilt for free downloadable information.

1 Layer, baste, and quilt your quilt, or take it to your favorite long-arm machine quilter for finishing.

2 Using the 2½"-wide bias strips, make and attach binding.

Family Gathering

This quilt was inspired by Ionne's memories of growing up in the country and attending great gatherings for dances, parties, and especially weddings. Along with the brides' white dresses and the groomsmen's dark suits, many colors danced across the polished floors of those country halls. What fun!

"Family Gathering," designed and made by Ionne McCauley and Sharon Pederson

Finished quilt: 48" x 54"   ◆   Finished block: 3" x 3"

Materials

Yardage is based on 42"-wide fabric.

1⅓ yards of white tone on tone for blocks and setting squares

1 yard *total* of assorted medium-gray tone on tones and hand-dyed fabrics for blocks and setting squares

⅞ yard *total* of assorted dark tone on tones for blocks with white background

⅔ yard *total* of assorted medium tone on tones for blocks with medium-gray background

½ yard of dark-gray print #1 for blocks and setting squares

½ yard of dark-gray print #2 for top and left side borders and binding*

½ yard of medium-gray print for bottom and right side borders and binding*

¼ yard *total* of assorted light tone on tones for blocks with dark-gray background

3 yards of fabric for backing

52" x 58" piece of batting

If you prefer to cut your binding from one fabric, you'll need ½ yard for binding and ¼ yard each of the two different fabrics for the borders.

Cutting

All measurements include ¼"-wide seam allowances.

From the white tone on tone, cut:
6 strips, 3½" x 40"; crosscut into 66 squares, 3½" x 3½"
9 strips, 1½" x 40"; crosscut into 68 rectangles, 1½" x 5"
3 strips, 1¾" x 40"; crosscut into 68 rectangles, 1½" x 1¾"

From the assorted dark colors, cut:
68 rectangles, 1½" x 5", and 68 rectangles, 1½" x 3¼", in matching pairs from the same fabric

From the assorted medium-gray tone on tones and hand-dyed fabrics, cut a *total* of:
48 squares, 3½" x 3½"
48 rectangles, 1½" x 5"
48 rectangles, 1½" x 1¾"

From the assorted medium colors, cut:
48 rectangles, 1½" x 5", and 48 rectangles, 1½" x 3¼", in matching pairs from the same fabric

From dark-gray print #1, cut:
2 strips, 3½" x 40"; crosscut into 13 squares, 3½" x 3½"
2 strips, 1½" x 40"; crosscut into 12 rectangles, 1½" x 5"
1 strip, 1½" x 40"; crosscut into 12 rectangles, 1½" x 1¾"

From the assorted light colors, cut:
12 rectangles, 1½" x 5", and 12 rectangles, 1½" x 3¼", in matching pairs from the same fabric

From the medium-gray print, cut:
3 strips, 2" x 40"
3 strips, 2½" x 40"*

From dark-gray print #2, cut:
3 strips, 2" x 40"
3 strips, 2½" x 40"*

Cut 6 strips from one fabric if you are not using 2 fabrics to make a pieced binding.

Making the Blocks

1 Sew a 1½" x 5" white strip to a 1½" x 5" dark-colored strip; press the seam allowances toward the darker fabric.

2 Sew a 1½" x 3¼" strip of the same colored fabric to the other side of the white strip. Press the seam allowances toward the dark fabric.

3 Sew a 1½" x 1¾" white rectangle to the 5" colored strip; be sure to sew the longer side of the rectangle to the colored strip. Press toward the darker fabric.

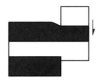

4 Crosscut the unit into three 1½"-wide segments as shown.

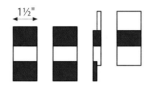

5 Sew the three segments together as shown, pressing toward the outside of the block.

6 Repeat steps 1–5 to make 68 blocks with white background fabric and dark-colored squares, 48 with medium-gray background fabric and medium-colored squares, and 12 with dark-gray background fabric and light-colored squares.

Assembling the Quilt Top

1 Referring to the quilt diagram, lay out the Nine Patch blocks and setting squares in 17 rows.

2 Sew the blocks and squares together in rows, pressing the seam allowances toward the setting squares.

3 Sew the rows together. Press the seam allowances in one direction.

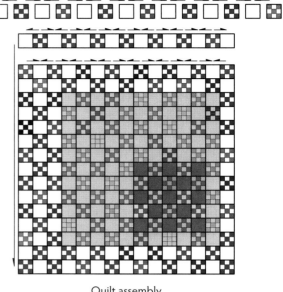

Quilt assembly

Adding the Borders

To balance the dark square in the lower-right corner of the quilt, Ionne and Sharon added a border in two values of gray—a medium and a dark. They placed the dark borders on the top and left edges of the quilt and the light-gray on the bottom and right edges. It's a subtle difference, but it adds interest and seems to counterbalance the darker areas of the quilt.

1 Sew the three 2" x 40" medium-gray border strips together end to end. Measure the quilt through the center horizontally, cut a strip to that measurement, and sew it to the bottom of the quilt. Press the seam allowances toward the border.

2 Measure the quilt through the center vertically. Cut the remaining medium-gray strip to fit and sew it to the right side of the quilt. Press the seam allowances toward the border.

3 Repeat steps 1 and 2 to add the 2"-wide dark-gray border strips to the top and left edges of the quilt. Press the seam allowances toward the border.

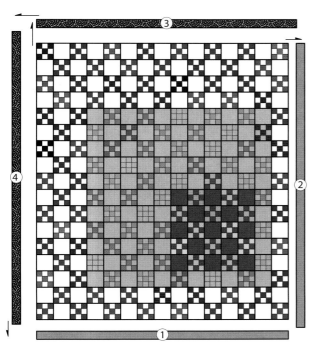

Adding the borders

Finishing the Quilt

For help with any of the finishing steps, go to ShopMartingale.com/HowtoQuilt for free downloadable information.

1 Layer, baste, and quilt your quilt, or take it to your favorite long-arm machine quilter for finishing.

2 Using the 2½"-wide medium-gray and dark-gray strips, make and attach binding (refer to "Adding a Pieced Binding" below).

Adding a Pieced Binding

To attach a binding that "matches" the borders of this quilt, you will need to sew on each side separately and butt the corners of your binding.

1 Sew the three binding strips of each color together using a diagonal seam to make one long strip. Cut the strips in half.

2 Cut two strips, 2½" x 4", off the end of one of the darker binding strips. Sew one to the end of each of the lighter binding strips using a straight seam. Press the seam allowances open.

3 Press the four binding strips in half lengthwise with wrong sides together.

4 Sew the shorter dark binding strip to the top of the quilt using a ¼" seam. Pin a pieced lighter binding strip to the bottom of the quilt, aligning the seam of the darker piece with the border seam. Sew and then trim the ends of the binding even with the quilt top. Press the binding strips away from the quilt.

5 Sew the remaining dark binding strip to the left side of the quilt. Pin a lighter pieced binding strip to the opposite side of the quilt, aligning the seam with the border seam as before. Sew and press the binding away from the quilt. Trim the ends, leaving an extra ¼" beyond the ends of the top and bottom binding.

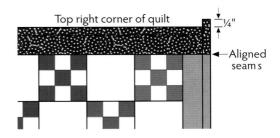

6 Fold the ¼" ends over, and then fold the binding strips to the back of the quilt, one side at a time, and hand sew them as for regular binding.

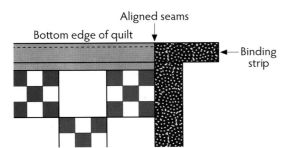

String Beans

Calling all colors! *Collect "string beans," or strips, from your favorite fabrics to create this cheerful cuddle-up quilt. Sewing string beans onto a foundation square will keep your bias under control. It's a good way to get your veggies!*

"String Beans," designed and made by Mary Jacobson and Barbara Groves

Finished quilt: 71" x 75" ◆ **Finished block:** 10" x 10"

▶ Materials

Yardage is based on 42"-wide fabric. Fat quarters are 18" x 21".

36 assorted fat quarters for blocks

4 yards of white muslin for block foundations

⅝ yard of pink print for border

⅝ yard of green print for border

½ yard of yellow print for border

½ yard of orange print for border

¾ yard of multicolored stripe for binding

5 yards of fabric for backing

79" x 83" piece of batting

▶ Cutting

All measurements include ¼"-wide seam allowances.

From *each* of the assorted fat quarters, cut:
2 strips, 2¾" x 20" (72 total)
2 strips, 2¼" x 20" (72 total)
2 strips, 1¾" x 20" (72 total)
2 strips, 1¼" x 20" (72 total)

From the white muslin, cut:
12 strips, 11" x 40"; crosscut into 36 squares, 11" x 11"

From *each* of the yellow and orange prints, cut:
2 strips, 5¾" x 40" (4 total)

From *each* of the pink and green prints, cut:
2 strips, 7¾" x 40" (4 total)

From the multicolored stripe, cut:
8 strips, 2¼" x 40"

Making the Blocks

1 Place a fat-quarter strip of any width right side up diagonally across the center of an 11" muslin foundation square.

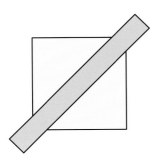

2 With right sides together, place another fat-quarter strip on top of the center strip; align the side edges. Make sure your strips always extend beyond the muslin foundation.

3 Stitch using a ¼" seam allowance along the edge through all layers. Flip and press toward the corner.

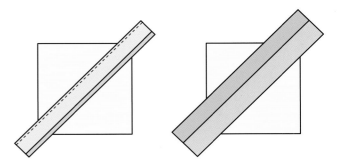

4 Continue adding strips to each side of the center strip until the muslin foundation is completely covered. Be creative; use different widths and colors so that no two blocks are the same.

5 From the back side, trim the blocks (including both the muslin foundation and the top fabrics) to measure 10½" square. The muslin foundation helps control the bias edges. Save the trimmed-off pieces for use in other projects, if you wish. Make 36.

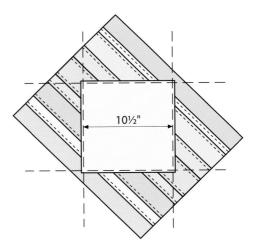

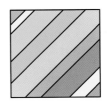

Make 36.

Assembling the Quilt Top

1 Arrange the blocks into six rows of six blocks each, rotating the blocks as shown in the quilt layout diagram below.

2 Sew the blocks in each row together, and then join the rows to complete the quilt top. The quilt should now measure 60½" square.

Adding the Borders

1 Piece the two 5¾" x 40" yellow strips end to end and piece the two 5¾" x 40" orange strips end to end. Press the seam allowances open.

2 Measure the quilt from top to bottom through the middle. From each pieced strip, cut a side border to the measured length. Attach the yellow strip to the left side of the quilt top and the orange strip to the right side.

3 Piece the two 7¾" x 40" pink border strips end to end and piece the two 7¾" x 40" green border strips end to end.

4 Measure the quilt from side to side through the middle, including the side borders. From each pieced strip, cut a border to the measured length. Attach the pink strip to the top of the quilt and the green strip to the bottom.

Finishing the Quilt

For help with any of the finishing steps, go to ShopMartingale.com/HowtoQuilt for free downloadable information.

1 Layer, baste, and quilt your quilt, or take it to your favorite long-arm machine quilter for finishing.

2 Using the 2¼"-wide striped strips, make and attach binding.

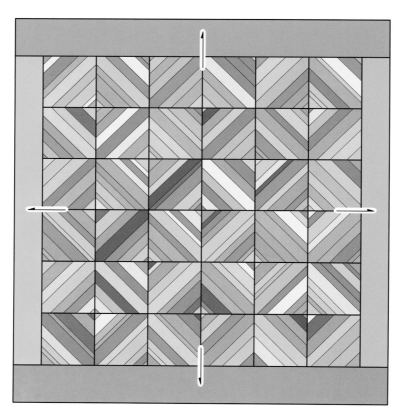

Quilt layout

Past and Present

Each block in this quilt is constructed using four 6½"
units. Instead of making full blocks, try experimenting with
the arrangement of the smaller units to create unique settings.

"Past and Present," designed and made by Kim Brackett
Finished quilt: 61½" x 73½"　◆　**Finished block:** 12" x 12"

Materials

Yardage is based on 42"-wide fabric.

2 yards of large-scale floral for outer border and binding

⅓ yard of blue print for inner border

40 strips (10 per color), 2½" x at least 30", of assorted dark prints in red, blue, green, and brown for blocks

40 strips, 2½" x at least 30", of assorted tan prints for blocks

4¼ yards of fabric for backing

65½" x 77½" piece of batting

Cutting

All measurements include ¼"-wide seam allowances.

From *each* of the 40 assorted dark-print strips and 40 assorted tan-print strips, cut:

2 rectangles, 2½" x 6½" (80 total dark and 80 total tan)

6 squares, 2½" x 2½" (240 total dark and 240 total tan)

From the blue print, cut:

6 strips, 1½" x 42"

From the large-scale floral, cut:

7 strips, 6" x 42"

8 strips, 2½" x 42"

Cutting from Scraps

If you prefer to use scraps, follow the instructions below. See "Cutting" above for instructions on cutting the borders and binding.

From assorted tan prints, cut:

80 sets of:
  1 rectangle, 2½" x 6½"
  3 squares, 2½" x 2½"

From assorted dark prints, cut:

80 sets of:
  1 rectangle, 2½" x 6½"
  3 squares, 2½" x 2½"

Making the Blocks

1 Select one 2½" x 6½" rectangle and three 2½" squares *each* from a single dark print and a single tan print. Using the folded-corner technique, make a half-square-triangle unit by drawing a diagonal line on the wrong side of a tan 2½" square. Layer the marked square, right sides together, with a dark 2½" square, matching the corners. Sew on the drawn line. Trim the excess fabric, leaving ¼" for seam allowance. Open the unit and press the seam allowances toward the dark triangle.

2 Sew a tan 2½" square and a dark 2½" square to opposite sides of the half-square-triangle unit as shown. Press the seam allowances toward the squares.

3 Make a folded-corner unit by sewing a tan 2½" square to a dark 2½" x 6½" rectangle along the diagonal of the square. Trim the excess fabric from the corner, leaving ¼" seam allowance, and press the unit open.

4 Make a folded-corner unit using a tan 2½" x 6½" rectangle and a dark 2½" square.

5 Join the units from steps 2, 3, and 4 to complete one-quarter of the block as shown. Press the seam allowances away from the center. Make 80 units.

Make 80.

6 Join one each of the red, brown, green, and blue units from step 5 to construct one block as shown. Press the seam allowances in a counterclockwise direction. Make 20 blocks.

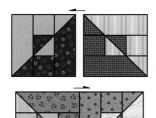

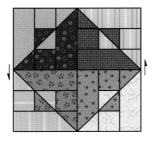

Make 20.

Assembling the Quilt Top

1 Arrange the blocks in five rows of four blocks each as shown in the quilt assembly diagram.

2 Sew the blocks together in rows, pressing the seam allowances in opposite directions from row to row. Sew the rows together. Press the seam allowances in one direction.

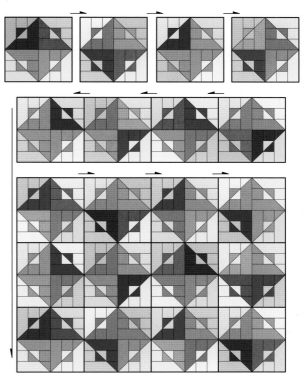

Quilt assembly

Finishing the Quilt

For help with any of the finishing steps, go to ShopMartingale.com/HowtoQuilt for free downloadable information.

1 Layer, baste, and quilt your quilt, or take it to your favorite long-arm machine quilter for finishing.

2 Using the floral 2½"-wide strips, make and attach binding.

Stars of Freedom

Dig out your red and blue scraps for this fun quilt. Although it may look complicated, it simply consists of triangles put together into rows. Careful placement of the blue and red triangles forms the stars. What a great way to show your patriotism!

"Stars of Freedom," designed and made by Evelyn Sloppy

Finished quilt: 57½" x 79½" ◆ **Finished block:** 6⅝" equilateral triangle

▶ Materials

Yardage is based on 42"-wide fabric. Fat quarters are 18" x 21".

2⅞ yards *total* of assorted red scraps *or* 12 fat quarters for triangles

2⅞ yards *total* of assorted blue scraps *or* 12 fat quarters for triangles

2⅞ yards of light print for background

⅝ yard of fabric for straight-grain binding *or* 1 yard for bias binding

5¼ yards of fabric for backing

65" x 87" piece of batting

▶ Cutting

All measurements include ¼"-wide seam allowances.

From the assorted red scraps or fat quarters, cut:
Approximately 119 strips that vary in width from 1" to 2½" and are at least 18" long

From the assorted blue scraps or fat quarters, cut:
Approximately 119 strips that vary in width from 1" to 2½" and are at least 18" long

From the light print, cut:
14 strips, 6½" x 42"

From the binding fabric, cut:
7 strips, 2½" x 42", for straight-grain binding, or enough 2½"-wide bias strips to make 282" of bias binding. If you choose to make rounded corners as in the quilt shown, you must use bias binding.

Making the String-Pieced Triangles

1 Use the red strips to make 17 string-pieced units that measure at least 6½" wide and 18" long, staggering the strip ends about ½". In the same manner, make 17 blue string-pieced units. Press the seam allowances in one direction. Trim each unit so that it measures exactly 6½" wide.

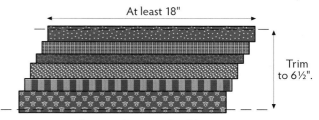

Make 17 red units and 17 blue units.

2 To cut the triangles, line up the 60°-angle mark on your ruler with the bottom of a string-pieced unit. Cut along the left edge of the ruler. Turn the ruler over and position it so that the 60°-angle mark lines up with the bottom of the unit and the ruler right edge aligns with the upper edge of the previous cut as shown. Cut along the right edge of the ruler. Continue rotating the ruler in this manner to cut the triangles from the blue and red string-pieced units. Each string-pieced unit will yield 4 triangles. Cut 66 red triangles and 66 blue triangles.

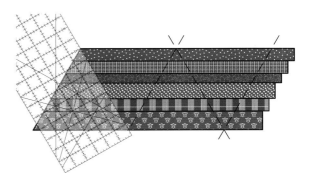

Cut 66 red triangles.   *Cut 66 blue triangles.*

3 Refer to step 2 to cut the light-print strips into triangles. Each strip will yield 9 triangles. Cut 118. Mark the bottom of each triangle with a chalk pencil or straight pin so you will know which edge is on the straight of grain. The straight-grain edge will be placed on the quilt outer edges when the triangles are assembled.

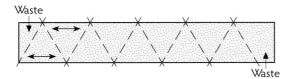

Assembling the Quilt Top

1 Sew the triangles into vertical rows as shown in the quilt assembly diagram below. Make sure the straight-grain edge of the light-colored triangles is

parallel to the outer edge of the top. Press the seam allowances in opposite directions from row to row.

2 Sew the rows together. Press the seam allowances in one direction. Trim the top and bottom edges ¼" beyond the tips of the red and blue triangles.

Finishing the Quilt

For help with any of the finishing steps, go to ShopMartingale.com/HowtoQuilt for free downloadable information.

1 Layer, baste, and quilt your quilt, or take it to your favorite long-arm machine quilter for finishing.

2 Using the 2½"-wide strips, make and attach binding.

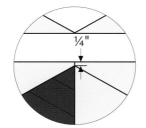

Trim top and bottom edges, leaving a ¼" seam allowance.

Quilt assembly

Days of '47

This quilt features the Salt Lake City block. Nancy made this quilt to honor her Mormon pioneer ancestors, who entered the Salt Lake Valley in 1847. The sashing simplifies the assembly, because you don't have to match points on all sides of the block. The block's large center square is an opportunity to feature a favorite large-scale print.

"Days of '47," designed and pieced by Nancy Allen, machine quilted by Catherine Timmons
Finished quilt: 61½" x 61½" ◆ Finished block: 10" x 10"

Materials

Yardage is based on 42"-wide fabric.

2 yards *total* of at least 16 assorted prints for blocks*

2 yards of multicolored print for outer border**

1¾ yards of cream solid for sashing, inner border, and pieced middle border

1 yard of black tone on tone for block backgrounds, sashing squares, and pieced middle border

⅝ yard of fabric for binding

4 yards of fabric for backing

70" x 70" piece of batting

A fat-eighth bundle of a complete fabric line will give you plenty of coordinated prints to mix and match. It will be more fabric than needed, but will offer flexibility when piecing your blocks.

**If you prefer to piece your border rather than use a lengthwise cut, you will need only 1 yard.*

Cutting

All measurements include ¼"-wide seam allowances.

From the assorted prints, cut a *total* of:
16 squares, 5½" x 5½"
16 sets of 4 matching squares, 2¼" x 2¼"

From *each* of 16 of the assorted prints, cut:
1 square, 6¼" x 6¼"; cut into quarters diagonally to yield 4 triangles (64 total)
2 squares, 3⅜" x 3⅜"; cut in half diagonally to yield 4 triangles (64 total)

From the black tone on tone, cut:
4 strips, 3¾" x 42"; crosscut into 32 squares, 3¾" x 3¾". Cut into quarters diagonally to yield 128 triangles.
3 strips, 3⅜" x 42"; crosscut into 32 squares, 3⅜" x 3⅜". Cut in half diagonally to yield 64 triangles.
3 strips, 2¼" x 42"; crosscut into 40 squares, 2¼" x 2¼"
1 strip, 2" x 42"; crosscut into 9 squares, 2" x 2"

From the cream solid, cut on the *lengthwise* grain:
4 strips, 3¼" x 54"; crosscut into:
  2 strips, 3¼" x 45"
  2 strips, 3¼" x 50½"

From the remaining cream solid, cut:
24 rectangles, 2" x 10½"
40 squares, 3⅜" x 3⅜"; cut in half diagonally to yield 80 triangles
4 squares, 3" x 3"

From the multicolored print, cut on the *lengthwise* grain:
4 strips, 3½" x 72"; crosscut into:
  2 strips, 3½" x 55½"
  2 strips, 3½" x 61½"

From the remaining multicolored print, cut:
20 squares, 3¾" x 3¾"; cut into quarters diagonally to yield 80 triangles

From the binding fabric, cut:
7 strips, 2¼" x 42"

Making the Blocks

1 Sew two black tone-on-tone quarter-square triangles to an assorted-print 2¼" square. Make four. Press the seam allowances toward the triangles.

Make 4.

2 Sew two matching assorted half-square triangles to a pieced unit from step 1 as shown. Press the seam allowances toward the triangles just added. Make two. If necessary, trim this unit to 3" x 5½", making sure to leave ¼" seam allowance above and below the square.

Make 2.

3 Sew two matching assorted quarter-square triangles to a pieced triangle from step 1 as shown. Press seam allowances toward the triangles just added. Make two.

Make 2.

4 Sew the pieced rectangles from step 2 to opposite sides of a 5½" square. Press the seam allowances toward the square.

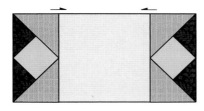

5 Sew the units from step 3 to the remaining sides; press the seam allowances open.

6 Sew a black tone-on-tone half-square triangle to each of the four corners. Press the seam allowances toward the corners. The block should measure 10½" square.

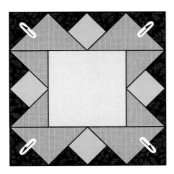

7 Repeat steps 1–6 to make a total of 16 blocks.

Assembling the Quilt Top

1 Lay out the blocks in four rows of four blocks each. Sew a cream 2" x 10½" sashing strip between the blocks in each row. Press the seam allowances toward the sashing.

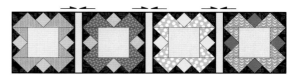

Make 4 rows.

2 Make a horizontal sashing row by joining four cream 2" x 10½" sashing strips and three black tone-on-tone 2" squares. Press the seam allowances toward the cream sashing strips. Make three rows.

Make 3.

3 Join the block rows and sashing rows as shown in the quilt assembly diagram on page 256. Press the seam allowances toward the sashing rows. The quilt center should now measure 45" x 45".

Adding the Borders

1 Sew cream 3¼" x 45" border strips to the left and right sides of the quilt; press the seam allowances toward the border. Sew cream 3¼" x 50½" border strips to the top and bottom of the quilt; press the seam allowances toward the border. The quilt should now measure 50½" x 50½" square.

2 To make the pieced border, sew two multicolored-print quarter-square triangles to a black tone-on-tone 2¼" square. Press the seam allowances toward the triangles. Sew cream half-square triangles to the left and right sides of the pieced triangle. Press the seam allowances in opposite directions as shown. By pressing the seam allowances in this manner, you'll be able to "nest" the seams when you sew the units together in the next step. Make 40. If necessary, trim these units to 3" x 5½", making sure to leave ¼" seam allowances above and below the square.

Make 40.

3 Sew 10 pieced units together end to end. Press the seam allowances open. Make four pieced border strips. Sew cream 3" squares to both ends of two of the border strips. Press the seam allowances toward the corner squares.

Make 2.

Make 2.

4 Join border strips without corner squares to the left and right sides of the quilt center. Press the seam allowances toward the cream inner border. Join border strips with corner squares to the top and bottom of the quilt center and press toward the cream inner border. The quilt should now measure 55½" x 55½".

5 Sew multicolored 3½" x 55½" border strips to the left and right sides of the quilt and 3½" x 61½" border strips to the top and bottom of the quilt; press all seam allowances toward the outer border. The quilt should now measure 61½" x 61½".

Finishing the Quilt

For help with any of the finishing steps, go to ShopMartingale.com/HowtoQuilt for free downloadable information.

1 Layer, baste, and quilt your quilt, or take it to your favorite long-arm machine quilter for finishing.

2 Using the 2¼"-wide strips, make and attach binding.

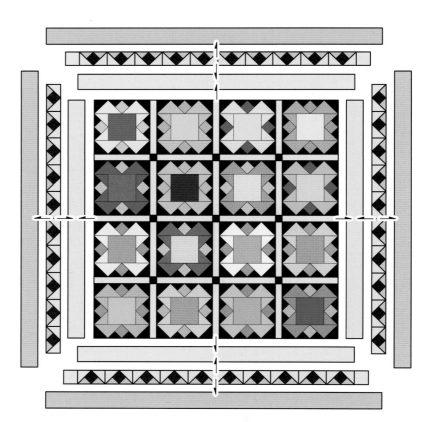

Quilt assembly

Very Varied Values

The use of very light, clear fabrics makes some of the blocks in this quilt seem to "glow." By adding blocks using five light squares and four medium squares, and blocks with five very dark squares and four medium squares, Lynn created a stunning quilt that's a lesson in the value of value.

"Very Varied Values," designed and made by Lynn Roddy Brown

Finished quilt: 73½" x 90½" ◆ Finished block: 6" x 6"

Materials

Yardage is based on 42"-wide fabric.

2⅞ yards of medium-green print for blocks, setting triangles, and pieced inner border

2½ yards of dark-green print for pieced inner border, outer border, and binding

1⅓ yards *total* of medium scraps for blocks

⅞ yard *total* of very light scraps for blocks

⅞ yard *total* of dark scraps for blocks

⅔ yard of dark-blue floral for blocks

6 yards of fabric for backing

82" x 99" piece of batting

Cutting

All measurements include ¼"-wide seam allowances.

From the medium scraps, cut:
63 sets of 4 matching squares, 2½" x 2½" (252 total)

From the dark scraps, cut:
32 sets of 5 matching squares, 2½" x 2½" (160 total)

From the very light scraps, cut:
31 sets of 5 matching squares, 2½" x 2½" (155 total)

From the dark-blue floral, cut:
8 strips, 2½" x 42"

From the medium-green print, cut:
16 strips, 2½" x 42"

7 squares, 11" x 11"; cut into quarters diagonally to yield 28 side triangles

2 squares, 6½" x 6½"; cut in half diagonally to yield 4 corner triangles

8 squares, 9¾" x 9¾"; cut into quarters diagonally to yield 32 border triangles

From the dark-green print, cut:
9 squares, 9¾" x 9¾"; cut 7 of the squares into quarters diagonally to yield 28 border triangles and cut 2 of the squares in half diagonally to yield 4 corner triangles

9 strips, 3" x 42"

9 strips, 2½" x 42"

Making the Nine Patch Blocks

The Nine Patch blocks in this quilt consist of two different value configurations as shown. The O block pairs a very light fabric with a medium. The X block pairs a dark fabric with a medium. The medium fabric is in the same position in both blocks. Value placement is very important.

O block   X block

1 Select five matching light 2½" squares and four matching medium 2½" squares. Lay out the squares as shown. Make certain the light and medium fabrics are in the correct positions. Sew the squares together in rows; press the seam allowances toward the medium fabric. Join the rows and press. Make 31.

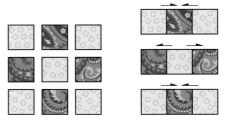

Make 31.

2 Select five matching dark 2½" squares and four matching medium 2½" squares. Lay out the squares as shown, making certain the light and

medium fabrics are in the correct positions. Sew the squares together in rows; press the seam allowances toward the dark fabric. Join the rows and press. Make 32.

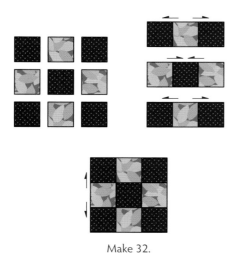

Make 32.

Making the Rail Blocks

Sew a medium-green 2½" x 42" strip to each long side of a dark-blue floral 2½" x 42" strip. Press the seam allowances toward the medium-green strip. Make eight strip sets and cut the strip sets into a total of 48 segments, 6½" wide.

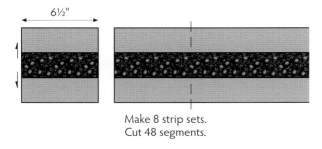

6½"

Make 8 strip sets.
Cut 48 segments.

Assembling the Quilt Top

1 Working on a design wall and referring to the quilt assembly diagram above right, arrange the X Nine Patch blocks, the O Nine Patch blocks, and the Rail blocks in diagonal rows. Note that the Nine Patch blocks alternate. The first and last rows begin and end with an X block. Alternate the direction of the Rail blocks to form a diagonal pattern.

2 Add the side triangles to the layout. Join the blocks and side triangles in diagonal rows. Press the seam allowances toward the Rail blocks. Join the rows and press the seam allowances open. Add the corner triangles; press the seam allowances outward.

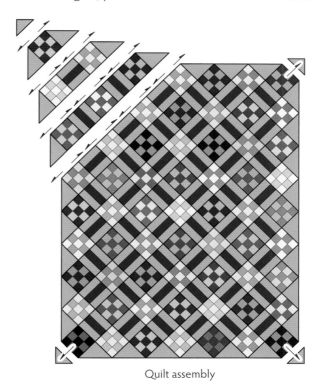

Quilt assembly

3 Trim the quilt on all four sides, leaving a ¼" seam allowance.

Adding the Borders

1 Sewing the triangles for the pieced border is much easier if the triangle points are trimmed. To trim the points, you can use a special point-trimmer ruler or a rotary ruler with ⅛" marks. Align the ⅜" line with a short edge of the triangle. Position the ruler so the corner is just touching the long edge of the triangle as shown. Trim the point. Rotate the triangle and trim the second point. Repeat for all 32 medium-green triangles and 28 dark-green triangles.

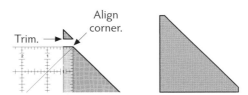

Align corner.

Trim.

2 Each pieced border starts and ends with a medium-green triangle. To join the border triangles, place a medium-green triangle right sides together with a dark-green triangle as shown. Notice the position of the ¼" seamline in relation to the trimmed point. Sew the seam and press the seam allowances open.

3 Join seven medium-green triangles and six dark-green triangles for the top/bottom border; make two. Piece a side border using nine medium-green triangles and eight dark-green triangles; make two.

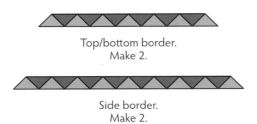

Top/bottom border.
Make 2.

Side border.
Make 2.

4 Add the side borders using pins and a steam iron if necessary to adjust the fit. Press the seam allowances open. Add the top and bottom borders. Press the seam allowances open. Add the dark-green corner triangles and press outward.

5 To make the dark-green side borders, cut one 3" x 42" strip into two equal lengths. Using diagonal seams, join two full-width strips and a half strip to make each side border. Using a diagonal seam, join two dark-green 3" x 42" border strips for the top outer border and two for the bottom outer border. Add the outer borders to the quilt top.

Finishing the Quilt

For help with any of the finishing steps, go to ShopMartingale.com/HowtoQuilt for free downloadable information.

1 Layer, baste, and quilt your quilt, or take it to your favorite long-arm machine quilter for finishing.

2 Using the dark-green 2½"-wide strips, make and attach binding.

Cabin Cozy

Embrace your frugal nature and use the tiniest saved scraps of your favorite prints in this quilt with classic appeal. Best of all, clever placement of your neutrals provides an unexpected and pleasing secondary design, letting your scrappy blocks shine.

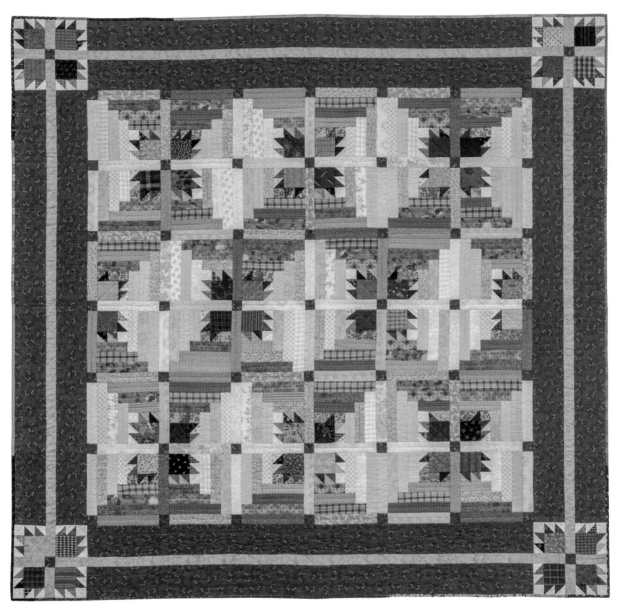

"Cabin Cozy," designed and made by Kim Diehl
Finished quilt: 57½" x 57½"   ◆   Finished block: 6" x 6"

Materials

Yardage is based on 42"-wide fabric. A fat quarter is 18"x21".

1½ yards *total* of assorted tan prints for blocks and sashing

1½ yards *total* of assorted cream prints for blocks and sashing

1⅓ yards of cranberry print for sashing squares and border

1¼ yards *total* of assorted prints for blocks and binding

⅓ yard of dark-tan print for border

1 fat quarter of cream print for border corner blocks

3½ yards of fabric for backing

64" x 64" piece of batting

Cutting

All measurements include ¼"-wide seam allowances. Cut pieces across the width of the fabric unless otherwise indicated.

From the assorted tan prints, cut a *combined total* of:
36 squares, 1⅞" x 1⅞"; cut in half diagonally to yield 72 triangles
18 squares, 1½" x 1½"
18 rectangles, 1½" x 3½"
36 rectangles, 1½" x 4½"
36 rectangles, 1½" x 5½"
62 rectangles, 1½" x 6½"

From the assorted cream prints, cut a *combined total* of:
36 squares, 1⅞" x 1⅞"; cut in half diagonally to yield 72 triangles
18 squares, 1½" x 1½"
18 rectangles, 1½" x 3½"
36 rectangles, 1½" x 4½"
36 rectangles, 1½" x 5½"
58 rectangles, 1½" x 6½"

From the assorted prints, cut a *combined total* of:
104 squares, 1⅞" x 1⅞"; cut in half diagonally to yield 208 triangles
52 squares, 2½" x 2½"
Enough 2½"-wide strips in random lengths to equal 238" of binding when pieced together end to end

From the fat quarter of cream print, cut:
32 squares, 1⅞" x 1⅞"; cut in half diagonally to yield 64 triangles
16 squares, 1½" x 1½"

From the cranberry print, cut on the *lengthwise* grain:
8 strips, 3½" x 43½"

From the remaining cranberry print, cut:
53 squares, 1½" x 1½"

From the dark-tan print, cut:
6 strips, 1½" x 42"; crosscut 1 of the strips into 8 rectangles, 1½" x 3½"

Achieving a Perfectly Sized Block

If you find that your pieced blocks are consistently just a skosh small, even when using a quarter-inch foot, here's a quick little trick that may make a difference in your accuracy. For sewing machines with incremental needle positions, try setting the needle just one notch to the right of the center position. Sew a test block and measure your results—this slight adjustment can be just enough to compensate for the thread or two that is lost to the fold of fabric when your seam allowances are pressed.

Making the Half-Square-Triangle Units

Sew all pieces with right sides together unless otherwise indicated.

1 Join an assorted-print 1⅞" triangle and an assorted tan-print 1⅞" triangle along the long bias edges. Press the seam allowances toward the assorted print. Trim away the dog-ear points. Repeat for a total of 72 tan-print half-square-triangle units.

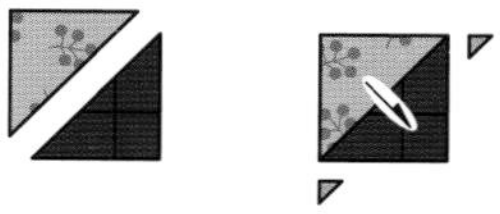

Make 72.

2 Repeat step 1 using the assorted-print 1⅞" triangles and assorted cream-print 1⅞" triangles to make a total of 72 assorted cream-print half-square-triangle units.

3 Repeat step 1 using the assorted-print 1⅞" triangles and cream-print 1⅞" triangles to make a total of 64 cream-print half-square-triangle units.

Making the Bear's Paw A Units

1 Lay out two tan-print half-square-triangle units and one assorted tan-print 1½" square. Join the pieces. Press the seam allowances toward the tan-print square. Repeat for a total of 18 tan-print pieced rectangles.

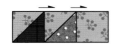

Make 18.

2 Join two assorted cream-print half-square-triangle units. Press the seam allowances toward the assorted print. Join this rectangle unit to an assorted-print 2½" square. Press the seam allowances toward the assorted-print square. Repeat for a total of 18 assorted cream-print units.

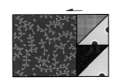

Make 18.

3 Join a tan-print pieced rectangle from step 1 to a cream-print unit from step 2. Press the seam allowances toward the cream-print unit. Repeat for a total of 18 bear's paw A units measuring 3½" square, including seam allowances.

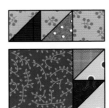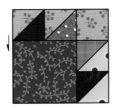

Unit A.
Make 18.

Making the Bear's Paw B Units

1 Lay out two assorted cream-print half-square-triangle units and one assorted cream-print 1½" square. Join the pieces. Press the seam allowances toward the cream-print square. Repeat for a total of 18 assorted cream-print pieced rectangles.

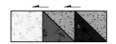

Make 18.

2 Join two tan-print half-square-triangle units. Press the seam allowances toward the assorted print. Join this rectangle unit to an assorted-print 2½" square. Press the seam allowances toward the assorted-print square. Repeat for a total of 18 tan-print units.

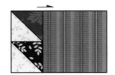

Make 18.

3 Join a cream-print pieced rectangle from step 1 to a tan-print unit from step 2 as shown. Press the seam allowances toward the tan-print unit. Repeat for a total of 18 bear's paw B units measuring 3½" square, including seam allowances.

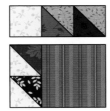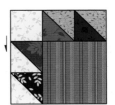

Unit B.
Make 18.

Making the A and B Blocks

1 Lay out an A unit and the assorted tan and assorted cream pieces in order as shown. Join the assorted cream-print 3½"-long strip to the A unit. Press the seam allowances toward the cream-print strip. Join and press the assorted tan-print 4½"-long strip to the unit in the same manner. Continue joining and pressing the cream and tan strips in the order shown. Repeat for a total of 18 Bear's Paw A blocks measuring 6½" square, including seam allowances.

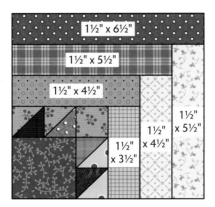

Block A.
Make 18.

2 Lay out a B unit and the assorted tan and assorted cream strips as shown. Sew and press the block in order in the same manner as for the A block. Repeat for a total of 18 Bear's Paw B blocks measuring 6½" square, including seam allowances.

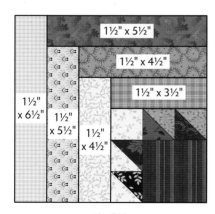

Block B.
Make 18.

Making the Block Rows

1 Lay out seven cranberry-print 1½" squares and six assorted tan-print 1½" x 6½" strips. Join the pieces. Press the seam allowances toward the tan-print strips. Repeat for a total of four tan sashing rows.

Make 4.

2 Lay out seven cranberry-print 1½" squares and six assorted cream-print 1½" x 6½" strips. Join the pieces. Press the seam allowances toward the cream-print strips. Repeat for a total of three cream-print sashing rows.

Make 3.

3 Lay out three B blocks, three A blocks, four assorted cream-print 1½" x 6½" strips, and three assorted tan-print 1½" x 6½" strips as shown. Join the pieces. Press the seam allowances toward the sashing strips. Repeat for a total of four A block rows.

Block A row.
Make 4.

4 Lay out three A blocks, three B blocks, four assorted tan-print 1½" x 6½" strips, and three assorted cream-print 1½" x 6½" strips as shown. Sew and press the pieces as instructed in step 3. Repeat for a total of two B block rows.

Block B row.
Make 2.

Assembling the Quilt Top

Lay out the sashing rows and block rows as shown to form the quilt center. Join the rows. Press the seam allowances toward the sashing rows.

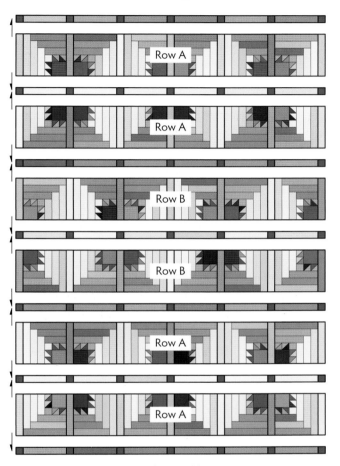

Quilt assembly

Adding the Borders

1 Referring to steps 1–3 of "Making the Bear's Paw A Units" on page 263, use four cream-print half-square-triangle units, one cream-print 1½" square, and one assorted-print 2½" square to make a bear's-paw unit. Repeat for a total of 16 bear's-paw border units measuring 3½" square, including seam allowances.

2 Cut and piece the dark-tan 1½" x 42" strips to make four border strips measuring 1½" x 49½". Press the seam allowances to one side.

3 Referring to the border assembly illustration on page 266, sew cranberry-print 3½" x 43½" strips to the top and bottom edges of the quilt center. Press the seam allowances toward the cranberry print. Sew a bear's-paw border unit from step 1 to each end of a cranberry-print 3½" x 43½" strip as shown. Repeat for a total of two strips. Join these strips to the right and left sides of the quilt center. Press the seam allowances toward the cranberry strips.

4 Join dark-tan 1½" x 49½" strips to the top and bottom edges of the quilt top. Press the seam allowances toward the tan strips. Join a cranberry-print 1½" square to each end of the remaining 49½"-long strips. Press the seam allowances toward the dark tan. Join these pieced strips to the right and left sides of the quilt top. Press the seam allowances toward the tan strips.

5 Lay out and join two dark-tan 1½" x 3½" rectangles, two bear's-paw border units from step 1, and one cranberry-print 3½" x 43½" strip as shown. Press the seam allowances away from the bear's-paw units. Repeat for a total of four pieced strips. Join two of these strips to the top and bottom edges of the quilt top. Press the seam allowances toward the cranberry strips. Join a bear's-paw border unit to each end of the remaining pieced strips. Press the seam allowances away from the bear's-paw units. Join these strips to the remaining sides of the quilt top. Press the seam allowances toward the cranberry strips. The pieced quilt top should now measure 57½" square, including seam allowances.

Finishing the Quilt

For help with any of the finishing steps, go to ShopMartingale.com/HowtoQuilt for free downloadable information.

1 Layer, baste, and quilt your quilt, or take it to your favorite long-arm machine quilter for finishing.

2 Using the assorted-print 2½"-wide strips, make and attach binding.

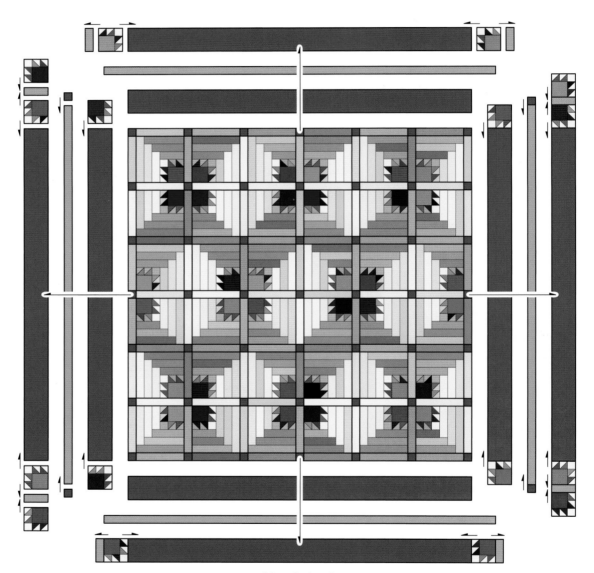

Adding the borders

Pinwheels Revisited

Inspired by a wonderful antique pinwheel quilt a friend found at an estate sale, Lynn made it her goal to reproduce the quilt as closely as possible. This quilt gave her permission to do all the things she hadn't done in other quilts, such as use inconsistent values, put the same fabrics or colors next to each other, and piece blocks with stripes going in different directions. She found this very liberating!

"Pinwheels Revisited," designed and made by Lynn Roddy Brown
Finished quilt: 68" x 76"　◆　**Finished block: 6" x 6"**

Materials

Yardage is based on 42"-wide fabric.

3⅛ yards *total* of medium and dark scraps for blocks and setting triangles

3⅛ yards *total* of light scraps for blocks and setting triangles

2¼ yards of black-and-gray print for border

⅔ yard of black-and-white check for binding*

5¼ yards of fabric for backing

76" x 84" piece of batting

For bias binding, you'll need 1¼ yards to make a total length of 300".

Cutting

All measurements include ¼"-wide seam allowances.

From the medium and dark scraps, cut:
85 matching pairs of squares, 4¼" x 4¼" (170 total)
6 matching pairs of squares, 4¼" x 4¼" (12 total)
7 squares, 6" x 6"*

From the light scraps, cut:
85 matching pairs of squares, 4¼" x 4¼" (170 total)
6 matching pairs of squares, 4¼" x 4¼" (12 total)
7 squares, 6" x 6"*

From the black-and-gray print, cut on the *lengthwise* grain:
2 strips, 4½" x 64"
2 strips, 8½" x 72"

From the black-and-white check, cut:
8 strips, 2½" x 42"

Cut 1 square to match each pair of 4¼" squares. The seventh square can be any print.

Making the Pinwheel Blocks

The quilt has about 59 of Pinwheel block A, about 25 of block B, and one of block C for a total of 85 blocks. The difference between the blocks is simply the value placement. Scattered randomly across the quilt surface, these blocks will create alternate patterns. Most of the blocks use two fabrics. A few odd blocks, such as block C, use additional fabrics and are made with half-square-triangle units arranged in other patterns. The instructions are written for two fabrics with the values positioned as shown in block A. Reverse the values in your blocks to create as many of block B as you like, and throw in a block C if desired. It's up to you to decide how scrappy you want your quilt. Note that in blocks A and B, the half-square-triangle units are simply positioned in different ways when sewn together. This opposite placement of the half-square-triangle units creates pinwheels that turn in opposite directions.

Block A   Block B

Block C

For each block you'll need two matching (or not) medium or dark 4¼" squares and two matching light 4¼" squares.

1 Draw a diagonal line on the wrong side of each light square. Place a light square right sides together with a medium or dark square, and sew ¼" from each side of the drawn line. Cut apart on the line. Press the seam allowances toward the darker fabric and trim the units to 3½" square. Make 85 matching sets of four.

Make 85 sets of four.

2 Arrange four matching units as shown. Make certain the lighter and darker fabrics are in the correct positions. Sew the units together in rows, and press the seam allowances open. Join the rows, and press the seam allowances open. Feel free to make a few blocks with unmatched units or blocks with the units in odd positions. Make a total of 85 blocks.

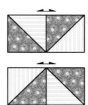

Make 85.

Making the Pieced Setting Triangles

In the original antique quilt, some of the setting triangles were pieced as one half of a Pinwheel block. These were probably extra blocks that were cut in half. The instructions are written for the most efficient use of fabric—half Pinwheel blocks made in sets of four. This will give you three sets of four identical triangles as shown in triangle A. Feel free to vary them as the original quiltmaker did, shown in triangles B, C, and D.

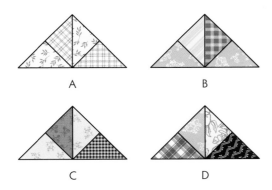

For each set of four setting triangles, you'll need:
   Two matching 4¼" squares and one 6" square of the same medium/dark fabric
   Two matching 4¼" squares and one 6" square of the same light fabric

1 Draw a diagonal line on the wrong side of each 4¼" light square. Place a light square right sides together with a 4¼" medium or dark square, and sew ¼" from each side of the drawn line. Cut apart on the line. Press the seam allowances toward the darker fabric and trim the units to 3½" square.

Make 4.

2 Cut both of the 6" squares into quarters diagonally to yield eight quarter-square triangles. Using a half-square-triangle unit from step 1, one light quarter-square triangle, and one medium/dark quarter-square triangle, arrange the units as shown below. Note that the quarter-square triangles are slightly oversized.

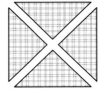

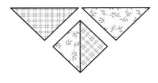

3 Matching the corners, sew a medium or dark triangle to the half-square-triangle unit. Press toward the triangle. Trim the point. Add the light triangle as shown. Press outward. Make four.

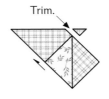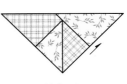

Trim.

Make 4.

4 Repeat steps 1–3 to make a total of 24 side setting triangles.

Making the Pieced Corner Triangles

For four corner triangles using the same fabrics: Pair a light 6" square with a medium or dark 6" square. Referring to step 1 of "Making the Pieced Setting Triangles," make two identical pieced squares. Press the seam allowances open. Don't trim the units. Cut the units in half diagonally, across the seam.

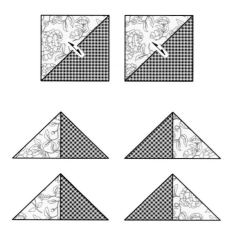

For four corner triangles using different fabrics: Join odd quarter-square triangles cut from 6" squares as shown. Press the seam allowances open.

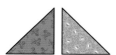 

Assembling the Quilt Top

1 Referring to the quilt assembly diagram, arrange the blocks, pieced setting triangles, and pieced corner triangles in a diagonal setting on a design wall. Rearrange the blocks until you are pleased with the layout. When identical fabrics or similar values touch, alternate patterns will form. The more this happens, the scrappier looking the quilt.

2 Sew the pieced side setting triangles and blocks together into diagonal rows. Press the seam allowances open. Join the rows and press the seam allowances open. Add the corner triangles; press the seam allowances outward.

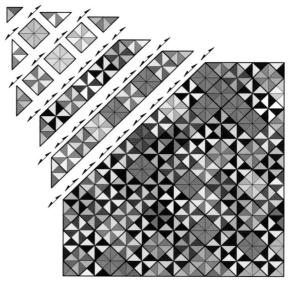

Quilt assembly

3 Trim the quilt on all four sides, leaving a ¼" seam allowance.

4 Join the 4½" x 64" black-and-gray strips to the sides of the quilt top. Add the 8½" x 72" black-and-gray strips to the top and bottom of the quilt top to complete the border.

Quilt layout

Finishing the Quilt

For help with any of the finishing steps, go to ShopMartingale.com/HowtoQuilt for free downloadable information.

1 Layer, baste, and quilt your quilt, or take it to your favorite long-arm machine quilter for finishing.

2 Using the 2½"-wide black-and-white strips, make and attach binding.

Chain Link

The interlocking effect of this quilt design is actually deceptively easy. Nancy Page offered this block in a newspaper advertisement in the 1930s for "three cents and a self-addressed, stamped envelope." Ah, for the good old days. Rotary cutting 2"-wide strips makes this a quick project in both cutting and assembly. With the addition of prairie points and pretty hand quilting, you're done!

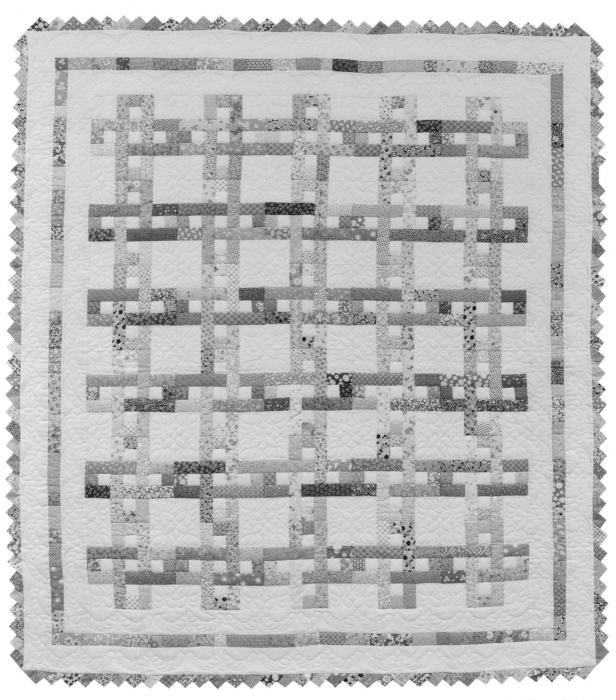

"Chain Link," designed by Kay Connors and Karen Earlywine, pieced by Kay Connors, quilted by Karen Earlywine

Finished quilt: 72" x 82½" (including prairie points)   ◆   **Finished block:** 10½" x 10½"

▸ Materials

Yardage is based on 42"-wide fabric except where noted.

4¾ yards *total* of assorted 1930s reproduction prints for blocks, middle border, and prairie points

3½ yards of unbleached muslin for blocks and borders

2½ yards of 90"-wide muslin for backing*

78" x 89" piece of batting

*If using 42"-wide unbleached muslin, you'll need 5½ yards (2 widths pieced vertically).

▸ Cutting

All measurements include ¼"-wide seam allowances.

From the assorted 1930s reproduction prints, cut a *total* of:
44 strips, 2" x 42"; crosscut 37 of the strips into:
   120 rectangles, 2" x 6½"
   120 rectangles, 2" x 3½"
   120 squares, 2" x 2"
146 squares, 4" x 4"

From the unbleached muslin, cut:
8 strips, 3¾" x 42"
8 strips, 3½" x 42"
11 strips, 3½" x 42"; crosscut 120 squares, 3½" x 3½"
8 strips, 2" x 42"; crosscut 150 squares, 2" x 2"

Making the Blocks

Each block consists of four rectangular units sewn to a center square using a partial-seam technique.

1 Sew a muslin 2" square to each print 2" square. Press the seam allowances toward the print square. Make 120.

Make 120.

2 Sew a print 2" x 3½" rectangle to the left side of each unit from step 1. Press the seam allowances toward the print rectangle. Make 120.

Make 120.

3 Stitch a muslin 3½" square to the left side of the print rectangle as shown. Press the seam allowances toward the rectangle. Make 120.

Make 120.

4 Stitch a print 2" x 6½" rectangle to the bottom of the unit from step 3. Press the seam allowances toward the print rectangle. Make 120 rectangle units.

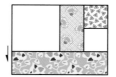

Make 120.

5 Arrange four rectangle units and one muslin 2" square as shown. Sew one rectangle unit to the center square, stopping in the center of the square. Press all seam allowances away from the center square.

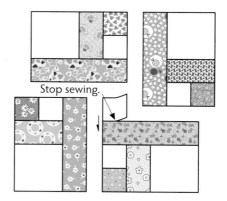

Stop sewing.

6 Sew a rectangle unit to the unit from step 5 as shown; press.

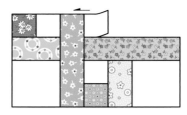

7 Sew the third rectangle unit to the unit from step 6; press.

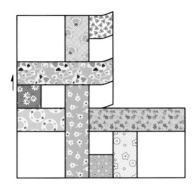

8 Sew the final rectangle unit to the block; press. Sew the small open section of the center-square seam closed to complete the block; press. Make a total of 30 blocks.

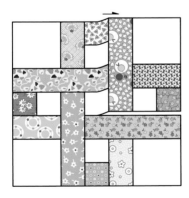

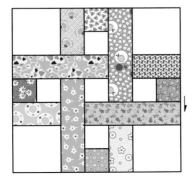

Make 30.

Assembling the Quilt Top

1 Arrange the blocks in six rows of five blocks each as shown in the quilt assembly diagram on page 274. Rearrange the blocks until you are pleased with the color placement.

2 Sew the blocks into rows. Press the seam allowances in alternate directions from row to row. Stitch the rows together. Press the seam allowances in one direction.

Adding the Borders

1 Sew two muslin 3½"-wide strips together end to end to make a long strip. Make four long strips. Measure, cut, and sew the strips to the quilt top for the inner border. Press the seam allowances toward the border.

2 Using the remaining print 2"-wide strips, cut pieces 2" to 5" long. Randomly sew the pieces together end to end to create two middle-border strips at least 75" long and two middle-border strips at least 60" long.

3 Measure, cut, and sew the shorter strips from step 2 to the top and bottom of the quilt top and the longer strips to the sides of the quilt top for the middle border. Press all seam allowances toward the newly added borders.

4 Repeat step 1 to sew the muslin 3¾"-wide outer-border strips to the quilt top. Press.

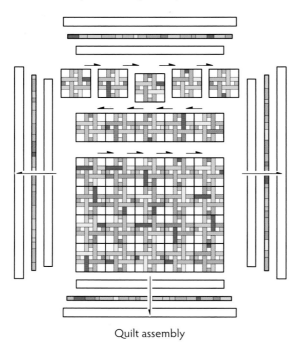

Quilt assembly

Finishing the Quilt

For help with any of the finishing steps, go to ShopMartingale.com/HowtoQuilt for free downloadable information.

1 Mark the quilting lines for your favorite quilting design.

2 Layer the quilt top with batting and backing, and then baste.

3 Hand quilt following the marked lines. Make sure no quilting stitches lie within ½" of the quilt edges to allow for the placement of the prairie points.

Adding the Prairie Points

Once your quilt has been quilted, you will add the prairie points.

1 Trim the batting and backing so that they extend about ⅜" beyond the quilt top on all sides.

2 To make the prairie points, fold each 4" print square in half diagonally, wrong sides together. Fold the square diagonally again, forming a smaller triangle. Make 146 prairie points.

Make 146.

3 Overlap each prairie point by tucking the fold of one point into the opening of the next one. Quiltmakers Kay and Karen like a deep overlap, so they overlap each point about half the length of the previous one. This creates a heavy, strong border that lies smooth. You can use fewer prairie points, if you prefer, by not overlapping them as much; just be sure to have the same number of points on each side and the same number of points on the top as on the bottom of the quilt top.

4 Start by placing one point in the center of one side of your quilt, aligning the long cut edge of the triangle with the cut edge of the quilt front. Place a prairie point at each end of the quilt side, making sure that the folded edges of the triangles aim in the same direction as the first one. Arrange prairie points between the triangles until the side of the quilt is full. The quilt shown has 34 points each on the top and the bottom and 39 points on each side of the quilt. Pin the prairie points along the edge of the quilt top only.

Center

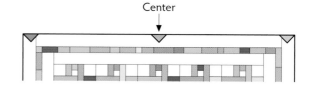

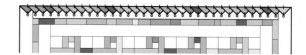

5 On the corners of the quilt, place two points as shown, so that they fit together side by side. They should not overlap. Pin the backing out of the way. Sewing through the quilt top and batting only, stitch the prairie point to all four edges of the quilt using a ¼"-wide seam allowance.

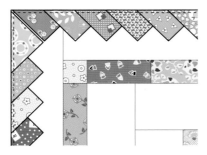

6 Trim the batting close to the stitching. Fold the prairie points out, turning the seam allowances toward the batting, and lightly press on the right side.

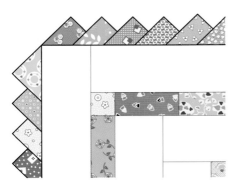

7 Turn the seam allowance of the backing under, covering the seam allowance and the line of stitches on the prairie points, and pin in place. Trim excess fabric at the corners as needed. Finish the back of the quilt using a blind stitch. Add quilting stitches along the edges of the quilt if necessary.

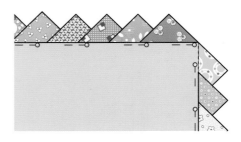

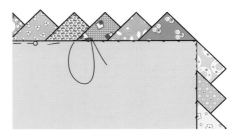

Jack and Jill

This quilt design is the perfect choice for using up those fat quarters you've collected. Divide your fat quarters into two color groups, add two neutral colors, and you'll be off and running to make a quilt for your lucky Jack or Jill!

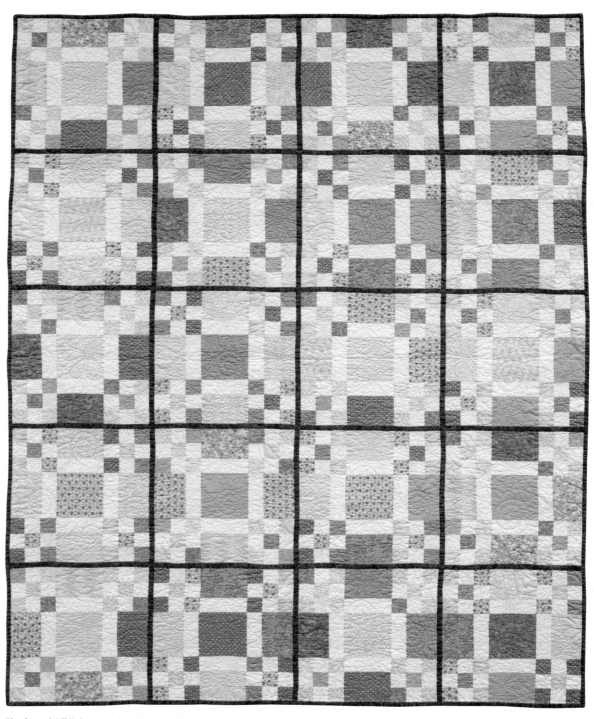

"Jack and Jill," designed and pieced by Jeanne Large and Shelley Wicks, machine quilted by Colleen Lawrence

Finished quilt: 56½" x 70"   ◆   **Finished block:** 13½" x 13½"

Choosing Pink or Blue

The materials, cutting, and assembly instructions are all based on making the pink "Jill" version of this project. To make a "Jack" quilt, simply substitute seven blue fat quarters for the pink ones, and then cut the blue fabrics as described for the pink version.

Materials

Yardage is based on 42"-wide fabric. Fat quarters are 18" x 21".

2 yards of white solid for blocks

7 fat quarters of assorted pink fabrics for blocks

7 fat quarters of assorted green fabrics for blocks

1 yard of brown solid for sashing and binding

3⅝ yards of fabric for backing

64" x 78" piece of batting

Matching or transparent thread for appliqué

Cutting

All measurements include ¼"-wide seam allowances. Cut strips across the width of the fabric unless otherwise indicated. Cut fat quarters perpendicular to the selvage (20" long).

From the 7 assorted pink fat quarters, cut a *total* of:
20 strips, 2" x 20"
11 strips, 5" x 20"; crosscut into:
   10 squares, 5" x 5"
   40 rectangles, 3½" x 5"

From the 7 assorted green fat quarters, cut a *total* of:
20 strips, 2" x 20"
11 strips, 5" x 20"; crosscut into:
   10 squares, 5" x 5"
   40 rectangles, 3½" x 5"

From the white solid, cut:
16 strips, 2" x 42"; crosscut each strip into 2 strips, 2" x 20" (32 total)
4 strips, 5" x 42"; crosscut each strip into 20 rectangles, 2" x 5" (80 total)

From the brown solid, cut:
14 strips, 1" x 42"; crosscut 8 of the strips into 2 strips each, 1" x 14" (16 total; 1 will be extra)
7 strips, 2½" x 42"

Making the Blocks

1 Sew a pink 2" x 20" strip to each long side of a white 2" x 20" strip to make a strip set. Press the seam allowances toward the pink strips. Make a total of eight strip sets. Cut each strip set into 10 segments, 2" wide (80 total).

Make 8 strip sets.
Cut 80 segments.

2 Sew a white 2" x 20" strip to each long side of a pink 2" x 20" strip to make a strip set. Press the seam allowances toward the pink strip. Make a total of four strip sets. Cut each strip set into 10 segments, 2" wide (40 total).

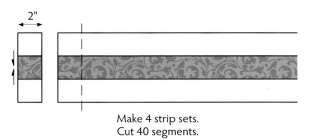

Make 4 strip sets.
Cut 40 segments.

3 Sew segments from step 1 to opposite sides of a segment from step 2 to make a nine-patch unit as shown. Press the seam allowances away from the center. Repeat to make 40 pink-and-white nine-patch units.

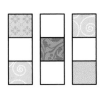

Make 40.

4 Repeat steps 1–3 using green and white 2" x 20" strips to make 40 additional nine-patch units.

Make 40.

5 Sew a white 2" x 5" rectangle to one long edge of each pink 3½" x 5" rectangle. Repeat with the green 3½" x 5" rectangles. Press the seam allowances away from the white rectangles. Make 40 units in each color (80 total).

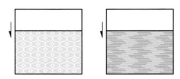

Make 40 each.

6 Arrange four pink nine-patch units, four green-and-white units from step 5, and a pink 5" square to form a block as shown. Sew into three rows, pressing the seam allowances as indicated. Sew the rows together and press toward the center row. Make 10 pink blocks.

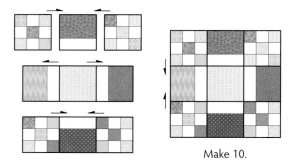

Make 10.

7 Repeat step 6 with the green nine-patch units, pink-and-white units from step 5, and green 5" squares to make 10 green blocks.

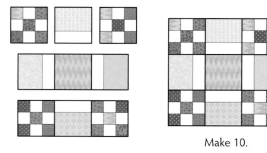

Make 10.

Assembling the Quilt Top

1 Arrange the blocks into five rows of four blocks each, alternating the color placement as shown in the quilt assembly diagram below.

2 Lay a brown 1" x 14" sashing strip between each block in a row. Sew the blocks and sashing strips together into rows. Press the seam allowances toward the sashing strips.

3 Sew the remaining brown 1" x 42" strips end to end to make one continuous strip. From this strip, cut four sashing strips, 1" x 56".

4 Sew the block rows and sashing strips together as shown. Press the seam allowances toward the sashing strips.

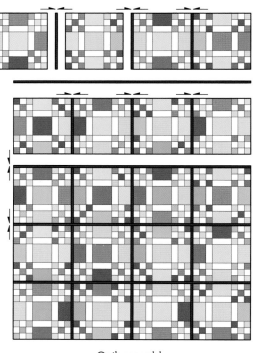

Quilt assembly

Finishing the Quilt

For help with any of the finishing steps, go to ShopMartingale.com/HowtoQuilt for free downloadable information.

1 Layer, baste, and quilt your quilt, or take it to your favorite long-arm machine quilter for finishing.

2 Using the brown 2½"-wide strips, make and attach binding.

Front Porch Blooms

The idea for the block in this quilt began with a picture of a bird feeder with a giant sunflower head in the center surrounded by layers of other yummy delights to entice the birds. For Joanna, it meant the beginning of a quilt. The block is strip pieced and straightforward to assemble.

"Front Porch Blooms," designed by Joanna Figueroa, pieced by Cheryl Hadley, quilted by Diana Johnson

Finished quilt: 63¼" x 63¼" ◆ **Finished block:** 11" x 11"

Materials

Yardage is based on 42"-wide fabric. You will need 16 different fabrics to make eight different pairs of fabric combinations. Choose a wide variety of colors and print sizes to give your stars visual interest. Make sure that you choose light, medium, and dark tones within your color palette so that the stars will stand out from one another and give your eyes a lot of variety to look at.

¼ yard *each* of 16 assorted peach, spring green, aqua blue, butter yellow, and faded brown prints for blocks and sashing squares (see "Fabric Selection" at right)

1⅛ yards of cream fabric for sashing

1⅛ yards of small-scale print for border

⅝ yard of fabric for binding

4 yards of fabric for backing

70" x 70" piece of batting

Cutting

All measurements include ¼"-wide seam allowances. Before you cut the block fabrics, separate them into pairs as instructed in "Fabric Selection" and keep the cut pieces for each pair together.

From *each* of the 16 assorted prints for blocks, cut:
1 strip, 7½" x 42"; crosscut the strip into:
   1 piece, 7½" x 6½"; trim to 6½" x 6½" (A)
   2 pieces, 7½" x 3¾"; crosscut each piece into 2 squares (4 total), 3¾" x 3¾". Cut each square into quarters diagonally to yield 16 triangles (B).
   4 pieces, 7½" x 2¼"; trim each piece to 6¾" x 2¼". Crosscut each piece into 3 squares (12 total), 2¼" x 2¼" (C).
   2 pieces, 7½" x 3"; trim each piece to 6" x 3". Crosscut each piece into 2 squares (4 total), 3" x 3" (D).
   4 pieces, 7½" x 2¼"; trim each piece to 6" x 2¼". Crosscut each piece into 2 pieces (8 total), 2¼" x 3" (E).

From the leftover block fabrics, cut a *total* of:
25 squares, 2¾" x 2¾"

From the cream fabric, cut:
3 strips, 11½" x 42"; crosscut into 40 sashing pieces, 2¾" x 11½"

From the small-scale print, cut:
8 border strips, 4½" x 42"

From the fabric for binding, cut:
7 strips, 2¼" x 42"

Making the Blocks

The instructions are for piecing two blocks at a time from one pair of fabrics.

1 Join one B triangle from each fabric to make a pair. Repeat with the remaining triangles from the two fabrics. Join two pairs to make an hourglass unit. Repeat to make a total of eight units. This will be enough for both blocks—they're identical to one another. Clip all the dog-ears.

Make 8.

2 Mark a diagonal line on the wrong side of a C square. Place a marked C square on the corner of the A square from the other fabric, orienting the square as shown. Sew along the marked line, press the C square toward the corner, and trim the excess fabric from behind it. Repeat to make one additional unit, reversing the fabric placement.

Make 1 of each.

3 In the same manner, join C squares to eight E pieces from the other fabric, orienting and sewing four squares with the fold line in one direction

and four squares with the fold line in the other direction as shown. Reverse the fabric placement and make eight additional units as shown.

Make 4.   Make 4.

Make 4.   Make 4.

4 Arrange the units from steps 1–3 and the D squares into three vertical rows for each of the two blocks. Be sure the star points are the same fabric as the A square in each block and that they are oriented correctly. Sew the pieces in each row together. Press the seam allowances as indicated. Sew the rows together. Press the seam allowances toward the outer rows.

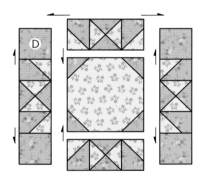

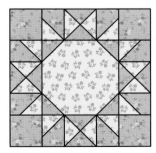 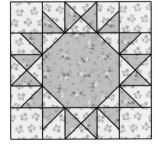

Make 1 of each.

Assembling the Quilt Top

1 To make the block rows, arrange the blocks in four rows of four blocks each, repositioning blocks as needed until you're satisfied with the arrangement. Be sure to notice the placement of the lighter and darker blocks to create a visual balance. Refer to the quilt assembly diagram to place a sashing piece vertically between each block. Join the blocks and sashing pieces in each row. Press the seam allowances toward the sashing pieces.

2 To make the sashing rows, join four sashing pieces and five 2¾" sashing squares as shown. Make five rows. Press the seam allowances toward the sashing pieces.

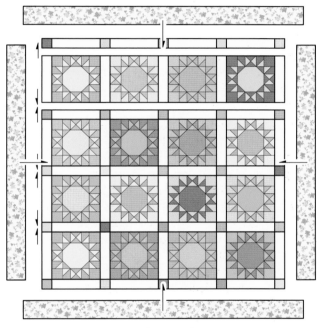

Make 5.

3 Join the block rows and sashing rows. Press the seam allowances toward the sashing rows.

4 Add the small-scale print 4½"-wide border strips to the quilt top, piecing the strips as necessary.

Quilt assembly

Finishing the Quilt

For help with any of the finishing steps, go to ShopMartingale.com/HowtoQuilt for free downloadable information.

1 Layer, baste, and quilt your quilt, or take it to your favorite long-arm machine quilter for finishing.

2 Using the 2¼"-wide strips, make and attach binding.

Spice Pantry

Blend a pinch of richly hued prints with a dash of traditional patchwork, and then sit back and enjoy the fruits of your labor as you wrap yourself within the whisper-soft folds of this charming lap quilt.

"Spice Pantry," designed by Kim Diehl, pieced by Pat Peyton, machine quilted by Deborah Poole
Finished quilt: 55½" x 64½"   ◆   **Finished block:** 13" x 13"

▶ Materials

Yardage is based on 42"-wide fabric. Fat quarters are 18" x 21" and fat eighths are 9" x 21".

20 fat eighths of assorted dark prints for patchwork units

10 fat quarters of assorted light-neutral prints for patchwork units

2 yards of orange print for border and binding

4 squares, 5½" x 5½", of assorted prints for border corner squares

4 yards of fabric for backing

62" x 71" piece of batting

▶ Cutting

All measurements include ¼"-wide seam allowances. Cut pieces across the width of the fabric unless otherwise indicated.

From the *length* of *each* of 16 assorted-print fat eighths, cut:
3 strips, 1½" x 21" (combined total of 48); keep the strips organized by print
1 strip, 3½" x 21"; crosscut into 6 squares, 3½" x 3½" (combined total of 96)

From the *length* of *each* of the 4 remaining assorted-print fat eighths, cut:
2 strips, 3½" x 21"; crosscut into 12 squares, 3½" x 3½" (combined total of 48)

From the *length* of *each* of 8 assorted neutral-print fat quarters, cut:
6 strips, 1½" x 21" (combined total of 48); keep the strips organized by print
2 strips, 3½" x 21"; crosscut into 6 rectangles, 3½" x 6½" (combined total of 48)

From the *length* of *each* of the 2 remaining assorted neutral-print fat quarters, cut:
4 strips, 3½" x 21"; crosscut into 12 rectangles, 3½" x 6½" (combined total of 24)

From the orange print, cut:
8 strips, 5½" x 42"
7 strips, 2½" x 42"

Making Double Nine-Patch Units

Sew all pieces with right sides together using a ¼" seam allowance unless otherwise indicated.

1 Select three matching assorted-print 1½" x 21" strips and three matching assorted neutral-print 1½" x 21" strips.

2 Join two neutral-print strips and one assorted-print strip along the long edges to make strip set A. Press the seam allowances toward the assorted print. Crosscut the strip set into 12 segments, 1½" wide.

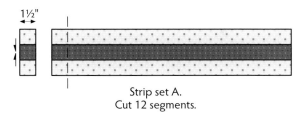

Strip set A.
Cut 12 segments.

3 Join the remaining two assorted-print 1½" x 21" strips and the neutral-print 1½" x 21" strip as previously instructed to make strip set B. Press the seam allowances toward the assorted prints. Crosscut the strip set into 12 segments, 1½" wide.

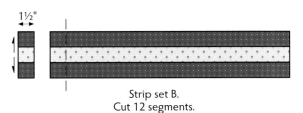

Strip set B.
Cut 12 segments.

4 Lay out two A segments and one B segment in three horizontal rows to form a nine patch. Join the rows. Press the seam allowances toward the middle row. Repeat to make a total of four pieced A units.

Unit A.
Make 4.

5 Lay out two B segments and one A segment in three horizontal rows to form a nine patch. Join the rows. Press the seam allowances away from the middle row. Repeat to make a total of four pieced B units.

Unit B.
Make 4.

6 Repeat steps 1–5 to make a total of 64 pieced A units and 64 pieced B units.

7 Select one A unit and one B unit, each from a different print. Join the units. Press the seam allowances open. Repeat for a total of 64 double nine-patch units measuring 3½" x 6½", including seam allowances.

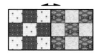

Make 64.

Making the Flying-Geese Units

1 Using a pencil and an acrylic ruler, draw a diagonal line on the wrong side of each assorted-print 3½" square.

2 Layer a marked square over one end of an assorted neutral-print 3½" x 6½" rectangle. Stitch the pair together on the drawn line. Flip the corner open, press, and trim the resulting corner triangle. In the same manner, sew, press, and trim a second prepared 3½" square to the remaining end of the rectangle, placing it in a mirror-image position. Repeat to make a total of 72 flying-geese units measuring 3½" x 6½", including seam allowances.

Make 72.

Assembling the Quilt Top

1 Select eight pieced flying-geese units and seven pieced double nine-patch units. Referring to the quilt photo on page 282, lay out the units in alternating positions to form a horizontal row. (Take care to reverse the direction of every other nine-patch unit, placing the first left-hand unit with the A unit on top as shown.) Join the units. Press the seam allowances toward the nine-patch units. Repeat for

a total of nine pieced rows. Please note that you will have one extra double nine-patch unit for added flexibility as you lay out the rows.

Make 9.

2 Using the pictured quilt as a guide, lay out the pieced rows to form the quilt center. Join the rows. Press the seam allowances open. The pieced quilt center should now measure 45½" x 54½", including seam allowances.

Adding the Borders

1 Join two orange-print 5½" x 42" strips end to end. Press the seam allowances open. Repeat to make four pieced strips.

2 Select a pieced strip. Use a pencil and acrylic ruler to mark a cutting line 27¼" out from each side of the center seam. Use a rotary cutter and acrylic ruler to cut away the excess strip length on the drawn lines. Repeat to make two border strips measuring 5½" x 54½". Join these strips to the right and left sides of the quilt center. Press the seam allowances toward the border strips.

3 Referring to step 2, mark and trim the remaining two pieced strips, measuring 22¾" out from the center seam to make two border strips measuring 5½" x 45½". Join an assorted-print 5½" square to each end of these border strips. Press the seam allowances away from the squares. Join these pieced strips to the remaining edges of the quilt center. The pieced quilt top should now measure 55½" x 64½", including seam allowances.

Finishing the Quilt

For help with any of the finishing steps, go to ShopMartingale.com/HowtoQuilt for free downloadable information.

1 Layer, baste, and quilt your quilt, or take it to your favorite long-arm machine quilter for finishing.

2 Using the orange-print 2½"-wide strips, make and attach binding.

Totally Decaffeinated

A relaxing palette evokes a peaceful feeling in this generous queen-size quilt. Rising Star blocks appear to float above a seashore of Stacked Logs blocks in dazzling blues, rich greens, and warm, sandy tones.

"Totally Decaffeinated," designed and made by Cathy Wierzbicki
Finished quilt: 98" x 110"   ◆   **Finished block:** 12" x 12"

Materials

Yardage is based on 42"-wide fabric.

5½ yards *total* of assorted light fabrics in cream, off-white, and tan for blocks and flying-geese border

3½ yards *total* of assorted dark-blue fabrics for blocks and flying-geese border

3½ yards *total* of assorted dark-green fabrics for blocks and flying-geese border

3¼ yards of blue-and-green print for outer border

¾ yard of dark-green fabric for inner border

1¼ yards of fabric for binding

102" x 114" piece of batting

Cutting

All measurements include ¼"-wide seam allowances. Cut pieces across the fabric width unless otherwise indicated. Each Rising Star block requires four different fabrics: one dark and one light for the inner star, and a different dark and a different light for the outer star. To help keep the pieces organized and keep the colors balanced throughout the quilt, cut the pieces for one Rising Star block and then stack the pieces together, set them aside, and cut the next block. Repeat this process until you've cut the pieces for each of the blocks required. Cut the pieces for the Stacked Logs blocks and borders first and then cut the pieces for the Rising Star blocks from the remaining assorted light and dark fabrics.

Cutting for the Stacked Logs Blocks, Borders, and Binding

From the assorted light fabrics, cut a *total* of:
36 strips, 2" x width of fabric
66 squares, 3⅞" x 3⅞"; cut in half diagonally to yield 132 triangles

From the dark-green fabric for inner border, cut:
10 strips, 2" x width of fabric

From the assorted dark-blue and dark-green fabrics, cut a *total* of:
60 strips, 2" x width of fabric
17 squares, 7¼" x 7¼"; cut into quarters diagonally to yield 68 triangles (2 are extra)

From the blue-and-green print, cut on the *lengthwise* grain:
2 strips, 6" x 87½"
2 strips, 6" x 110½"

From the binding fabric, cut:
11 strips, 2½" x 42"

Cutting for the Rising Star Blocks (repeat to cut pieces for 16 blocks)

From 1 light fabric, cut:
4 squares, 2" x 2"
1 square, 4¼" x 4¼"; cut into quarters diagonally to yield 4 triangles

From 1 dark fabric, cut:
1 square, 3½" x 3½"
4 squares, 2⅜" x 2⅜"; cut in half diagonally to yield 8 triangles

From a different light fabric, cut:
4 squares, 3½" x 3½"
1 square, 7¼" x 7¼"; cut into quarters diagonally to yield 4 triangles

From a different dark fabric, cut:
4 squares, 3⅞" x 3⅞"; cut in half diagonally to yield 8 triangles

Making the Rising Star Blocks

1. Using the pieces from one stack, sew dark 2⅜" half-square triangles to the short sides of each light 4¼" quarter-square triangle as shown. Press toward the dark triangles. Make four small flying-geese units for the inner star. Repeat with the remaining dark half-square triangles and light quarter-square triangles to make four large flying-geese units for the outer star.

Make 4.

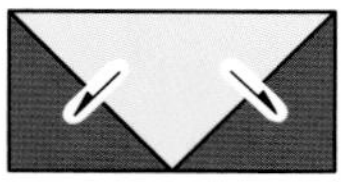

Make 4.

2 Arrange the four small flying-geese units from step 1, the four light 2" squares, and the dark 3½" square into three vertical rows as shown. Stitch the pieces in each row together and then stitch the rows together to complete the inner star unit.

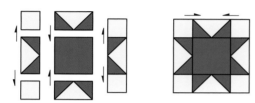

3 Arrange the four large flying-geese units from step 1, the four light 3½" squares, and the inner star unit into three vertical rows as shown. Stitch the pieces in each row together and then stitch the rows together to complete the block.

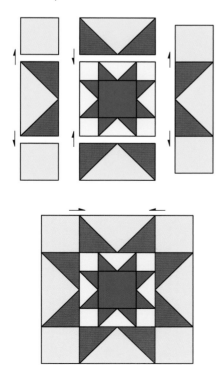

4 Repeat steps 1–3 with each of the remaining stacks to make a total of 16 Rising Star blocks.

Making the Stacked Logs Blocks

1 Randomly select two different light 2"-wide strips and stitch them together along the long edges to make a strip set. Press the seam allowances to one side. Make 18. Crosscut the strip sets into 192 segments, 3½" wide.

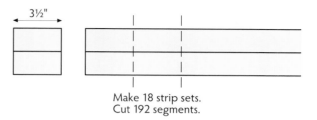

Make 18 strip sets.
Cut 192 segments.

2 Randomly select two different dark 2"-wide strips and stitch them together along the long edges to make a strip set. Press the seam allowances to one side. Make 30. Crosscut the strip sets into 320 segments, 3½" wide.

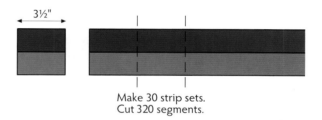

Make 30 strip sets.
Cut 320 segments.

3 Arrange 10 dark segments and six light segments into four rows of four segments each as shown. Pay close attention to the orientation of each segment. When the segments are positioned correctly, you will not need to match seams within each block or when sewing the blocks to each other. Sew the segments in each row together and then sew the rows together. Make 32 Stacked Logs blocks.

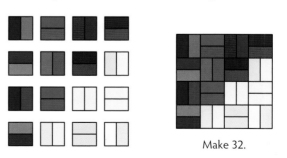

Make 32.

Assembling the Quilt Top

Arrange the Rising Star blocks and Stacked Logs blocks into rows, rotating the Stacked Logs blocks as shown. For a quilt this large, you may find it helpful to organize the quilt into more manageable units by assembling the quilt top in quarters. For each quarter, stitch the blocks in each row together, and then sew the rows together. Finish by sewing the quarters together.

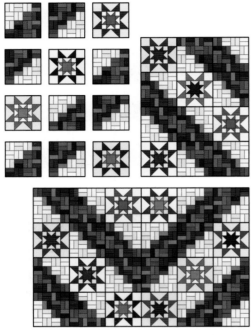

Quilt assembly

Adding the Borders

1 To make the inner border, stitch the dark-green strips together to make two strips, 2" x 72½", and two strips, 2" x 99½". Refer to the diagram at right to stitch the 72½"-long strips to the top and bottom edges of the quilt top. Sew the 99½"-long strips to the sides of the quilt top.

2 To make the flying-geese border, randomly select two light 3⅞" half-square triangles and stitch them to the short sides of each dark 7¼" quarter-square triangle as shown. Press seam allowances toward the dark triangle. Make 66 flying-geese units.

Make 66.

3 Stitch 33 flying-geese units together, orienting the points in the same direction. Make two strips. Stitch the strips to the sides of the quilt top.

Make 2.

4 Stitch the blue-and-green 6" x 87½" strips to the top and bottom edges of the quilt top, and then add the blue-and-green 6" x 110½" strips to the quilt sides to complete the outer border.

Adding the borders

Finishing the Quilt

For help with any of the finishing steps, go to ShopMartingale.com/HowtoQuilt for free downloadable information.

1 Layer, baste, and quilt your quilt, or take it to your favorite long-arm machine quilter for finishing.

2 Using the 2½"-wide strips, make and attach the binding.